Thomas Paine

Autographed mezzotint of a portrait of Thomas Paine by an unknown artist.

Thomas Paine

A Collection of Unknown Writings

Collected, edited and introduced by
Hazel Burgess

First published 2010 by
PALGRAVE MACMILLAN

Palgrave Macmillan in the UK is an imprint of Macmillan Publishers Limited,
registered in England, company number 785998, of Houndmills, Basingstoke,
Hampshire RG21 6XS.

Palgrave Macmillan in the US is a division of St Martin's Press LLC,
175 Fifth Avenue, New York, NY 10010.

Palgrave Macmillan is the global academic imprint of the above companies
and has companies and representatives throughout the world.

Palgrave® and Macmillan® are registered trademarks in the United States,
the United Kingdom, Europe and other countries

ISBN 978-0-230-23971-5   ISBN 978-0-230-24533-4 (eBook)
DOI 10.1007/978-0-230-24533-4

A catalogue record for this book is available from the British Library.

A catalog record for this book is available from the Library of Congress.

10 9 8 7 6 5 4 3 2 1
19 18 17 16 15 14 13 12 11 10

Transferred to Digital Printing in 2011

*This book is dedicated to my husband,
John, with love and gratitude.*

Without him, it would not have happened.

CONTENTS

ACKNOWLEDGEMENTS

The editor and publisher wish to thank The National Portrait Gallery, London for *A Portrait of Thomas Paine* by Laurent Dabos (*circa* 1791); and the Norfolk Record Office for permission to photograph a mezzotint of a portrait of Thomas Paine by an unknown artist, from W. G. Clarke's *Notes on the Thomas Paine Centenary* (1909) MS 120.

FOREWORD

I have been watching at a distance, admiringly and not without excitement, as Dr Hazel Burgess has carried out her artful detective work on Thomas Paine's opus. There is something about research, admittedly, that can combine benefit with annoyance; just when we think we have got it right, along comes new evidence. There has been a handsome cluster of in-depth studies about the controversial Paine over the last quarter-century, but Burgess has now made the provocative and well-substantiated claim that the great radical published rather more than we thought we knew. We are all forced back to our drawing boards, especially because, if her arguments are correct, Paine (1737–1809) was an author with many faces. He was a remarkable survivor, who was ready to receive payment to write and act for quite a variety of causes, so long as they were not too out of line with his famously democratic proclivities. In other words, he was an articulate polemicist who allowed himself to be used. This helps explain why he was the only great Enlightenment thinker embroiled in the two great revolutions of his time. Both, to be sure, proved his undoing; as the virtually unknown expatriate Englishman who penned *Common Sense* (1776), a veritable literary catalyst for the thirteen colonies of America to rise up against their British masters, he had to fight hard to be paid off for his services to the American Revolution. Before long, a deputy in France's (early revolutionary) National Convention, his presence as a foreigner in an increasingly tumultuous Paris landed him in jail at the Luxembourg Palace, which had been converted to a penitentiary. It was there that he wrote *The Age of Reason, Part Two*, which was published on his release in 1796. He later fell out with George Washington, with whom he had worked so closely during the War of Independence. The British establishment found him a very uncomfortable figure, and the rapid rise of Napoleon Bonaparte left no place for him in European affairs. On returning to America, his last years were bitter-sweet. Of Quaker stock, his roles had been too unpacifistic to allow a space in his desired Quaker burial ground, and even after his friend, Madame Marguerite Bonneville, saw him buried in a corner of his farm, his bones were disinterred by the devoted English radical William Cobbett and apparently distributed among faithful supporters of Radicalism in England!

It was in connection with the last part of this story that Burgess's keen interest in Paine was first made plain to me. She was intrigued with the issue of Paine's remains, their whereabouts and what they could tell us. Little did I know that, within ten years of my first learning about her interest, she would have acquired enough information to write a lengthy work on these material questions, let alone would have acquired a doctorate at the University of Sydney (2002) for her brilliant reconstruction of Paine's remarkable career. Still less did I realize, because Burgess was shy about the matter herself, that there were unrecognized works of the great radical she was uncovering in the course of her researches, all waiting to enter the scholarly light of day. Now the results of her patience and trained perceptivity are here before us, ahead of both the promised biography and an investigation of Painean relics; and it is my great honour, as an historian of social and political thought myself, to introduce them to the public.

The collection that follows is a miscellany, as one might expect, including letters that other editors of Paine's works – those by Moncure Daniel Conway and Philip S. Foner especially – have missed, and pamphlets that only skilled detection can reveal as his. Among the most interesting in the collection is the substantial piece under the title 'Reflections on the Present State of the British Nation' (1791), which in its defence of just laws and popularly based government and its assaults on tyranny is complementary to *Rights of Man* (1791–2) and surely very characteristic of the Paine we all think we know. On the other hand, at least two items, 'For the Times' (1789) and 'A Letter from Common Sense to the King and People' (1791), do not seem to fit the bill, the former making too many concessions to the very idea of monarchy when Paine is notoriously disdainful of royalty, and the second being rather too uncritically defensive of both the existing British constitution and glorious empire. But Burgess knows her Paine only too well. Apart from the fact that the English *provocateur* was strongly opposed to the regicide of France's Louis XVI, she has established that he simply had to make a living by writing and he would readily tailor his writing to suit his patrons if it meant surviving economically – but, of course, never with such compromise that he became some kind of Tory or utter turncoat. The possibility of his owning slaves was perhaps the furthest he veered to the right.

In any case, Burgess leaves us with a much more intelligible, less idealized Paine than others have done; a man who lurched from opportunity to opportunity while attempting to maintain the profile of liberty's staunch defender and consistent opponent of tyrannical power and unjust institutions. I heartily recommend this collection to all those interested in the history of liberty and the constant need to guard her from lurking enemies.

Garry W. Trompf
Emeritus Professor in the History of Ideas
The University of Sydney

PREFACE

When I first embarked on researching the life and times of that great pamphleteer of the eighteenth century, Thomas Paine, little did I realize that it would lead me on a path of significant discoveries. That path determined the contents of this book. At that time, I noted all of his works as edited and presented in the late Philip S. Foner's laudable two-volume work, *The Complete Writings of Thomas Paine*.[1] In itself, making that list in chronological order would have been a pointless exercise, but by inserting dated works mentioned by other writers on Paine, I discovered there were some not included in Foner's work. Without my list, this present collection would not have come about. It was with excitement that I found I was able to add to the known corpus. Early collections, partly published material and peripheral literature furnished further matter, and later discoveries of my own from searches of library catalogues, with one exception, completed the work. (The one exception came about by of word of mouth.) From these sources, this eclectic offering now brings together, in one volume, both works of substance and pieces of an ephemeral nature.

Collections of Paine's writings have frequently been heavily edited, so I sought out and utilized originals of his known work from newspapers of his time or, in the case of manuscripts, repositories sourced by other writers. It seemed to me that the original publications or earliest reproductions evoked the urgency of matters, which, in their time, were of pressing concern; I read the works as Paine himself wrote them and as the addressees read them. Fieldwork in Britain and the United States yielded rewards in bringing pieces to light, but the bulk of my work was researched from Australia.

All finds were thrilling experiences; the privilege of reading what nobody else has seen in over 200 years provided sweet satisfaction, regardless of its subject. I think the most exciting of my discoveries came about early in my research when, through the Library of Congress, I located a manuscript at a New York library. It had been catalogued and stored, not to be handled again until I requested a copy. The Rare Books Librarian transcribed it for the first time for use in my work. It gave him great pleasure to find the library's 'long-lost Paine letter', which led to his informing a friend of his unexpected labour of love. Coincidentally, his friend was aware of the recent sale of a privately owned Paine manuscript to the Pierpont Morgan Library, New York. Both letters, re-transcribed with small differences, appear in this book, as does a further published piece found as the result of mention by Paine in one of the letters. It reveals a previously unknown pseudonym. Surprisingly, some writings signed by known pseudonyms, or even Paine's own name, have long lain in wait for their place in a collection of Paine writings. They were sought in likely publications and holdings.

My discovery, in 1996, of a photograph of an eighteenth-century mezzotint of a portrait of Paine provided a challenge in thinking and speculating on its history and that of the unknown, original painting; the photograph serves as the frontispiece to this work, and its story augments comment on a letter of the same date.

Yet another interesting discovery was found in a letter from Paine to the Mayor of New York. It revealed the fact that a well-known piece was not written in the year all commentators have noted, but the previous year. It was its subject matter, yellow fever, that prevented its publication at time of writing.

Paine's verse and private letters provide an insight into the man, while his longer pamphlets show that at times he did not baulk from offering different points of view on the same subject. Where I had some doubt about a writing actually being by Paine rather than by another adopting his pseudonym, I carefully checked and compared the language with that of his other works, paying attention to phraseology in general, and similes and metaphors in particular. I am satisfied that all included in this book originated from the pen of the enigmatic Paine.

The writings are described as unknown in the title of this book because most have not been reprinted since their first appearance during Paine's lifetime. Some few have appeared in collections of papers of others, for example, Robert Morris and De Witt Clinton. A few have been mentioned or appeared as short extracts from the whole within writings on Paine; they are here given in full for the first time. I have made every effort to ensure such is the case, and believe it to be so. In moving chronologically through political pamphlets, private correspondence and verse, this book offers an insight into Paine's thinking, location and feelings at the time of writing. With some few exceptions, which are noted, primary sources, either original or from microfiche, microfilm and databases, were consulted, transcribed and edited.[2]

In cases where Paine did not furnish a date for his writings, I have provided the date of publication; where both are known they are given in the text. Where only a date of publication is known, that is provided in the

Contents in place of the actual date of writing. His pamphlets, like books, merely gave a year of publication so, where necessary, I have inserted them where they seemed likely to have preceded or followed other pieces. In referring to his famous *Rights of Man*, published in two parts, I have not appended a part number to the earlier work. Throughout the text, but not in the notes, I follow Paine in referring to the second part as *Part the Second*. I have not given a descriptive title to any writings; they are listed only by date. During my research and checking for previous publication of items, I found the different titles given to the same article by various editors and writers to be confusing and time-consuming in my need to check their singularity, especially where dates also varied or were incorrect.

Where Paine or newspaper editors used unnecessary capitalization, I have replaced much of it with lower case, unless quoting supportive material from authors who have collected and edited works, or in cases of other supportive material. Where capitalization was intended as emphasis, I have used italics. Where Paine did not capitalize proper nouns, I have done, and, where he capitalized needlessly, I have edited those capitals out with the exception of those used in personification of human characteristics such as 'Folly' and 'Reason'. As a signature, the name of Thomas Paine is capitalized only as done in published writings, not in personal correspondence. I have corrected much, but not all, of Paine's punctuation and that of others. Spelling has been amended as required, but I have retained some older forms as quaint and of their time, one instance being Paine's use of *ph* where modern usage requires an *f*. I have not altered his inconsistencies of spelling; a subtle distinction is discernible between his and others' use of English on either side of the Atlantic with the passing of time. I have abandoned Paine's use of superscripts as was commonly used in such phrases as 'Your Ob^t Humble Serv$^{t'}$', replacing it with normal text. I have conformed with his occasional style of signing off letters to the left of the page. Where hyphenation was normal in the eighteenth century, as for example in 'New-York', I have complied with modern usage, unless it formed part of quoted material or the title of a newspaper or periodical. For interest, I have made few changes to Paine's grammar; it is clear that it varied considerably between personal, hurried, important and published writings. His handwriting similarly varied. Where he deleted words or sentences in manuscript material, I have omitted the deletion. When so spelled by others, I have retained the spelling of Paine as 'Pain', and the French spelling 'Payne'. Bible references are to the Authorized [King James] Version.

My introductions and comments on Paine's pieces are minimal, but sufficient to set each within its context. Further reading on particular or concurrent events is to be found in the several biographies of Paine, although a brief outline of his life is included in this work as an introduction for those not familiar with it. If some elements appear laboured, it is because they have not been presented until now and require more explanation than known material given in the accepted and repetitive biographies of the past.

With a background in anthropology and studies in religion, I have enjoyed my wanderings in the fields of eighteenth-century history, transatlantic politics, philosophy, economics and English literature. I am grateful to specialists in these disciplines who have generously given me time and shown interest in my work. It remains for them to analyse Paine's writings according to their individual theories and expertise.

Many academics, institutions and friends have demonstrated their support, friendship and expertise as they listened to what seems to be my only topic of conversation: Thomas Paine. In transcribing eighteenth-century English, I became so accustomed to its usage that I sometimes found myself writing, if not speaking it; I would ask readers to bear with any remnants apparent in my writing.

Of the academics, thanks are due to my special friends, Emeritus Professor in the History of Ideas, Garry W. Trompf, and Associate Professor Carole Cusack, both of the University of Sydney, who, in that order, were supervisors and associate supervisors of my doctoral candidature. Garry has always expressed deep interest in the ideas of Paine; he kindly wrote the foreword to this book. Carole developed yet another interest to add to an ever-increasing multiplicity of knowledge. Particular gratitude is due to Professor Eric Foner of Columbia University, whose valued advice and encouragement helped me on my way; he himself has added to the collection of works edited by his uncle, Philip S. Foner. The late Professor Alfred Owen Aldridge gave kindly encouragement.

Specialist librarians and curators at libraries in the United Kingdom, the United States and Australia have given of their time, knowledge and interest. Thanks are due to those of The Bodleian Library; The British Library, particularly Dr Christopher Wright of the Manuscripts Department; the Library of Congress; the Buffalo and Erie County Library, especially William H. Loos, former Curator of the Rare Book Room; the Library of Virginia; Princeton University Library; New York Public Library; the Rare Book and Manuscript Library, Columbia University; the Pierpont Morgan Library; and the James S. Copley Library. Special mention of their help is due to Mr Bruce Kirby, Manuscript Reference Librarian of the Library of Congress, who conducted an intensive search of their holdings, and to Mr Ed Lengel, Associate

Editor of the *Papers of George Washington*, and Mr David Haugaard, Reference Librarian of the Historical Society of Pennsylvania, whose joint efforts helped in locating the manuscript of a letter to Robert Morris thought to have been elsewhere; to Elizabeth Gallagher, Reference and Special Projects Librarian of the Manhattanville College Library, for providing me, in the year 2000, with a copy of an article that provided evidence of a manuscript letter from Thomas Paine to Robert Morris, of 1782, not to be missing; to Ann Okerson, Associate University Librarian, Collections and International Programs, Yale University; and to Sarah Huggins of the Library of Virginia for bringing an obscure footnote in a rare book to my attention; it helped with my introduction to Paine's publication of 9 July 1783. Over the years of my research, the Inter-Library Loans personnel of the University of Sydney at times performed the seeming impossible in procuring rare material for me, and Jillian Brown of the Audio-Visual Department was, and still is, ever helpful with her range of equipment and staunch friendship. Staff members of many other libraries have assisted me in my research, but as material from their collections does not appear in this publication, they are not here named. They will be in my planned future writings.

Specialists of the Department of Painting and Sculpture of the Smithsonian National Portrait Gallery and the Prints and Photographs Division of the Library of Congress, Washington, were helpful in answering my queries on the possible existence of a print of the photograph already mentioned.

The collections of the American Antiquarian Society have proved inestimably valuable to my research, as have collections of other newspaper and periodical resources made available through digitization, microfilm and microfiche. The searchable databases of the first have smoothed the way for relatively rapid discovery of items that, at the beginning of my research, sometimes took months to retrieve and then transcribe.

Members and staff of the Thetford Town Council warmly welcomed my husband and me, and provided access to their miscellaneous collection of Paine items. It was at their offices at the King's House that I located one letter published in this collection. Norfolk Record Office also kindly provided material found in the following pages. The Royal Commission on Historical Manuscripts, London, directed me to a letter, hitherto unknown, published here for the first time. The National Portrait Gallery, London, and the National Portrait Gallery, Washington, DC, have shown keen interest and offered comments on portraits of Paine. Christie's, London accommodated my request to transcribe material not otherwise available from one of their sale catalogues. The New Hampshire Historical Society went to trouble on my behalf, and Jason D. Stratman of the Missouri Historical Society searched their records for information on a fire said to have destroyed many of Paine's papers. Phil McGahan, bursar of Thetford Grammar School, kindly answered my queries regarding Paine's attendance at the school, and, when visiting the school in 1996, the then headmaster, John Weeks, kindly and proudly showed us the schoolroom in which Paine would have studied, and the new library named for him.

The Thomas Paine Society in England has been of great help and support, especially in the persons of the hard-worked Robert Morrell and the late Eric Paine. Members of the Thomas Paine National Historical Association of New Rochelle, New York, kindly offered their facilities, and provided friendly and comfortable accommodation during research in the United States; their generosity is much appreciated. From a distance, David Alden efficiently organized and undertook the task of photographing an old image held by the Norfolk Record Office. I am grateful to him.

More individuals than can be named have assisted me along the way. George, 8th Marquess of Lansdowne, generously gave permission to consult the Lansdowne Papers. I suspect that the late Jim Deacon, local historian of Thetford, spent more time than I know in making sure he gave me the right answers to the many questions I put to him; Thetford is a poorer town for his passing. Carol Gill of Canterbury looked up parish records for me when resources did not allow me to visit the Cathedral Archives; her assistance added to the Paine story. Robin Mingay helped with information on his ancestor, James Mingay, and Bob Solly kindly supplied information on his ancestor, Richard Solly.

Warm thanks are given to my loyal friends. In alphabetical order, worthy of special mention, are the ever-helpful Don Barrett; my brother-in-law Robert Burgess, who has always accommodated and shared his village life with us in East Sussex; Shirley Maxwell, who patiently proofread some of my writing; my friend of many years, the late Jean Morris of London, who provided accommodation while I visited several institutions my research demanded; Patricia Tunbridge of Surrey, an avid reader who let me know of any news or book reviews that mentioned Paine; Vikki J. Vickers with whom, since we were both completing our doctoral degrees, I have shared correspondence; and Sally Williams, of West Sussex, who took great personal interest in my topic and also kept me informed of any mention of Thomas Paine that appeared in British newspapers and magazines. There are many more not named who are deserving of thanks; they know who they are and how their input has been appreciated.

Final mention goes to my family. My sons David and Philip, after many years of living with their mother's apparent obsession, now see words in print. Despite living with it through their youth into manhood, their patient listening and interest have never wavered. Thank you both.

Hazel Burgess

INTRODUCTION

THOMAS PAINE – REVOLUTIONARY WORDSMITH

Until one day in 1778 when he stepped away from his pseudonym of 'Common Sense', the title of his first major pamphlet in America, and revealed his true identity as author of all writings under that signature, Thomas Paine was a literary nonentity.[3] Prior to that revelation, the man who was to become famous as a radical writer on both sides of the Atlantic during the last decades of the eighteenth century, and to fade out of the spotlight in the early years of the nineteenth, was known only to the British Board of Excise and those concerned with it. Paine was an Excise man who had been dismissed from his position at Lewes, Sussex. The reason for his dismissal was 'having quitted his Business, without obtaining the Board's Leave for so doing, and being gone off on Account of the Debts which he hath contracted'.[4] Paine had taken time out to write and present a petition to Parliament on behalf of all Excise men in the land. It described their distress and set out the need for a higher salary. Printed as an unpublished petition at Lewes in 1772 and bearing no mark of authorship, it remained unknown. It was published in 1793 following the author's rise to fame.[5]

All who have written on Paine have given the date of his birth as 29 January 1737 at the town of Thetford, Norfolk. They have told of his father, Joseph Pain,[6] being a humble Quaker stay-maker to whom Thomas was apprenticed at the age of 13 following his schooling at Thetford Grammar School. Strange as it may seem for a man of whom many biographies have been written, it is not possible to say with certainty that he was the child born to Joseph Pain and his wife, Elizabeth. Every biographer and writer who has mentioned his childhood and early adult life has depended upon the first, Francis Oldys, alias George Chalmers,[7] and repeated his story with embellishments. That story has proved to be the stuff of which legends are made. Nobody has questioned the initial account of the first

1

37 years in the life of Paine, the Englishman, whose writings, which first appeared during his middle age, aided in prompting and stirring cataclysmic changes in the Western world. At present, despite there not being a shred of evidence to suggest he ever lived at Thetford, there is no evidence to refute it. Only twice in his writings did he refer to his schooling: once in *Rights of Man, Part the Second*, and again in *The Age of Reason*. In the first, he wrote of a master whom he named in a footnote as 'Rev. William Knowles',[8] and in the second, he wrote of having attended a grammar school, with a footnote identifying it as 'The same school, Thetford in Norfolk, that the present counsellor Mingay went to, and under the same master'.[9]

None of Paine's known personal correspondence mentions his beginnings in Norfolk, and the little he mentioned in footnotes, with no significant bearing on the text, presents a problem. James Mingay KC, to whom he referred, was born on 9 March 1752, 15 years after the birth of Paine. It was not possible for both of them to have studied under William Knowles,[10] because Knowles was not associated with Thetford Grammar School until 1756,[11] when Paine was 19 years old. The little biographical material that exists on James Mingay tells of his being at the school under John Cole Galloway, who succeeded Knowles in 1764.[12] All knowledge of Paine's childhood emanated from Chalmers, none of which Paine denied, but of which he only wrote following publication of Chalmers's biography. There are no parish records, school records or records of any other kind referring to Paine at Thetford, although there are records of Pains living in the town, so it is impossible to write about his childhood of which he told nothing until the Pains of Thetford were dead. As shown, that which he did write, here given in totality, does not accord with official records.[13]

Of his youth, Paine left a brief record of having been imbued with the 'false heroism' of William Knowles, 'who had served in a man of war', and of joining the crew of a privateer but of his being rescued from a seafaring career by the intervention of a 'good father'.[14] Nevertheless, he wrote of embarking unhindered on another privateer, the *King of Prussia*, on a mission that was to last seven months.[15]

Paine told no more of his early manhood and no contemporaries ever wrote of him, so reliance must be placed on Chalmers's scathing story of truths and falsehoods, his title and accounts varying, augmenting and embroidering with each edition of his tale to suit the market.[16] It is, therefore, necessary to draw from the first edition, that which would have been read and not refuted by Paine. According to Chalmers, the young Paine moved to London[17] and, in later editions of his work, told of him working there as a stay-maker for Mr Morris of Hanover Street, Longacre.

In 1758, he moved to Dover, Kent, where he worked for another stay-maker and unrewardingly courted his employer's daughter. From there, in 1759, he moved to Sandwich where he set up as a master stay-maker. It was there that he met Mary Lambert, 'a pretty girl of modest behaviour'. She was the orphaned daughter of a dismissed Excise man and his wife, both of whom died in 1753, who worked as a waiting woman to Maria Solly, wife of an 'eminent woollen draper'.[18] Chalmers did not mention the fact that the woollen draper, Richard Solly, had formerly been a twice-elected mayor of Sandwich.[19]

At the age of 22, Thomas married Mary at St Peter's Church, Sandwich, on 27 September 1759. A handwritten copy of the entry, long thought to be the original, is held on loan by the Thetford Library;[20] the original of the printed church register is in fact held in the Canterbury Cathedral Archives.[21] Chalmers told of Paine, heavily in debt, and his young wife fleeing from Sandwich to nearby Margate.[22] The biographer passed on gossip of the 'fate' of Mary:

> By some she is said to have perished on the road of ill usage, and a premature birth. The women of Sandwich are positive, that she died in the British Lying-in Hospital, in Brownlow-street, Long-acre; but the register of this charity, which is kept with commendable accuracy, evinces, that she had not been received into this laudable refuge of female wretchedness.[23]

In 1819, Francis Westley, in a short, hostile biography, picked up the gossip reported by Chalmers and, virtually word for word, related it as fact, adding that Paine and his wife had set out from Margate for London. In the same year two admiring biographers, Thomas Clio Rickman and W. T. Sherwin, both merely stated that Mary died at Margate in 1760.[24] Many biographers since have written that Mary died in childbirth.

None of those stories can be true. There is no entry in the parish registers at Canterbury bearing evidence of Mary's death with mention of a possible child, and, it appears, nobody has sought one. However, in the records of the Parish of St Lawrence, Thanet, close to Margate where Rickman and Sherwin wrote of Mary dying, is an entry of baptism in 1760: 'Pain – Sarah Dr of Thomas and Mary – Dec: 7' and, in the following year, a poignant, one-line, burial entry, 'Pain – Sarah Dr of Thomas and Mary Pain – Sept. 12'.[25] The fact that Mary was not mentioned as deceased in either entry suggests that she was alive in 1761.

Paine kept details of his early life to himself. If there was any record of Mary in the manuscripts he left behind, none is known to have survived.

It is possible that she was alive in 1791, when Chalmers published his derisive biography, but nothing more of her is known beyond the time of the infant Sarah's death. It is unlikely that her fate will ever be known.

Of Paine himself little is known other than his being twice employed and dismissed by the Board of Excise. It is only in the Board's records that official documentation of his life begins; the truth of the written account cannot be verified. Having begun his service in 1762, Paine was first dismissed in 1765 for falsely claiming he had completed duties that he had not. On 3 July 1766, applying to be reinstated, he apologized for his earlier behaviour and, surprisingly, added that 'no complaint of the least dishonesty, or intemperance, ever appeared against me'.[26] More surprising still, he was reinstated the following day. The Excise Board made a note: 'July 4, 1766. – To be restored on a proper vacancy. S.B'.[27]

It was not until February 1768 that Paine accepted an appointment at Lewes, but, during the interval between postings, an extraordinary metamorphosis befell him. Having humbly applied for reinstatement, he had the confidence to decline a vacancy when one was offered in Cornwall; he had resided in London where he had attended lectures in philosophy; had taught at two London schools;[28] and had met with men not normally associated with tradesmen or Excise men. By the time he had completed his *Case of the Officers of Excise*, he had married and separated from a second wife and returned to London. Before long, he was given two references by Benjamin Franklin, who was in Britain attempting to reconcile the struggle for power between Parliament and the colonies. One reference was addressed to Franklin's son-in-law, Richard Bache:

> The bearer, Mr. Thomas Paine, is very well recommended to me as an ingenious, worthy young man. He goes to Pennsylvania with a view of settling there. I request you to give him your best advice and countenance, as he is quite a stranger there. If you can put him in a way of obtaining employment as a clerk, or assistant tutor in a school, or assistant surveyor, (all of which I think him very capable,) so that he may procure a subsistence at least, till he can make acquaintance and obtain a knowledge of the country, you will do well, and much oblige your affectionate father.[29]

There was no mention of Paine's background in either stay-making or the Excise.

Paine wrote of arriving in America late in 1774, so ill that he was unable to present his reference to Richard Bache for six weeks.[30] At the time, many of the colonists were agitating over matters concerning British rule, particularly their being subject to taxation but without representation. Minor skirmishes had escalated into conflict with British troops. It was the spillage of blood at the Battle of Lexington and Concord on 19 April 1775 that stirred Paine into action. From this point on, his life and many of his works are known to some extent, but until now have remained, and yet remain, in need of further research.

Paine acquainted himself with the situation of his new country to a remarkable degree. By May 1775, he had established himself as an anonymous contributor to the new *Pennsylvania Magazine: or American Monthly Museum*. Prior to its publication, when proposed, its Scottish editor, Robert Aitken, described it as including a wide range of subjects extending to 'the whole circle of science, including politics and religion as objects of philosophical disquisition', exclusive of controversy.[31] According to Paine, who claimed to have taken no part in the first issue, he was approached by Aitken for assistance in establishing the journal, with the result, for which Paine took credit, of raising subscribers from 600 to 1,500 within a few weeks.[32] The full extent of his contributions is not known, and several works have been wrongly ascribed to him by admirers. Much of the literature printed in American magazines of the time had already been published in English journals, some rewritten and some signed with pen names.[33] The result was that the authorship of numerous pieces has remained cloaked in anonymity and wrongly ascribed.

Works for which Paine has been given undue credit are 'Reflections on Unhappy Marriages' and 'An Occasional Letter on the Female Sex'. The first of these, published in *The Pennsylvania Magazine* of June 1775, was introduced by a columnist as a dissertation he had 'accidentally hit upon' and transcribed; he styled himself 'The Old Bachelor'. It was clearly not by Paine. The second, a plea on behalf of women, was proved in 1931 by Frank Smith to have been just part of the introduction to a two-volume English translation of Antoine Léonard Thomas's *Essai sur le caractère, les moeurs et l'esprit des femmes dans les différens siècles*, which was published in Paris in 1772.[34] The English translation was padded out to fill two volumes.[35] Based on the short piece in *The Pennsylvania Magazine*, for more than a century since the piece was attributed to Paine by Moncure Daniel Conway,[36] many have accepted him as a champion of the cause of women. It appeared in the last major collection of Paine's works 'because it indicates his interest as editor of the magazine in the subject, and because some of the language of the essay is his'. There is, in fact, no credible evidence to demonstrate that Paine was, as stated by many commentators, editor of Aitken's magazine.

Only one mention of his being so by a contemporary is to be found in a letter from Benjamin Rush, a former member of the Continental Congress and a signer of the Declaration of Independence, to James Cheetham who solicited information from him for his derogatory biography of Paine.[37]

More cruelly, to this day Paine is acknowledged as the author of an essay on black slavery in America, again first attributed to him by Conway.[38] He was not. Published on 8 March 1775 in the *Pennsylvania Journal and the Weekly Advertiser*, a rival publication to Aitken's magazine, his authorship has been accepted on the basis of Rush's response to Cheetham, in which he recalled and recounted a vague memory. He told Cheetham of having met Paine in Philadelphia in 1773 and of having been told by him that the essay 'was the first thing he had ever published in his life'.[39] Based solely on Rush's letter, Conway claimed the piece for Paine.

The essay was printed along with its accompanying note to the publishers, William Bradford and his son, Thomas: 'Please to insert the following, and oblige yours, A.B.' Of Paine's known acquaintances of the time, the initials A.B. have no significance in the sense of a friend submitting an article on Paine's behalf. However, the initials do indicate that the essay was written by the well-known Quaker abolitionist Anthony Benezet, who had already written on the subject of slavery and slave trading.[40] The signature to the essay, which was written from a strongly Christian perspective by one 'not sympathetic to the grievances of the colonists', a description inappropriate to Paine, was 'Justice and Humanity'.[41] The author of the essay mentioned that prominent men had already proved that enslavement was 'contrary to the light of nature, to every principle of Justice and Humanity, and even good policy'. He named those men, including John Locke, in a footnote.[42]

In later years Paine claimed never to have read Locke.[43] Few commentators have followed such reasoning through to the logical conclusion that the writer was not Paine. In attributing the essay to him, both he and descendants of African slaves have been dealt a severe injustice. Paine was claimed as an advocate of abolition and, in that, accorded unjustified honour. Generations of African Americans have been misled to look upon him as a proponent of their rights.

It was probably in about June or July 1775 that Paine's employment by Aitken ended. No pieces certainly attributable to him appeared in *The Pennsylvania Magazine* after that date, but he then had his mind on a work that was to have an impact of major proportions, the work in which he took greatest pride for the rest of his life. Such was his pride that towards the end of his life he asked that his headstone be engraved with his name followed by 'Author of Common Sense'.

Common Sense, Paine's *tour de force*, an argument for separation from Britain, first published in Philadelphia on 9 January 1776, became an instant best-seller.[44] The first edition of this momentous pamphlet gave the name of no author. The publisher, Robert Bell, and Paine argued over profits so they parted company but, within days, Bell published a reprint, the title page of which revealed the fact that it was 'Written by an Englishman'. It sold edition after edition and became the talk of the colonies, reaching out to all, both the literate and the illiterate, to whom it was read. While not the sole contributing factor that led to the colonists declaring their independence from Britain, as noted by A. Owen Aldridge, its significance can be gauged by its incorporation with three other documents in a Library of Congress publication, *Fundamental Testaments of the American Revolution*. It is bound with the Declaration of Independence, the Articles of Confederation and the Treaty of Paris of 1783.[45] The acclaim with which it was greeted in America defied superlatives, but it was not without its critics. Nevertheless, it set its anonymous author on the road to fame and a place in revolutionary history.

Following the course recommended in Paine's pamphlet, war between Britain and the colonies followed within months, as did the Declaration of Independence. Having helped enormously to galvanize the colonists' resistance to British rule, Paine shouldered a musket and joined their ranks in the field as aide-de-camp to General Nathaniel Greene. During the darkest days of defeat and surrenderings of Washington's army, when victory seemed an impossible goal, the former stay-maker again reached for his persuasive pen. In a 'passion of patriotism',[46] he wrote the first number of his *American Crisis* series, which opened with words possibly more evocative than any others he ever wrote:

> These are the times that try men's souls: The summer soldier and the sunshine patriot will, in this crisis, shrink from the service of his country; but he that stands it now, deserves the love and thanks of man and woman. Tyranny, like hell, is not easily conquered; yet we have this consolation with us, that the harder the conflict, the more glorious the triumph. What we obtain too cheap, we esteem too lightly. It is dearness only that gives every thing its value.[47]

The rousing, patriotic language appealed to the masses in the colonies, and convincingly rallied troops and civilians alike to fight for freedom from the restrictions of British rule. As were all the *Crisis* pamphlets, it was signed 'Common Sense'. The last of the series, based on glory not despair, appeared in 1783 when peace prevailed. They had been, in effect, a running history of events of the American Revolution, and the writings of 'Common Sense' were known throughout the then United States of America. The unknown author was hailed as a hero.

Thomas Paine was also an inventor. With the coming of peace, he retired, as it were, to his small house on five acres of land at Bordentown, New Jersey, close to the property of his friend Colonel Kirkbride.[48] There he immersed himself in a new obsession: designing an iron arch bridge. Its model was admired, but a full-scale bridge was never built in America.

On 26 April 1787, again with a reference from Benjamin Franklin in his pocket, Paine sailed for France, where he arrived at Le Havre de Grace on 26 May in the earliest days of the French Revolution. He travelled several times between France and England where he was to publish his next major work, *Rights of Man*, in 1791.

Just as his *Common Sense* became a *sine qua non* for the success of the American Revolutionary War, *Rights of Man* was published in England with similar impact, especially among the working class, but without the desired outcome. Furthering sentiments articulated in *Common Sense*, the work was reverentially dedicated to George Washington. The title page named the author as 'Thomas Paine, Secretary for Foreign Affairs to Congress in the American War', a position he never held.[49]

More than he had in his earlier work, Paine criticized the monarchical system and the British traditions so strongly defended by Edmund Burke in his *Reflections on the Revolution in France*.[50] It was expected that Paine would be prosecuted, but his judicious use of language could not be shown to be seditious. The work was expensive at 3 shillings, but it sold out in three days. Thousands of copies were produced and authorities feared that the less literate of the population might be seduced into revolutionary thinking.

Intoxicated with the success of *Rights of Man*, Paine worked in France on its sequel. Like its precursor, it sold to the masses in thousands. To the authorities it screamed promulgation of revolution. Denouncing the monarchy and the British Constitution, Paine went further in proposing measures, complete with figures, which might be applied to ameliorate the miserable conditions endured by the underclass; at the same time, his suggested scheme would pay off the National Debt, thereby improving the economy of the nation. By use of metaphors of spring and summer, he concluded by forecasting a snowballing change of unprecedented magnitude in a revolution of the world:

> What pace the political summer may keep with the natural, no human foresight can determine. It is, however, not difficult to perceive that the

spring is begun. Thus wishing, as I sincerely do, freedom and happiness to all nations, I close the SECOND PART.[51]

On publication, for the audaciousness of *Rights of Man, Part the Second*, Paine was charged with seditious libel, but by the time he was to be heard he had fled to France, where he had been elected to a seat in the National Convention. Tried *in absentia*, he was found guilty and declared an outlaw. *Rights of Man* was suppressed in the land of the author's birth to which he would never return, but France welcomed the exile, where, yet again, he wrote on behalf of the oppressed.

Paine arrived in France soon after abolition of the monarchy and witnessed the heady days of the beginning of the French Republic. The atrocities perpetrated against the nobles appalled him and in the Convention, he pleaded for the life of Louis XVI and his family. As history has shown, his efforts were in vain. As events were overtaking manageable government, Paine moved from his lodgings in Paris to the then small town of Saint-Denis where he continued his political writings and, in March 1793, the work that led to his ultimate obloquy, *The Age of Reason*, was translated and printed in French by his friend François-Xavier Lanthenas. The work was suppressed; it is not known why. It was published in England in 1794.

In short, Paine's new work denounced the Bible as not being the word of God, but merely a collection of ancient myths supported by the writings of men. It denounced the virgin birth of Jesus as impossible, and told of the unprecedented and never-repeated circumstance of the resurrection of Christ. It promoted deism – belief in the existence of a god – and dismissed as impossible not only Christianity but also any form of revealed religion.

The French Revolution continued to escalate into the Reign of Terror. Under the limitless powers of the Committee of Public Safety, the rule of the guillotine began. Paine himself feared for his life as he had unsuccessfully pleaded for banishment of Louis XVI rather than execution. Following a decree excluding foreigners from the Convention, he was arrested on 27 December 1793. The next day he was imprisoned in the Luxembourg Palace, which had been converted to a prison. Prisoners were taken away on a nightly basis to meet their fate at the guillotine. Paine was spared that fate, but, despite the entreaties of his American friends for his release, remained incarcerated until the fall of Robespierre.

Part 2 of Paine's *Age of Reason* was published in 1796, and he published one further major work in France. Similar in nature to *Rights of Man, Part the Second*, *Agrarian Justice* was a dissertation on equitable distribution of wealth and abolition of poverty, providing a scheme for effecting change.

Unlike his previous major compositions, the essay was addressed to the rulers, the Directory, on behalf of the masses. The language was not that of the common people, yet it rang with the certitude and powerful prose of the writings that had preceded it. On the basis of this essay, Paine has been credited by many as having been the first to propose measures of social security. The English edition was published in 1797, 'the little piece' having been 'written in the winter of 1795 and 96'.[52] Paine's work was clearly addressing the situation in France, which had experienced the heights and depths of revolution, but, in concluding, he foresaw his scheme as completing the revolution and spreading throughout 'civilization':

> It is a revolution in the state of civilization, that will give perfection to the revolution of France. Already, the conviction that government, by representation, is the true system of government, is spreading itself fast in the world. The reasonableness of it can be seen by all. The justness of it makes itself felt even by its opposers. But when a system of civilization, growing out of that system of government, shall be so organized, that not a man or woman born in the republic, but shall inherit some means of beginning the world, and see before them the certainty of escaping the miseries, that under other governments accompany old age, the revolution of France will have an advocate and an ally in the heart of all nations.
>
> An army of principles will penetrate where an army of soldiers cannot – it will succeed where diplomatic management would fail – It is neither the Rhine, the Channel, nor the Ocean, that can arrest its progress – It will march on the horizon of the world, and it will conquer.[53]

For Paine, revolution could begin the world anew. In *Common Sense* he had written:

> We have it in our power to begin the world over again. A situation, similar to the present, hath not happened since the days of Noah until now. The birthday of a new world is at hand, and a race of men, perhaps as numerous as all Europe contains, are to receive their portion of freedom from the events of a few months.[54]

These words applied to the American colonists, but in writing *Agrarian Justice*, his sights were set on distant horizons.

The Age of Reason had offended the sensibilities of many of Paine's former admirers on both sides of the Atlantic, but he added to his widely held public disgrace in the United States by lashing out in fury at George Washington. He never forgave the President for not claiming him as an American citizen and negotiating his release from imprisonment in France. In 1796, he wrote a vituperative attack on Washington, which he submitted for publication in the American pro-Republican press. Benjamin Franklin Bache, grandson of Benjamin Franklin and editor of the *Philadelphia Aurora*, published excerpts of the letter in the months prior to the election of John Adams as successor to Washington as President. The entire letter appeared as a pamphlet in February 1797 and incurred the wrath and hatred of the majority of Americans towards Paine, the once revered, anonymous author of *Common Sense*; they were unforgiving of his attack on Washington who was known as 'The Father of His Country'.

Having witnessed the frenzied years of revolution in France, delayed his return to America due to fear of capture at sea by British ships, and having survived the Terror, Paine returned to the United States in 1802, where he was now regarded as an infidel. His friends were few, but he continued with his political writings and social commentaries. He died at Greenwich Village, New York, on 8 June 1809, and was buried on his farm at New Rochelle the following day. In death, he was not to rest in peace. Ten years later the English political writer William Cobbett disinterred his remains and took them to England, where he planned a grand burial for the man he had come to admire through reading one of his writings. Lack of subscriptions to fund the event and the death of Cobbett led to the bones being held by a series of custodians[55] and subsequently to their loss, an incongruous ending to the story of a man who played a major part in two revolutions that shook the Western world. He would have wished for more.

Wherever there were subversive whisperings of changing the status quo, particularly where this involved matters of rights, during the known years of his life, Thomas Paine was on the scene. Once, at a time when he thought it possible, with a mix of solemnity and humour, he proposed a toast to 'the revolution of the world'; the pun would not have been lost on the company.[56]

UNKNOWN WRITINGS BY
THOMAS PAINE

18 DECEMBER 1778

Published 21 December 1778

The following letter, never printed within the Paine canon, was published by the New-York Historical Society towards the end of the nineteenth century.[57] The original appeared within days of a public address from Thomas Paine to Silas Deane, a Connecticut delegate to Congress, which was printed in the *Pennsylvania Packet or the General Advertiser* of 15 December 1778. It was in response to a piece published by Deane, who had been sent to France in March 1776 in an attempt to gain official recognition of the United States in the form of an alliance or aid in the war against Britain. France had already given unofficial aid, but, despite being received by the Comte de Vergennes, Minister of Foreign Affairs, Deane negotiated with American sympathizers, particularly Pierre-Augustin Caron de Beaumarchais. Together with Arthur Lee, agent of the Continental Congress, Beaumarchais had formed a spurious business, known as Roderique Hortalez and Company. The kings of both Spain and France had contributed considerable sums to the company to assist in providing supplies to America. Louis XVI of France did not wish to be seen by the British as being involved in such a matter so, for him, this arrangement was convenient. Congress believed the supplies to be a gift, but Beaumarchais was intent on making a profit and attempted to sell arms to America at enormous gain to himself.[58] Three shiploads of supplies were despatched, but two were captured by the British.

Late in 1777, a commercial agent arrived in Philadelphia and presented Congress with vouchers and bills of lading amounting to 4,500,000 livres from Hortalez and Company. He also presented a letter from Deane certifying the correctness of the account that should be paid to Beaumarchais. The bemused Congress, having assumed the aid to be gifts, recalled Deane, who arrived in Philadelphia in the summer of 1778. He carried testimonials of his fine services to America from Vergenne and Benjamin Franklin, who was then in France.[59] The two were closely connected, but Franklin feigned ignorance of the matter. There is no evidence suggesting he was involved, but he later returned to America with a considerable fortune.[60]

Congress became divided into factions – those who supported Deane and those who did not. The doubters demanded his accounts, but were astonished to learn that he had left them in France. Heard by Congress on 15, 17 and 21 August,[61] but dismissed and thereafter required to state his case in writing on several occasions without doing so, Deane published his case in the *Pennsylvania Packet* of 5 December 1778. He accused those members of Congress who did not support him of being disposed towards reconciliation with Britain. The president of Congress, Henry Laurens, finding it inconsistent with his own principles to remain in the House, resigned without notice on 9 December.[62] Paine, as secretary to the Committee for Foreign Affairs, knew from the correspondence of its members that the supplies which Deane and Beaumarchais avowed they had purchased 'were a present from the court of France, and came out of the king's arsenals'.[63] Paine, although incensed, wished to 'preserve the honor of Congress', so published a restrained reply to Deane on 15 December.[64] The following self-explanatory letter was last published in 1889 in a collection of the Silas Deane papers.[65]

Mr Dunlap[66]

In your paper of Thursday last is the following Note: 'Be pleased to inform the public that Common Sense will be answered by a person under the signature of Plain Truth on Saturday next. Plain Truth contends to prove that almost the whole of the elaborate Address to Mr Deane is a gross misrepresentation of facts.[67] Whether this proceeds from ignorance, or a worse cause, the public will hereafter determine.'

As Common Sense has the dates of Mr Deane's letters, and the dates of the resolutions of Congress, in his hands, and rests his proof on those dates and letters, and the resolutions they refer to, he, therefore, says, it is impossible to prove *him* wrong; and feeling that perfect tranquillity which arises from conscious integrity, he is wholly indifferent who or how many may reply, or what they may say. He has not, nor ever had, any interested connection with either Mr Deane or Mr Lee, nor ever corresponded with either of them; and whether Mr Deane is wrong, or Mr Lee wrong, or both wrong, is alike to him as to personal favor or interest. He *believes* the whole affair to be an inflammatory bubble, thrown among the public to answer both a mercantile end and a private pique. He is well acquainted with, and truly ashamed of, the illiberal combination that was formed a few nights ago, for purposes very dishonorable to themselves; and is more surprised, because one, who, he believes, was on that affair, ought to have acted a direct contrary part.[68]

Common Sense could have said a great deal more in his first address if he had thought proper, but as he expected to be replied to, and even abused, by those who had an immediate interest in the matter, or a revenge to gratify, he therefore reserved himself at that time, and the remainder, which will be his *last on this bubble of the day*, will appear in a succeeding paper; after which he shall employ himself on more important matters, if any thing can be more important than to prevent a public being misled and made tools of.

COMMON SENSE

Philadelphia, Dec. 18, 1778

The matter escalated beyond 'a bubble of the day'; Paine found himself heavily embroiled in what became known as the 'Silas Deane Affair'. A series of unrestrained letters to the public flowed from his pen, in which he informed the people of America of the inappropriate dealings and connivings of certain members of Congress.

PUBLISHED 24 DECEMBER 1778

As promised in his notice inserted in the *Pennsylvania Packet* of 17 December 1778,[69] 'Plain Truth' published a reply to Paine's public letter to Silas Deane on Saturday 21 December, the same day that Paine's letter dismissing the matter appeared. 'Plain Truth', who proved to be one Matthew Clarkson, recently resigned auditor of accounts in the army,[70] wrote on behalf and in defence of Silas Deane. He was unrestrained in his accusations against Paine and argued in support of Deane with a wit and venom that struck and incensed Paine. 'Plain Truth' ridiculed him for hiding behind his *nom-de-plume* of 'Common Sense', the only name by which Paine was known to the public, the name so highly regarded by the many who had been persuaded by his pamphlet of that name that it was in the best interests of the colonies to separate from Britain. Clarkson made it known that his own name had been 'left with the printer'. He wrote of his hopes that Paine would clear Deane's name, but it became clear to him that Paine had no such intention. 'Plain Truth' wrote effusively of Deane's merits and service to his country, and of it being the aim of 'Common Sense' to deceive the public. On 24 December 1778, Paine published his intentions.[71]

For the *Pennsylvania Packet*

The author whose signature is Common Sense, has not, on any occasion, held out falsehood in the place of truth; therefore the public will not hastily form an opinion to his prejudice, founded on the assertions or insinuations of the author who signs himself Plain Truth. The friends of Common Sense wish and expect he will lay the facts fairly, with his usual candor, before the public.

Paine became engaged in a newspaper war of words which was to cost him his job within days, the price he was to pay for publishing material 'inconsistent with his official character and duty'.[72]

PUBLISHED MAY 1779

When Thomas Paine published the following article, which appeared under the head 'Foreign Affairs', in *The United States Magazine: a Repository of History Politics and Literature* of May 1779,[73] it was just four months after his resignation from the position of secretary to the Committee for Foreign Affairs. However, as Congress was about to take steps towards his dismissal when his letter of resignation was received on 9 January 1779, he was deemed to have been dismissed on grounds of having informed the public of state secrets in his writings against Silas Deane.[74] Paine had gone beyond discretion in revealing his identity and offering to display evidence. In a letter to the public in the *Pennsylvania Packet* of 2 January 1779, he had written the following.

If Mr Deane or any other gentleman will procure an order from Congress to inspect an account in my office, or any of Mr Deane's friends in Congress will take the trouble of coming themselves, I will give him or them my attendance, and show them in a hand writing, which Mr Deane is well acquainted with, that the supplies he so pompously plumes himself upon were promised and engaged, and that, as a present, before he even arrived in France and the part that fell to Mr Deane was only to see it done ....'[75]

The article was read in Congress on 7 January.[76]

There was no stopping Paine in his attempts to prove Deane's guilt. In the following piece, he printed information gleaned from his knowledge of Congressional papers. This was an arrogant move on his part as, on 16 January, Congress had resolved 'that the Committee of Foreign Affairs be directed to take out of the possession of Thomas Paine, all the public papers entrusted to him as secretary to that committee, and then discharge him from that office'.[77] His quotation from the letter alluded to in this piece suggests that either he still had the letter or that he had made a copy of it, and probably others, related to the Deane Affair.

The war Paine mentions was that of the Bavarian Succession, a short-lived conflict (July 1778–May 1779) in which Frederick II of Prussia thwarted the efforts of Joseph II of Austria to take Bavaria. James Rivington, also mentioned, was a New York Loyalist who, throughout the Revolutionary War, took pride in being 'printer to the King's Most Excellent Majesty'. He edited several newspapers, including *Rivington's New-York Gazette*, a controversial paper that ran from 1777 to 1783. Despite his paper being regarded by patriots as frighteningly loyal to the British cause, it is known that he was a double-agent, who gathered intelligence for Washington's secret service.[78] His short-lived Philadelphia magazine, in which the following piece appeared, was edited by Hugh Breckenridge whom Rivington parodied.[79] The two were politically opposed and the following, introduced to the Paine canon for the first time, is a reply to an article in the *Gazette*.

The peace lately concluded between the Emperor of Germany and the King of Prussia is, in its present state, a field for political speculation.[80] The New-York papers, from which the account of the peace is taken, have endeavoured to represent it as a circumstance favourable to Britain, but until Mr Rivington can furnish his readers with some sufficient grounds for such a conjecture, his simple opinion of the matter will signify but little.[81] Those who please may believe Mr Rivington; but as the case at present stands, it admits of an opinion directly contrary to that which he has endeavoured to circulate.

In order to form some judgment concerning the consequences of the peace, it is necessary, in the first place, to go back to the state of things before the war broke out between those two powers. Secondly, what were the hopes and expectations of Britain respecting that war. And thirdly, by what means the peace was accomplished.

The good disposition of both those powers towards America so late as March 1778, is, or ought to be, very well known here, and as their difference arose, about a month afterwards, on a measure no ways connected with America, there is no reason yet to suppose that any new grounds have been since produced to change either their disposition or line of politics with respect to us. Mention was made in our papers last summer, that Prussia would be the second power in Europe to acknowledge our independence; the information was founded on no less authority than that of a state officer of the first rank of the Prussian court, and transmitted here by one of our commissioners, but the rupture happening almost immediately after, naturally occasioned at that court a cessation of all other politics.[82] The disposition of the Emperor of Germany at that time towards America may be easily collected from his connections with the court of France. Therefore, nothing that happened prior to the rupture has any thing in it favourable towards Britain.

The rupture broke suddenly out a few days after the treaty between France and America was signed,[83] and the apprehensions which the several powers on the continent of Europe were under, as to the probable extent and consequences of the quarrel, seem in a great measure to have restricted their operations respecting America, by calling their attention more immediately to themselves. And it appears to have been the hope and expectation of Britain, that the contest between the Emperor and King of Prussia would, in the end, involve France, and probably Spain. For a confirmation of this opinion, I shall give an extract of a letter from a gentleman of high character in France, dated Feb. 28, 1778.

'I am sorry to inform you there is now an appearance of an approaching rupture between the Emperor and the King of Prussia, relative to the possessions of the late Emperor of Bavaria's estates. Great Britain, you may be sure, will endeavour to instigate the King of Prussia to go on, because if war ensues, France will most probably be drawn in to take a part; but I still hope that peace will be maintained by negotiation'.[84]

It has happened according to the writer's wish. Peace has taken place between the Emperor and the King of Prussia, and that through the mediation of *France* and *Russia*. It does not appear, even by the New York account, that the court of London had anything to do in compromising the dispute, and as it is easy to see that her hope was in the continuance and probable consequences of the quarrel, it is natural to conclude that she must feel herself disappointed by the peace. That the peace is an agreeable event to France is deduced with certainty from the part which she took in promoting it; and as it relieves her from the apprehensions of a war on the continent of Europe, it leaves her at liberty to prosecute the object of the alliance.

COMMON SENSE

27 AND 28 JULY 1779

Published 29 July 1779

Continuing to expose Silas Deane in the papers, Paine's patriotism was called into question by the pro-Deane faction in Congress and anonymous writers of public letters. He was attacked, harangued and accused of blocking French aid as, contrary to his oath of secrecy, he disclosed the contents of Congressional papers to inculpate Deane. He was intent on proving his own honour. Many years later, in 1835, Congress paid $38,000 to the heirs of Deane; his own statement of his case, found among his papers, and Franklin's assertion of his integrity, had convinced Congress that Deane had been wronged. By the mid-nineteenth century, when all parties concerned were dead, letters from George III to his Prime Minister, Lord North, revealed that Deane was in British employ.[85] One letter stated: 'I think it perfectly right that Mr Deane should so far be trusted as to have three thousand pounds in goods for America'.[86] Paine, it seems, was right in suspecting not only Deane's motives but also his patriotism. The mystery and complicated intrigues of the affair have not yet been satisfactorily unravelled and are usually lightly skirted around by Paine commentators.

These items, a note to John Dunlap and a letter to Silas Deane, John Nixon and James Wilson, are the last here offered on the Deane Affair and its consequences.[87] By their nature, reproduction of the small article containing them, which was printed in the *Pennsylvania Packet* of 29 July and a follow-up letter that has been previously published, is necessary in order that the new material be seen in context.[88] At this stage, the affair had blown out to proportions, which, beyond splitting the government, also divided public opinion. Deane was claiming justice and Paine continued to protest his credibility.

An introduction to the cast of characters is required: Charles Willson Peale was an American artist who had studied in Britain, and is best remembered for his portraits of significant leaders of the American Revolution. In 1778, Henry Laurens commissioned him to paint a portrait of Paine, with whom Peale enjoyed a life-long friendship. Unfortunately, after Peale's death, his little-known likeness of his friend was sold, along with others in the collection of 'American Heroes', to the Boston Museum by his son Rembrandt Peale. The portrait of Paine was rejected on religious grounds, and sold to a private buyer on whose death it was sold to Joseph Jefferson, an eminent nineteenth-century actor. The painting was destroyed when his house burned to the ground.[89] Fortunately, a copy of it had been made, reproductions of which have appeared in some few works on Paine.[90] Peale served in the Philadelphia militia, and fought at the Battle of Princeton where the patriots outmanoeuvred the British. From 1779 to 1780, he represented the Whigs in the Pennsylvania Assembly.

John Nixon was a leading army officer throughout the years of the American Revolution. Following the signing of the Declaration of Independence on 8 July 1776, he read it aloud to the crowds gathered in the yard of the State House, now known as Independence Hall, at Philadelphia. He and James Wilson were strong supporters of Silas Deane. Wilson was a lawyer and one of the signers of the Declaration of Independence. In the politically turbulent year of 1779, he was appointed advocate general for France, which meant that he represented France in matters arising from the French alliance with the American states.

Mr Dunlap,
Please to publish the following letter of Mr Deane to Capt. Peale, which was left with him by Silas Deane, John Nixon, and James Wilson, Esquires, together with my answer to their demand.

THOMAS PAINE

Mr Peale
Philadelphia, July 27, 1779

Sir,
You declared yesterday to the citizens met at the Coffee-house, that a bribe, or salary, had been offered Mr Thomas Paine, to engage him not to write or publish anything respecting me or my affairs. As such an assertion must tend to prejudice my character and conduct with my countrymen and fellow citizens, I now call on you for the name of the person or persons who made this offer to Mr Paine. Justice to the public, as well as to my own character, requires that their names should be known and authorizes me to make this demand of you.

I am, Sir,
Your most obedient humble servant,
SILAS DEANE

Market Street, July 28th, 1779

Gentlemen,

Capt. Peale having this morning shown me the above letter, and named the gentlemen who accompanied Mr Deane, and as the matter relates particularly to me, I have to reply, that as I was not present at the Coffee house at the time to which Mr Deane refers, I cannot be a judge of what particular conversation passed; but if anything there spoken referred to an offer made to me last winter, which, for sundry reasons, I thought it my duty to decline, I shall in justice to Capt. Peale as a friend, as well as for the satisfaction of the public, publish in next Saturday's paper the whole transactions respecting the offer in question.

I would likewise observe, that I was coming down Market Street, at the time Mr Deane, Mr Nixon and Mr Wilson were standing at Capt. Peale's door, and as some of them saw me, they might have had the satisfaction from me, which they required, had they waited till I came up which was within a few minutes of their going away.

I am, Gentlemen, your obedient humble servant,
THOMAS PAINE[91]

Silas Deane
John Nixon   } Esquires
James Wilson

Philadelphia, July 28th, 1779

Mr Deane

Sir,

Mr Paine had been grossly abused in a public paper by an anonymous author whose name had been concealed, and believing Mr Paine to be a firm friend to America, and my personal acquaintance with him gives me an opportunity of knowing that he had done more for our common cause than the world, who had only seen his publications, could know, I thought it my duty to support him, and gave to the public the intimation which you mention in your letter.

That letter I have put into the hands of Mr Paine and he will publish the whole of the transaction by which means you as well as the public will obtain in due time the fullest information. I am Sir, your most humble servant,

CHARLES WILLSON PEALE

To Silas Deane, Esq.

In the event, the piece that Paine sent for the Saturday paper did not adequately answer Deane's demand. It was printed by Philip S. Foner, but is inserted here to assist the reader.[92]

Mr Dunlap. Please to insert the following.

T.P.

Silas Deane, John Nixon, and James Wilson, Esquires, having called on Capt. Peale, and left with him a letter signed Silas Deane, dated the 27th instant, respecting intimations used by him, Capt. Peale, at the Coffee-house on the morning of the 26th instant, relative to some pecuniary offers made to me, and Capt. Peale having shewn me that letter, which together with my and his answer thereto, were published in the *Pennsylvania Packet* of Thursday last, in which answer of mine I engaged to give the information required in this day's paper.

On examining Mr Deane's letter, a second time I see the request is for the *name* or *names* only, and not for circumstances of the affair in question. To give the one without the other, might be made an ill use of, and to give both in the present situation of things, without first referring the matter to Congress, might, as far as I am able to foresee, produce considerable inconvenience.

So far as respects the three gentlemen in question I shall give such answers as ought to suffice them, and that part which may be supposed to belong more generally to the public, I entreat them to leave to my discretion. Had there been no peculiar nicety in this affair, I undoubtedly should for my own sake have published it before now, because in any light in which it may be viewed, it will add to my reputation.

Therefore, it is sufficient on my part that I declined the offer; and it is sufficient to Mr Nixon and Mr Wilson that they were not the persons who made it, or, I believe knew anything about; and on the part of Mr Deane, it is somewhat extraordinary that he should stir about *this only* who has taken every thing else so quietly. It is likewise more extraordinary that he should stir at *this* particular time, because I cannot suppose he is ignorant of a letter of mine to Congress dated so long ago as the 23d of April where I mentioned the same affair to which, I presume, Capt. Peale alluded; and I give my consent that Mr Thomson should shew Mr Deane that letter, upon condition that he does not commence a quarrel with Mr Carmichael for dubbing him at Nantz [Nantes] with the title of a ——.[93]

After informing Congress that an offer had been made to me, I added 'that however polite the proposal might be, or however friendly it might be designed, I thought it my duty to decline it, as it was accompanied with a condition which had a tendency to prevent the information I had since given and should still give on public affairs'.

The offer was made both before and after I made my resignation on the 8th of January. It was first put in general terms, afterwards in particular ones, was pressed on me with a great deal of anxiety, and amounted to more than twice my salary in Congress.

I cannot possess myself of the mind of the gentleman who proposed it, so as to declare what every intention of his might be, but I well know that the acceptance of it would at that time as effectually have prevented the publication I gave in Mr Dunlap's paper of the 16th of February, respecting the supplies and the loss of the dispatches, as if my silence had been made the express condition of my acceptance.[94]

Having said thus much, I think it a prudent step in me to refer the affair first to Congress. If they please to call on me for particulars, I will furnish them, and I am persuaded the honest and well-wishing part of the public rest satisfied with this, as there are matters connected with it which might, either by mistake or design, be made a very ill use of.

There is not a man in the Thirteen States, so far as his powers and abilities extend, that will go further or do more in supporting the cause of America than myself, or of any country connected with her. This, every one knows, who has any intimate acquaintance with me; and according to my opinion of things and principles; a man needs no pecuniary inducement to do that, to which the twofold powers of duty and disposition naturally lead him on.

Having thus far satisfied Mr Nixon and Mr Wilson, I take the liberty of asking Mr Wilson, if he is or was not directly or indirectly a partner in the Foreign Commercial Company, in which Mr Deane with several Members of Congress at that time, and others were concerned.

And exclusive of all other questions to Mr Deane, I desire him to inform the public, for what purpose it was that he remitted over to Mr Samuel

Wharton, of London, 19,520 livres, eleven days after the Treaty of Alliance was signed.[95] I presume he will not undertake to contradict the fact, if he does, I can prove it.

THOMAS PAINE

P.S. As to Whitehead Humphreys, I give him my full and free consent to publish whatever and whenever he pleases, and under any signature he likes best, promising, on my part, to make no reply thereto, if he, Whitehead Humphreys, will, to each of his future pieces, add at the bottom the following words, viz.

'This is published by the same person who inserted several libellous productions under the signature of "Cato," in Benjamin Towne's Evening Post, of July, 1779, which were so infamously false that the author or carrier of them, in order to avoid the shame and scandal of being known, tied the Printer down to such strong obligations to conceal him, that "nothing but a halter could extort it from him".'

Philadelphia, July 30, 1779.[96]

Having divulged much over the previous months, Paine became coy about providing the information he had promised to publish without consulting Congress. He thought it sufficient on his part to let the public know that he had declined the offer because, several months earlier, he had written to Congress informing members that an offer had been made to him. His reason for declining was that, had he accepted, he would not have been able to present to the public the information on state affairs that he had done or still wished to do. Paine had indeed written to Congress on 23 April enclosing a copy of the letter containing the offer. Apparently, he had no reply as he publicly called upon Congress to approach him in order that he might furnish them with particulars. As far as Paine was concerned, Congress had no wish to engage with him in what had become a sizzling, public newspaper war of accusatory words.[97]

As it transpired, Peale was not aware that the offer in question had been made by Conrad Alexandre Gérard, the French ambassador to America. Paine had not mentioned the name of the person who made the offer, and Peale jumped to the conclusion that it was Silas Deane. The already complicated matter became even more so.[98]

23 NOVEMBER 1779

The following letter, never published, was discovered as a copy at the King's House, Thetford, Norfolk, in 1996.[99] Colonel Peabody, a member of Congress, to whom the letter was addressed, was a delegate from New Hampshire.[100] With the radicals in power in the Pennsylvania government, in November 1779, Paine had been appointed its clerk. From that position, with a seeming sense of self-importance, he effected an introduction on behalf of a stranger. According to Congressional records, the name of the subject of the letter was Baron de Miklasewicz.[101] On 22 December 1779, a memorial from him was read to Congress, where it was ordered that Paine's letter be referred to the Board of Admiralty.[102] Peabody had accepted Paine's reference and Miklasewicz had taken his advice to delay.

Philadelphia Nov. 23d, 1779

Dear Sir,
The bearer of this is the Baron de Mehlazaiel whom I spoke to you of at the State House. He is a stranger with all the appearance of a gentleman, and has honorable credentials with him, and your favorable notice of him will I hope be recompenced on his part by an attention to deserve it. He has some thoughts of applying to Congress for a captaincy of marines, but I have advised him to delay it for a few days till he shall have an opportunity of making himself known to some of the Members, and your advice to him on that subject will be a favor done to

Your obedient humble servant
Thomas Paine

Honorable Colonel Peabody
Member of Congress
Chestnut & Front Sts.
[Philadelphia]

It seems possible that an autographed mezzotint of a portrait of Paine accompanied the letter to Colonel Peabody, when it was handed to the bearer. Whether the picture passed to the addressee or remained with the subject of the letter is not clear because the original letter is held at the Library of Congress, but there is no enclosure with it. As mentioned, a photocopy of the letter is held in the collection of Paine memorabilia at the King's House, Thetford, and a photograph of the probable mezzotint was discovered at the Norfolk Record Office in nearby Norwich. It is in the form of an illustration cut from an unknown magazine and pasted in an exercise book.[103] It seems likely that either the mezzotint, if that is what it was, was given to the subject of the letter at the time of Paine's writing a reference for him, or that Paine enclosed it with the letter to the addressee from which it became separated; both bear the same date, 23 November 1779. This was within a year of Paine revealing his identity, and the Deane Affair was still very much in the public consciousness. Paine was then a man of note who took great pride in his work, and his autograph would have been sought by admirers. If the likeness is of an American portrait of the 1770s, it does not appear to have been reproduced since.

It is not inconceivable that when Paine travelled from America to Europe in 1787, he took with him two works of art: a model of the bridge he had designed, which he wished to have erected in Europe and America,[104] and a splendid portrait of himself. Such a painting might well have been what the French artist Laurent Dabos based his portrait of Paine on, which emerged from the obscurity of private ownership in 2006.[105] If the Norwich photograph was of a dated mezzotint, there is no possibility of the two paintings being by the same artist, yet, at first glance, the image appears to be of Dabos's portrait, painted in about 1792–93 when Paine was a member of the National Convention.[106] The face seems to be of an older man. If the item found at Norwich was a print, there are no records or copies of it at the Library of Congress or the National Portrait Gallery, Washington, DC, the National Portrait Gallery, London, or the Louvre, Paris. It is, of course, possible that a photograph of both the portrait and the autograph were combined to form a single image, rather than it being, as it appears, a late eighteenth-century American proof before inscription signed by Paine himself.

Interestingly, details of the picture differ: in what may have been the earlier work, the face appears full; the eyes larger; the full-lipped mouth smiles gently and less proudly; the fingers are spread more widely; the hairline is low, the hair thick; and the cravat is tied differently. The most noticeable differences are in the chair: the carving and gilding of the rococo design is more apparent, and the upholstery fabric is patterned. Unlike the chair in Dabos's painting, its arm rests elegantly on the wooden base of the chair, rather than on the seat, which gives it an awkward, poorly crafted appearance. Further small disparities are evident.

Dabos was a fine copyist of his own work; another of his paintings, a bust portrait of Thomas Paine, also privately owned, was unknown until it was purchased by the National Portrait Gallery, Washington in 2008. It is almost a precise copy of the head and shoulders of the painting in London so it is probable that they were both painted from the same sketch.

Differences in details of the two images in question do not necessarily mean that the possible mezzotint is not of Dabos's painting; allowance must be made for artistic licence, but, if the photograph at Norwich is of a painting of an earlier date, it is possible that the painting was executed by Charles Willson Peale. It is known that he painted two portraits of Paine, the fate of which only one, already mentioned, is known; the whereabouts of the other, if it still exists, is a mystery. Moncure Daniel Conway wrote of there having been an early engraving from one of Peale's pictures, because John Hall, an acquaintance of Paine, told of a print of 'Common Sense' being available in 1786, but that it bore the name Tom, not Thomas. Conway asked: 'Can there be a portrait lost under some other name?'[107] He later wrote of a French engraving of a portrait which was a variant of one of the two by Peale, then hanging in Independence Hall.[108] A print of that engraving was exhibited at the Thomas Paine Exhibition held in London in 1895.[109] Conway's writing on the portraits is somewhat confused, but, by the French description, he was obviously referring to an engraving of the Dabos portrait. At this stage, there is wide scope for further research on portraits of Paine, both those accounted for and those believed to be lost.

PUBLISHED 28 JUNE 1780

As the war with Britain raged and worsened, Thomas Paine, as clerk, read to the Pennsylvania Assembly a letter addressed to its president, Joseph Reed. It was from George Washington who was then leading a demoralized, hope-bereft army against superior British forces on the battlefront at Morristown, New Jersey. That letter, dated 28 May 1780, has been termed 'the gloomiest letter George Washington ever wrote'[110] and followed close on the heels of the surrender of Charleston, South Carolina, on 12 May. Washington wrote of the deprivations suffered by his men, who were desperately short of supplies and showing 'the most serious features of mutiny and sedition'.[111] The chamber filled with despair.

There was little in the Treasury, but sufficient for Paine to draw immediately upon his salary. He took matters into his own hands and wrote to a wealthy merchant and moderate radical, Blair McClenaghan, declaring his wish for 'the merchants and traders of Philadelphia to set an honorable example, and enter into a subscription to raise three four or five hundred men'. He enclosed $500 as his own contribution, promising, if that was not sufficient, he would double the amount.[112]

McClenaghan rallied to the cause and, following a meeting of Philadelphia merchants he had called at the coffee house, managed to raise a subscription which brought an amount of £400 'hard money'; a further £101,360 'continental' was promised within a day.[113] A second meeting was held at the City Tavern on 17 June, where it was resolved 'to open a security-subscription, to the amount of £300,000, Pennsylvania currency, in real money; the subscribers to execute bonds to the amount of their subscriptions, and to form a bank thereon for supplying the army'.[114] A list of subscribers was published in the *Pennsylvania Gazette* of 5 July; Paine's name was not included.[115] From these beginnings, the Bank of North America gradually evolved.

There was criticism from a few radicals who thought the planned bank was a ploy to embarrass the Pennsylvania government. In the following article, not printed since original publication in the *Pennsylvania Gazette* of 28 June, 'Common Sense' points out the advantages of the bank to both government and citizens.[116]

For the *Pennsylvania Gazette*

There never was a public spirited measure yet entered into at any time or place that did not excite the envy of little minds, and the opposition of the ignorant. Some find fault as an excuse for their own want of merit and spirit. They, forsooth, do not like such a measure because they have not hearts to promote it.

I could not help being led to these reflections on hearing that two or three persons (whose contrivances will never set the river on fire) were making their remarks on the proposal of the merchants and others of this city, for raising a Bank to the amount of Three Hundred Thousand Pounds hard money, for the immediate purpose of supplying the army.[117] It is done, say they, to lessen the dignity of government. But I wish to ask such persons what they suppose the dignity of government consists in, and what sort of a figure the dignity of government in England or any other country would cut in time of war if left unassisted by the aid of individuals or collective bodies of them? Is not the Bank of England an aid to government? Does not it lend its credit to government; and is it not the same with every established Company in that country? Are not the voluntary subscriptions of the city of London and other places, to give additional bounties to seamen and recruits, and aids to government? Have not whole regiments been raised even by individuals as aids to government? Is the revenue of any country in Europe equal to the immediate expences of war, without being aided by the extra credit of public spirited men? And do not all these aids by tending to the support, tend likewise to the dignity of government. For what constitutes the dignity of government but the attachment of the country to its measures, and a cheerful determination to exert every endeavour to carry them into effect? In short, all voluntary aids are so many honors to government. They are honors likewise to those who do them; and at this particular time when the treasuries are drained by demands on one hand, and weakened by the depreciation on the other, and require a respite from expence, that the monies collecting in may accumulate. Such voluntary aids are of the utmost service, and truly deserving the highest applause.

C. S.

13 MARCH 1782

In December 1780, Congress agreed that Colonel John Laurens, son of the former president of Congress, Henry Laurens, be elected minister for the special purpose of seeking aid from Louis XVI of France. Paine accompanied him ostensibly as secretary, but, having paid his own expenses, returned in August 1781 desperately in need of an income. He found himself 'worse off than ever'.[118] On 30 November, he wrote a confidential letter to George Washington, then in Philadelphia, expressing a wish to meet with him. He told of his hopeless plight and of the lack of appreciation by the United States to one who had given his all to its cause in his writings, even forgoing all profits usually taken by authors.[119]

Washington 'became affectionately interested' in Paine's distress and 'concerted with a friend or two'.[120] One of those friends was Robert Morris, a signatory of the Declaration of Independence and member of the Pennsylvania legislature. He had been of the pro-Deane faction during the Silas Deane Affair and was later to become known as the financier of the American Revolution; he founded the Bank of North America. The other friend was the newly appointed Secretary for Foreign Affairs, Robert Livingston. The three agreed to pay Paine an annual sum of $800 in return for writings that were to serve the interest of the country. He was to be paid from the secret service funds furnished by Morris who, with Livingston and Washington, drew up and signed an agreement.

> The Subscribers, taking into consideration the important Situation of Affairs at the present Moment, and the Propriety and even necessity of informing the People and rousing them into Action; considering also the Abilities of Mr Thomas Paine as a Writer, and that he has been of considerable Utility to the common Cause by several of his Publications: They have agreed that it will be much for the Interest of the United States that Mr. Paine be engaged in their Service for the purposes abovementioned...[121]

The agreement was formally entered into on 10 February 1782, but news of Paine's engagement was never released because it was thought that the publications might lose their persuasive force if it became known that the writer was paid for them by the government. Paine's brief was 'to prepare the minds of the people for such restraints ... as are absolutely necessary for their own welfare', and to comment favourably on military transactions, civil officers or citizens who served their country well.[122]

In an undated letter, probably written on 18 February 1782, Paine told Robert Morris of his plan 'to get out a piece tomorrow on the King of England's speech' and of how he had contacted all the printers to secure places in the Wednesday papers of the following week. He also advised that he would consult with Morris and his unrelated assistant, Gouverneur Morris.[123] The manuscript of that letter was missing from the Morris papers, but was located during research for this work.[124]

Paine worked diligently. The two instalments of his article 'On the King of England's Speech' were published within days. The article was a response to George III's speech at the Opening of Parliament on 27 November 1781, when he assured his subjects that he was determined to continue with the war.[125] That piece was the first of several Paine was to write to the satisfaction of his employers.

One week after publication of Paine's *Crisis Number X*, which was written according to his secret agreement, he wrote the following brief letter to Robert Morris.[126]

March 13th 1782

Sir

I enclose you the receipt signed agreeable to proposal. If you can conveniently find a leisure half hour either this evening or any time tomorrow, I should be glad to consult with you on a matter, purely public, before General Washington goes out of Town.

Tomorrow will suit me better than today if it is equally as convenient to yourself.[127]

I am Sir
Your Obedient Humble Servant
Thomas Paine[128]

It would appear that Paine was looking forward to a further payment. The receipt he enclosed with the note to Morris has not been located.[129] As Paine was to be paid by the Secretary of Foreign Affairs 'out of Monies to be allowed by the Superintendant [sic] of Finance for Secret Services',[130] it is highly likely that the receipt was destroyed; both parties were satisfied with the deal done, which was to be kept secret, not only from the public of the time, but from posterity. The reason for the letter of 13 March not being held with the Morris papers, but in the Emmet Collection at the New York Historical Society, is probably that Thomas Addis Emmet was one of Paine's executors on his death; it is possible that the letter sent to Morris was returned to Paine. A further original manuscript, perhaps Paine's own copy, passed into the possession of Walter Morton, another of his executors.[131] Morris carefully preserved all his own papers, but the secrecy of the arrangement might have seen the return of Paine's correspondence on the matter to himself. He was not careful in preserving his records; he left very few personal papers, many of which were said by Moncure Daniel Conway to have been burnt in a St Louis fire.[132] However, searches by the Missouri Historical Society for information on the fire, both in their own and the fire department records, produced nothing, despite their holding vast records on the property where the fire is said to have taken place, the home of General Benjamin Bonneville, son of Paine's Parisian friends, Nicolas Bonneville and his wife Marguerite.[133] It is probable that any destructive fire was deliberate – an attempt to destroy evidence of Paine's secret dealings.

13 MAY 1783

On 25 March 1783, Paine called on Robert Morris offering congratulations on the recently proclaimed peace and about 'some Business'.[134] The first news of a general peace was delivered to the United States on 23 March by the commander of a French cutter. It was in the form of an abstract of preliminary articles signed in Paris on 20 January. On 11 April, cessation of hostilities was proclaimed, and, on the eighth anniversary of the Battle of Lexington, 19 April 1783, Paine published his final *Crisis* letter. Tense only changed, it began with the same ringing phrase that introduced the first: 'The times that tried men's souls' are over. Paine's secret agreement to write 'for the Interest of the United States'[135] might have come to an end, but it seems obvious that, for a short while, he continued writings, as agreed. He was distressed for want of money, and so was the young nation. The following letter, which has appeared only in *The Papers of Robert Morris,* was written from Philadelphia.[136]

Second Street May 13, 1783

Sir

You Mentioned the last time I saw you that you never was more distressed to raise Money than now. I have thrown together a few thoughts which occurred to me this Morning, perhaps they may be of some use – as in difficulties every thing may be worth a thought. As I go out of town tomorrow morning I shall take an opportunity of calling on you about twelve or one.

I am Sir
Your Obedient Humble Servant
Thomas Paine

Morris noted in his diary of that day that Paine had called 'with a Plan for raising Money'. The plan might have been transmitted verbally as nothing in writing to that effect has been found.[137]

19 MAY 1783

Some few sentences from the following letter were quoted by John Keane in his biography, *Tom Paine: A Political Life*.[138] Printed nowhere within collections of Paine's works, like the previous item, it also appeared in *The Papers of Robert Morris*.[139]

Unemployed, desperate for money and embarrassed to admit the fact, just six days after writing the 13 May letter to Morris, Paine sat down and wrote the following to a person unknown. It has been noted that mention of 'repossession' of 'your city' indicates that the letter was probably written to someone in New York, most likely Robert Livingston, who resigned from his position of Secretary of Foreign Affairs in June 1783.[140] Unaddressed, but endorsed by Morris, it was probably intended to come into his hands; it remains with his papers.[141] However, Paine's evident reluctance to disclose his circumstances to one where they might not have been understood, or heeded, suggests that the letter was intended for one who had no understanding or knowledge of the arrangement under which he had worked until the close of the war. The unaddressed letter, the same as an earlier letter from Paine to Washington,[142] was probably not written to Livingston, but, more likely, to a member of the then Continental Congress, perhaps James Duane.[143] Paine wrote as one who sought reward, probably on advice given by Morris when they met a few days earlier.[144] He wrote strongly and went so far as to threaten letting the world know that his efforts in gaining independence for the former colonies had not been recognized. He claimed the outcome of the war to have lain solely in his writing of that famous and persuasive pamphlet *Common Sense*.

Borden Town May 19th 1783

Sir

There are two reasons for my troubling you with this letter, the one is, because I find my mind exceedingly distressed, and the other, because I do not like to disclose it where, perhaps, it may neither be understood nor attended to;[145] besides which, I have never entered into conversation on the subject with any gentleman (except General Washington) so much as with yourself on a late occasion, some short time ago.[146]

While the war lasted and the issue was in doubt, all my anxieties were called away from myself, and tho' they would now and then make a private prey of me for a while, yet on any appearance of public difficulty or danger wherein I could see a way to be useful, they lost their hold and I felt no more of them, and so far from being discontented I have often been secretly pleased at the opportunities of sharing in the difficulties of the country.

But as the war is now over and happily closed the case is altered. The cessation of public objects has left leisure for private thinking, and I cannot help being sometimes seriously affected at the thoughts and prospect of my own situation. I look round and see a large and thriving world towards whose freedom and prosperity I have freely and honorably contributed, and yet I see no prospect for myself to live in it. The country that ought to have been to me a home, has scarcely been an Asylum. I sometimes ask myself, what am I better off than a refugee, and that of the most extraordinary kind, a refugee from the country I have befriended, to that which can owe me no goodwill. If this be not a precedent that must hereafter serve to kill all kind of public spirit in individuals, and to blemish the character of a country, then am I totally at a loss to understand mankind. I question whether there is a parallel instance to be produced in the world, of an individual, circumstanced as I have been, acting for years together, towards a country as I have done, and that country acting in return, as America has done by me. Neither am I so much affected at the personal inconveniencies it lays me under, as I am at the reproach she is exposing herself to; for the fact unfortunately rests on a person whose word will reach a great way and be believed.

I am fully persuaded that the Congress in 75 and 76, not only would not have ventured on, but were opposed to the idea of independence until they were called upon, and forced into it, by the voice of the country, and the country too were at that time, much in the same state. And the only act of public justice that I have met with is a general and candid acknowledgment that they formed their sentiment of independence on the publication of *Common Sense.* I did not reflect upon it at the time, but I can now see that I put myself in a very dangerous situation by that work, for had the measure failed I know not where my home could have been, and tho' it has succeeded I am not much better off.

The part I have acted was as necessary towards the revolution as any military operations in the field, because there was a necessity of changing the whole mind of the country before any active operations could be effectual, and this, tho' one of the principal links in the chain, and apparently as difficult as any, is the only one that has not only cost nothing, but to give it every possible chance, I relinquished all the profits.

That I have a popular interest throughout the states I cannot be insensible of yet I conceal my situation from the public for many reasons – I cannot tell it to them without telling it to all the world and the thing is too disgraceful to be told. Were the country in a state of want, and every civil deportment performed gratis, I could contentedly share that want, and act that part with them, and even rejoice in it; tho' in this case they would be better off than I should be, because they would serve by rotation and I should not so easily find others to take up my part. But the reverse of all this is the case, the country is rich, and her prosperity increasing, and under such circumstances patience is no longer a merit.

I might probably do very well in Holland, were it only by taking to myself the profits which the London booksellers are making out of the publications which in this country I am giving away or making nothing of, for I have no doubt but they have made more out of my letter to the Abbe Raynal, than my expences for seven years have amounted to.[147]

I might likewise do very well in the Emperor's Dominion as he is a man of a popular taste, and seems disposed to make people happy.[148] But here another difficulty arises, what account am I to give of myself or of America, for continuing with her through all her distresses and leaving her in her prosperity?

There is but one final resolution I have formed, which is that of not acting a little part, and I am certain that, in what ever country I may be cast, you will not hear anything mean of me. But I have a much better ground for this than a resolution, because it is not my nature to do otherwise, or I should have done it long ago.

I have obtained the rank of being reckoned among the founders of a new empire, yet if America has any idea of considering me as one of her citizens, she cannot think of retaining me by the conduct she pursues, because it amounts to banishment. And except the reputation I have gained, I am much worse off than when I first came, because then I had a home and now I have none. I am neither block nor marble and cannot enter on those reflections without suffering deeply from them. That same cast of mind that made me feel for others now makes me feel for myself.

After the business for which I accompanied Col. Laurens to France upon was settled, I told him, that as my situation in America had been so exceedingly distressing to me, I could have no thoughts of returning to it, and most earnestly requested him not to think of my going back with him. I repeated it over and over to him, with a positive assurance that I would never mention it, and that if any opportunity offered in Europe in which I might promote the cause of America I would freely do it. His entreaties to me to return with him were pressing and passionate.[149] He spoke to Doctor Franklin to advise me to go back, and he sent a nephew of the Doctor's, Mr Williams, to me, on the same account but in fuller terms, tho' the reasons for my unwillingness was concealed from both of them.[150] He felt, as he expressed it, ashamed of his country that I should have such reasons, and assured me that if they were not removed he would out of his own fortune remove them himself, which is what he meant in his last letter to me subsequent to that which you have, wherein he offered to participate equally with me in every thing which he possessed. But as I could not think of being a burthen upon him, and had too much experience of America, my intentions were not changed by the proposal, and I wrote a letter to Mr Izard which Col. Laurens was to have brought, stating my reasons for not returning. When Col. Laurens saw this letter he was more pressing than before. (The letter is now in Mr Izard's hands.)[151] I agreed however to accompany him to Brest, and see him on board, but when we came there, as he had no body else with him, and as it was not proper in case of accidents that he should be alone, I gave up to his request and getting again in the scene thought no more of it.[152] I am now in the same state of uncertainty as then, and see no end to it. I am sure that over and above a common share of difficulties I have had my mind most severely tryed – for what can try a man more than the ingratitude of those who from every motive of honor ought to be his friends, except, (which is my case) the necessity of concealing it. But the best disposition must in time wear out.

Yet amongst all those reflections I am still at a loss to understand the cause of what I complain. Every body I meet treats me with respect and assures me of their friendship. I am loaded with a profusion of thanks, and as modestly as I can I thank them again and here the matter ends. Almost every one joins in censuring each other, and frequently the whole reflection is thrown upon Congress. All this I every day hear and as soon as I can put a stop to the conversation.

I cannot blame the public, because they are not acquainted with the circumstances, neither have they, as a body, any means of knowing it but from me. I cannot on the other hand blame Congress because there is a nicety in the matter, and because they have not much in their power; but I cannot avoid blaming them for that thoughtlessness which they have shewn towards me. There has been an apparent want of disposition as well as means. A sort of desire to let the matter slip over. It is a deal I have put up with in point of temper, as well as in point of circumstances.

But I now wish to bring the matter to a clear issue. I am truly weary of my situation. It is to me like a dungeon without prospects. My hopes have nothing to rest on, and I feel myself left in a condition as dishonorable to the country as it is distressing to me.

In considering my own situation I take into the account every thing which is combined or connected with it. As the country is young and the governments still younger, there are many things yet to be done, and as the signature I use is that under which the sentiment of the country has been formed, and is the only one universally known I am careful in preserving its usefulness, and therefore I am no ways desirous of any dependence upon Congress for tho' something is due to me as a debt by all the laws of honor, gratitude, and service, yet I would not sacrifice my popularity, or deprive myself of the pleasure of being useful for the sake of obtaining it. Besides, every farthing that Congress can raise will be wanted for the army, and there would appear something of an awkwardness in my promoting the payment of taxes were I to receive any part of them for my own service tho' as I before mentioned it would be due to me by all those laws.

I think the more eligible way would be to do it by subscription. In the line in which I have served I stand a separate man, and there are certainly men of fortune and property enough in America, to make my situation what it ought to be, without throwing me either on Congress or on the public. I ought not to suppose others less honorable or less generous than myself and I am sure I have given away freely. Besides as mine has been a literary service there is a propriety in putting it in this line. Several persons have made me offers in this way, General Greene in a letter which is in Mr Morris's hand made me a handsome offer. Col Laurens was greatly beyond what I should have accepted had he lived.[153] A person in Market Street who is only a substantial trade man told me he would freely give fifty pounds, and old Ludwick the baker offered me £25[154] but I should not like to have a subscription hawked about the country as if it was for charity, because there are gentlemen enough to do it and to make my situation happy, and leave me to follow uninfluenced a disposition that has hitherto done good. I certainly deserve property in America, but hitherto I have none. Since beginning this letter, I have amused myself with calculating expences, and the sum of five or six thousand guineas, raised in the manner I mention would not hurt the subscribers, would make me easy and remove all difficulties, and if there is not spirit and honor enough to do this, then America and me are very different characters.[155]

But whatever method may be pursued respecting me, the first proper step that can be taken (as it appears to me) will be for Congress to appoint a Committee to enquire into the service and situation of Mr Paine from the Commencement of the War. I shall, in consequence, attend the Committee and deliver them in writing a concise account for each year, and this, I think is a necessary foundation, both on account of Congress and myself – for it will shew, in the first place, that I have not supported the measures of Congress by any *influence* of theirs or pecuniary reward from them, but that I have done it as the necessary measures of the Country – and on my own part it will shew that there is a debt of Honor and Gratitude due to me.

Besides Congress had much better do it themselves, than leave me to do it, because the former will have an honorable and the latter something of a dishonorable appearance.

Mr Rittenhouse shewed me some time ago a London Publication, (and I have seen the same idea thrown out several times) in which it mentions that when Congress have any measures to carry with the country which they are doubtful of, that 'this Author', say they, is set to work to sound the disposition of the people, and prepare the way.[156] Now as there has been no such thing, it would be but justice to themselves and me to remove the error, both abroad and at home, for the Rhode Islander talked much in the same manner.[157]

I have now, Sir, written you a long and I fear, a troublesome letter – but as you know my situation, and how unwilling I am to make disagreeable things public, & the necessity I am under of mentioning them to somebody I can trust them to, I think you will excuse it. If on consulting with such friends as you may think proper to disclose the subject to you should fall in with the ideas in this letter, I shall be much obliged to you to promote the appointment of a committee for the purpose I have mentioned, because until this is done, there will be no ground to go on in any thing.

There is one idea I wish to guard against, which is, that of keeping all expectations of a book out of sight – I mean it as retrospect and not a prospect. Besides, subscription for a book will answer me no good purpose, and if I must depend upon that I should make three times as much at it in England. Besides any thing for a service yet to be performed have on me a disagreeable effect.

I shall be glad to be favored with an opinion from you on these matters, a letter sent to my lodgings, or sent to the Borden Town Stage boat, at the Crooked Billet Wharf directed to me at Col. Kirkbride's at Borden Town will come safe to hand.[158] The stage boat goes twice a week Wednesday's and Sunday. Wishing you prosperity and a repossession of your city.

I am your Obedient Humble Servant
Thomas Paine

Until now, it has not been clear to Paine scholars why he accompanied John Laurens to France in 1781. He claimed at the time that he was accompanying him as his secretary, and that he would make every effort to secure cash and supplies for the United States and the troops. He always claimed to have paid his own fare. It also appears from this letter that he intended to remain in Europe; a few weeks prior to his departure with Laurens, Paine had written what appears to be a letter of farewell, suggestive of a longer time away from America than the few months he and Laurens spent abroad. He wrote to General Greene:

> I leave America with the perfect satisfaction of having been to her an honest, faithful and affectionate friend, and I go away with the hope of returning to spend better or more agreeable days with her than those which are past.[159]

As it happened, Paine's case was put to Congress. A committee appointed to consider it delivered a report on 15 August, proposing that he be appointed historiographer for the United States. It was agreed that the work should be undertaken 'by one ... who has been and is governed by the most disinterested principle of public good, totally uninfluenced by party of every kind'. His salary was to be determined at a later date. The report was read on 18 August and laid aside until 31 October, when it was referred to another committee.[160]

As shown in Paine's penultimate paragraph, he did not want future employment; rather, he sought cash or property.[161] On 3 December 1783, he wrote to James Duane telling of his long-held wish to write a history of the Revolution, but that Congress put it 'out of his power'.[162] Exactly what he meant is not clear, but it appears certain that his case was dropped by the appointed committee; Paine did not warrant a mention in Congress for a further two years.

9 JULY 1783

The following offering, which appeared on 9 July 1783, has been mentioned within the Paine *oeuvre* before,[163] but has never been reprinted there. It became evident that the piece was by Paine from a letter he wrote to Washington on 22 July 1783 introducing a former pupil from London.[164] That letter read:

Philadelphia July 22, 1783

Sir

The bearer of this Mr Darby who is introduced to this country by Mr Laurens, was a pupil of mine in London about twelve or fourteen years ago. His curiosity to see the great world of America has induced him to take the voyage and make the tour of it. As it is his intention to visit camp and wait on your greeting I presume in the liberty of adding this to other introductions he is furnished with to you.

Mr Darby's waiting for this will I hope apologize for its incorrectness.[165]

I enclose Your Excellency a copy of the Address of the Citizens to Congress which will I hope find a close to the affair.[166] It is signed by near a thousand of the principal merchants and inhabitants.

I send you the paper of today. The account of the entertainment given to the officers is concise. It will be follow[ed] in the papers of tomorrow. There were present: the President of the State, the French Minister and almost every person of note and rank in the city.

The voluntary was the best received I ever knew a toast in my life or none was ever more so.

I likewise enclose you a paper containing a letter to Fairfax respecting the instructions from that place.

As I have much to write to Your Excellency again I request you would not regard this as a letter but only as a line or two, on account of the gentleman who bears it and the opportunity of enclosing you a few papers.

I just now learn that five Spanish Officers have obtained furloughs for six months to visit Your Excellency and are in the River.[167]

I am Sir – with every wish for your happiness
Your Excellency's most obliged and Humble Servant
Thomas Paine

Compliments to the Gentlemen of your Family

His Excellency General Washington[168]

The entertainment of which Paine wrote took place on Friday, 18 July 1783 when, at the State House in Philadelphia, the citizens hosted an 'elegant entertainment' in honour of the army officers. In all, thirteen toasts were made:

1. The United States in Congress.
2. Our illustrious ally, the king of France.
3. The States of Holland.
4. General Washington and the Federal army.
5. The glorious Martyrs to our Liberty and Independence.
6. New strength to the Union, and new honors to its friends.
7. May our love of Liberty be shewn in the virtuous use of it, and in the just rewards of those who have gained it for us.
8. Our Ministers in Europe.
9. May we never forget that the only bulwark of a republic is virtue.
10. May honor and honesty ever triumph over meanness and ingratitude.
11. May all our soldiers be citizens, and our citizens soldiers; and may the plough be as prosperous as the sword has been successful.
12. Peace, Liberty and Happiness to the whole world.
13. The State of Pennsylvania.

The toasts were followed by a voluntary to the 'Honor and Immortality to the Principles of Freedom and Virtue, in General Washington's circular letter'.[169] The instructions from Fairfax to which Paine referred were written by George Mason, a former justice of the Fairfax County Court, who, on 30 May, on behalf of the Fairfax County Freeholders, wrote a letter of instructions to delegates of Virginia's General Assembly.[170] The first of the several instructions read:

And first, Gentlemen, we desire and expressly instruct you, that you give not your assent to, and on the contrary, that you oppose to the utmost of your power, the smallest infraction of the late Treaty of Peace, either with respect to the payment of debts, or in any other matter whatsoever, whereby the public faith, solemnly pledged by the American Commissioners duly authorized, may be violated, and this country again involved in the calamities of war, or the danger of reprisals.

The address was first published in the *Richmond Virginia Gazette* of 7 June 1783.[171]

The published letter to Fairfax that Paine enclosed with his letter to Washington was appended to a short paragraph in the *Pennsylvania Gazette* of 9 July 1783. The letter of 22 July, quoted above, reveals the writer of the whole, not just the introduction, as Thomas Paine although it was signed S.C., not his usual abbreviation, C.S. There would have been no point in his sending the paper to his friend if he had not written the piece himself. Until recently, not even the introduction has been attributed to him due, most probably, to the pseudonym, which was, in all likelihood, a printer's error. The letter concerns the complicated matter of the Continental Congress's appeal to the states to impose further taxes as a means of supporting the army and discharging the public debt. From the individual points of view of the dissentious states, Congress was seen to be attempting to undermine their constitutional right of being free and independent. Despite two attempts, the states would not agree to grant Congress the power to levy taxes. The piece in the *Gazette* ran as follows:

To the Printers throughout the United States

Gentlemen,

I am desirous of recommending to you the insertion of the following part of a letter. It was written by a gentleman of established honor and integrity, and a sincere friend to the cause and character of America, to his friend in Fairfax, in Virginia, and was occasioned by the instructions given from that place to their members in Assembly, the 30th May last, as you will see by the conclusion of it.[172] It has a turn of thinking and expression which is rather new, and though I sincerely hope there may be no occasion of applying them to any other place, than that to which they are addressed, yet it may serve as a beacon to others, to avoid the rock on which national reputation may be ship-wrecked.

I am, Gentlemen, yours, &c.

S.C.

'It now remains to be proved whether the people of America are an honest people or not, and whether they have in them the true principles of faith, honor and gratitude, or only the unsubstantial professions of what they do not possess; whether virtue be an empty, hackneyed name, prostituted to the purposes of passion, party and design; or whether it has a national existence among the citizens of this new world.

'There is now a crisis of the most delicate nature taking place: The crisis of moral and national reputation: and tho' I am ardent in my wishes for the issue, I should be exceedingly happy could I say I was equally as sanguine in my hopes.

'The cause of America was beyond exception just; it now remains to know whether the people are so: For it is on the union or disunion of those two points, that the character of the country will stand with lustre, or fall with disgrace.

'To be jealous of power, which is now, with some, the cant phrase of the day, and is very unmeaningly insinuated in your instructions, is a passion which may be possessed by the bravest or the basest mind, for the best or the worst of purposes. It belongs as much, and perhaps more, to the conspirator, than to the patriot. The envious wretch, who can bear no equal, and hates all merit but his own, is never free from it; and he who wants to avoid a duty, which the circumstances of his country calls for, will affect to be jealous of power, as a pretence for his delinquency. It is, therefore, in itself no virtue, and in its best stage is but a vice refined. I never knew man who had much of this jealousy of power in him, but I could discover a littleness of soul, an enviousness of heart, a fractiousness of temper, and a fondness for himself, at the bottom.

'But if we must deify a vice, and give it a place in the pantheon of America, pray let us, for our honor's sake, put it in the most obscure corner of the building, and never let its sneaky visage be seen until the amiable goddess *Confidence* gives some symptoms of sickness. He would be a fool and a wretch of a husband that should, the morning after his marriage, place the figure of jealousy in his house, to secure the fidelity of his wife.

'There is some consistency in being jealous of power in the hands of those who assume it by birth, or without our consent, and over whom we have no controul, nor the power of removal, as was the case with the Crown of England over America. But to be jealous of those whom we chuse, the instant we have chosen them, shews either the folly of our choice, or the absurdity of our politics; and that in the transition from monarchy to a republic, we have unfortunately bastardized our ideas, by placing jealousy where we ought to place confidence.

'If a man does not do his duty, remove him; if he transgresses it, punish him; but this little, mean, sneaking, and sneaky temper of jealousy, this poison to human happiness, and which in a thousand instances, for one to the contrary, is only the stalking horse of party and private design, ought either to be banished from among us, or admitted only with the utmost caution.

'But if we must be jealous, pray let us be jealous of our character and honor, lest, from our negligence of those things, or our disregard to them, the world should hereafter call us cheats, and say that our politics were managed to get and borrow every thing we could, and pay no-body.

'The independence of America has been very cheaply obtained, and besides this, she has received extraordinary helps, without any expence to her. A debt, then, of thirty or forty million of dollars at the end of eight years war, closing with every success she could wish for, and more than she expected, an universal trade, and in the sovereign possession of a country which before was added to the sovereignty of another, is, I say, compared with the advantages gained, a trifle.

'The less, then, this trifle is, the greater will be the disgrace not to adopt measures to discharge it. "But we are jealous of the power of Congress", says some cunning minded modern politician. No, sir, he is not jealous of the power of Congress but he wants to play the cheat, and he wants a pretence for doing it. He wants to draw his neck from the collar, and leave the burthen on other people's shoulders. He wants the blessings of independence at other people's expence, and the benefit of an universal trade without paying any thing for it; and most probably too he wants to get into power, by meanly and treacherously undermining those who have been preferred before him.

'But it is impossible the world can either be long duped or mistaken; the real character of the states must come out, and I most earnestly and devoutly wish it may be such as they may collectively and severally have cause to glory in.

' "O never fear it", say some; yes, but I do fear it, I see cause to fear it. This bug-bear of the power of Congress, which, God knows, and every one of us knows, is the most flimsy tale of a falsehood ever invented, can only be invented for a bad purpose. It is a trick contrived to cheat with, and nothing else.

'Congress, beset at all times with a thousand difficulties, have, nevertheless, gone through the war, and concluded a peace. In the course of it they have been obliged to borrow money in France, in Holland, and at home, and happy did America then think herself that Congress was able to procure it for her. They have been obliged to postpone a great part of the pay of the army, until the war should end, when the return of peace and the increase of trade should enable the country to do it more easily. France has not only lent money, but has given money, and joined her arms in the contest; and Holland, by lending us money, has involved herself in a war disastrous to her interest. This is a true and concise state of the case. Do you not, Sir, begin to feel a blush rising in your countenance, a tremulous apprehension beginning in your heart, lest that which is to follow should not be as honorable as that which is past.[173]

'Congress have now laid before the states the amount of the monies borrowed, and the debt contracted, and recommended to them means for discharging it.

'Had they not done this, the clamour would have been that they had suffered the honor of America to be stained for ever. That the people, proud of that honor, and determined to transmit it uninjured to posterity, and desirous of nothing so much, as securing their future peace and the good affections of the world, by a just and grateful discharge of their debts and obligations, were ready to rise up against them – and now they have done it, the clamour is reversed, at least with you, and as a pretence for not complying, the cry is, O the power of Congress! O the power of fraud and nonsense! Say I in return.

'If the character of America should be sacrificed in this instance, or her future happiness disturbed by it, the fault cannot be laid on those we call tories, it cannot be laid on the refugees, it must rest on the country itself, and on the whigs themselves, and therefore it becomes every one of them to reflect that his individual honor and that of his country is at stake.

'There is no such thing in the nature of our constitutions, either confederated or individual, or from the circumstances of them, as granting money to Congress. The idea is a false one, when applied to a republic. Whatever money is raised in a republic is for public service, and this which is now called for is to discharge a public debt. Does a man grant money when he pays his debts? Certainly not. A man's creditors may grant him indulgence, but he certainly grants them nothing by paying them.

'A grant means a gift, or present, done out of meer good will or good opinion. But here is a debt to be paid, which all America has contracted; and the states, in sending up their money for that purpose, grant nothing. They have a right, and ought to say to their several delegates entrusted with the payment of it, "There Gentlemen, is our part, and we direct you to see that it is applied, according to the purpose for which it is raised. We have tried very hard, but, however, we have done it; because, being our duty, we would have no reproach fall on us for not fulfilling it; neither can we bear the reflection of having it said, that we lay under obligations we do not discharge. You will immediately acknowledge the receipt of it, and furnish us with accounts of its applications. We have chosen you for this and other business of the state, because we had confidence in your integrity, and in discharging this trust, you will acquire our further confidence; but if you fail herein, your head, at least, and perhaps your estate, must pay for it.

'This would be an honest and peremptory way of speaking, and such as people who do *their* duty have a right to use. Now let us examine the contrary side.

'I am truly ashamed to begin upon it. There is something so exceedingly trickish, selfish, mean and low in it, that I feel soiled by it. A man never ought to act the rascal even in jest; and we have that in our natures, which unfits us for the imitation of characters not natural to our minds. I know I shall make a bungling hand of it. But the plain case is this:

'When a man wants to shift, he will set on foot a thousand inventions. It will not do to tell the world that he intends to be dishonest; but he will assign this excuse, that excuse, this pretence, that pretence, he will stretch a little, then a little more .... Something has disappointed him ... but you may be sure, Sir, ... you may rely on it, Sir, ... and so on, till all the changes are run through, and then, as the last resource, he grows impertinent ... calls himself a gentleman ... an independent gentleman ... keeps his doors locked ... abuses his friends ... and puts his creditors to defiance.

'Now, what more is necessary to understand the instructions of Fairfax, than to compare them with this kind of conduct.

'When the address of Congress, with the statement of the public debt, and the means for discharging it (which is one of the best principled and liberal performances which have, at any time, come from that body) arrived among the people of Fairfax, they, instead of expressing their gratitude for the extraordinary assistance they have received during the war, and instead of honestly and cheerfully entering into the measures recommended for the discharge of their debt, and the support of the public faith and character of America, instead, I say, of these things, which it was their duty to do, they attempt to shift that duty off in the following manner:

' "We like not", say they, in their instructions, "the language of the late address from Congress to the different states, and of the report of their committee upon the subject of revenue, published in the same pamphlet. If they are carefully and impartially examined, they will be found to exhibit strong proofs of lust of power. They contain the same kind of arguments which were formerly used in the business of ship money, to justify the arbitrary measures of the race of Stuarts in England".[174]

'The only remark necessary to be made on these instructions is, that they require no examination at all, to see that they are a most flimsy affectation of patriotism, flying in the face of truth, and calculated to cover one of the greatest frauds and most scandalous actions a people can commit.

'If truth, honor and justice are to prevail over falsehood, disgrace and dishonesty; if every thing which can inspire the mind with virtuous emulation can triumph over things which can debase it, the shiftiness of character, exhibited in those instructions, will every where be held in detestation. For either let men be honest, as they ought to be, or act their dishonesty in huff.

I am, Sir, &c. &c.'

The addressee of the letter is unknown but, without doubt, was highly respected by Paine.

3 JANUARY 1786

Having begun his career in his father's counting house, during the years prior to the Revolution, Thomas Willing, to whom the following letter was addressed, had filled several public offices. He had been a member of the Common Council of Philadelphia, judge of the City Court, Mayor of Philadelphia, a justice of the Supreme Court of Pennsylvania, a member of the Provincial Assembly, President of the first Provincial Congress of Pennsylvania and a delegate to the second Continental Congress. He played a major part in raising money for the Continental Army and, in 1781, became the first president of the Bank of North America, a position he held at the time Paine addressed the following letter to him. The situation was that the farmers of Pennsylvania were heavily in debt and hoped to increase the circulation of paper money. They were concerned that the bank might not accept paper money, so demanded the repeal of the bank's charter. Conversely, the wealthy merchants and artisans of Philadelphia were worried about inflation and opposed both the clamour for paper money and the repeal of the charter. The bank had not violated the terms of the charter, but the legislature of Pennsylvania repealed it. The bank's directors and stockholders refused to recognize it. Investors withdrew their money and the bank, barely surviving under its Congressional charter, appeared in imminent danger of collapse.

Walnut Street

January 3 1786

Sir

I enclose you something for your perusal respecting the affairs of the bank.[175]

Tho' I wish the Memorial to go forward as much as possible, as it shews the exceeding ill conduct and ill policy of the late House – yet I do not think that any charter the house can give will be of any real service to the bank, or worth its acceptance.[176]

It appears to me that the conduct of the late House in violating the Charter, especially in the manner they did it, shews that the power of an Assembly is no more than that of a committee if they stop for one year, and that therefore an assembly is incompetent to any business which requires a duration beyond that time, such as granting charters, contracting debts, fixing funds for the redemption of these debts, making money or any thing else which requires permanency. It would perhaps be best that the repealing law should take place, and that all the charters granted by former Assemblies should be reassumed on the ground of inadequacy, and that they should be refereed by a general Act for that purpose to continue (if it can continue) until the next convention when the mode of granting charters may be then fixed and made a part of the Constitution.

I intend getting out a Pamphlet on some of these subjects, against the time the Assembly meets. Had I been a member of the House I would have voted against Mr Morris's plan because I do not see how the government is to give the security to the bank, which the plan required and instead of Mr Whitehill's doubt of the bank, the doubt ought to have been on the government – for as they have assumed the power of violating engagements, they cannot now be trusted.[177]

Last spring I sent Mr Francis a copy of my Letter to Blair McClenachan.[178] I want to see it, if it can be found, for I have not the copy with me – it is I suppose at Borden Town among my papers.

I am Sir
Your Obedient Humble Servant
Thomas Paine

Thomas Willing Esquire[179]

Paine had turned his back on former friends, the radicals, who viewed the bank as a symbol of conservative wealth. He was about to make this public; in February he published *Dissertations on Government, the Affairs of the Bank, and Paper Money*. He followed that, until March of the following year, with letters to newspapers defending and expanding his views on the Bank of North America. The real issue was whether it was in order for a legislature to revoke a charter granted by another legislature if the terms of the charter had not been violated. Eventually, aided by Paine's pen, supporters of the bank were able to introduce a bill to revive the incorporation of the subscribers to the Bank of North America. It was passed on 17 March 1787, just ten days after Paine's last words on the subject were published.

PUBLISHED 1 NOVEMBER 1786

At the end of the American Revolutionary War, the soldiers of the Continental Army were demobilized with little or nothing in the way of reward for their services. Those of Massachusetts were desperately in need; the Continental notes with which they had been paid were exchanged at a hugely discounted rate. The farmers were also suffering from the depression, and petitions for relief were of no avail. The situation led to rebellion in August 1786, when, under the leadership of a former army captain, Daniel Shays, army veterans and soldiers banded together in protests against taxes, excessive salaries of state officials and concomitant grievances. In September, delegates from five states convened at Annapolis, Maryland, to address the nation's economic problems. The delegates found that little could be done to alleviate matters without changes to the Articles of Confederation, changes that they, representatives of only five states, did not have the necessary powers to make. They called on all states to send delegates to a constitutional convention during the summer of 1787, a convention designed to strengthen the governance of the United States.

Under such circumstances, in the midst of the protests, Paine, over the signature of 'Common Sense', published the following article in the *Worcester Magazine* of 1 November 1786. It was a reply to a letter signed 'A Member of Convention' in an earlier issue of the same magazine; Paine's response conveys the subject of the member's contribution.

For the *Worcester Magazine*

Mr Editor,

Having observed a piece in one of your late Magazines undersigned *A Member of Convention*, I wish to make a few remarks thereon, and present the same to you for publication, in your *free* magazine, and must expect to be gratified.[180]

The writer appears to me so destitute either of genius, judgment, or a good motive, that I should have passed him over with a single reflection of contempt, had he not betrayed a proud tyrannical disposition, and a visible attachment to principles unfavourable to the natural rights of mankind; I discover in his *reflections* upon one of the first characters in the commonwealth, the spirit of a haughty Spanish nobleman, who pluming himself upon the purity of his noble birth, looks with insulting contempt upon every man, who cannot trace his lineage through the loins of princes for five hundred years at least. To say in this country of freedom, this last asylum of expatiated liberty, that one citizen is inherently better than another, and to reproach a man now in an elevated station, for having been in one of less rank, is at once, an avowed dereliction to the fundamental principles of our free government, and an insult upon ninety-nine in a hundred, throughout the community; so many of them being, I presume, farmers and mechanicks: Now, if the *smut* of the latter renders them filthy and incapable of merit, the former being as often and as much covered with *smut* and dirt as the other, must necessarily, in the contemplation of the writer, be equally despicable and unworthy: With every sentiment of deference due to so exalted a character as the 'Member of Convention', I humbly apprehend that the whole human race, as soon as ushered into existence, are at that moment invested with the same equal, unalienable, and indefensible rights; and that no other distinctions can arise or be had among them, but those which proceed from the good or bad conduct of the individual; the position I now lay down, I know is incontrovertible, and so far as the real disposition of a man may be discovered by his manner of acting and speaking, so much am I convinced, that the member of Convention is secretly averse to those principles, upon which we have founded our system of civil policy: He certainly wishes to establish as a necessary maxim in politicks, that a man born, as he would term it, one of the prophane vulgar, is *ipso facto* excommunicated from every honour in the community, and ought never to presume to cultivate his understanding however brilliant and solid; in short that the common people should never aspire after learning and wisdom. If, Mr Editor, we look into biography, and read the lives of illustrious men, we shall almost every where find, that those who have rendered themselves the most conspicuous, have had no advantages from family or fortune, but on the other hand, have had to contend with every obstacle, which indigence and the want of friends could create; the celebrated Roman orator was a Tuscan plebeian, and the late Earl of Chatham was born in an obscure village of the kingdom of Great-Britain;[181] yet they were honoured and esteemed by their respective contemporaries, and posterity will never cease to regard them as the most perfect models of human virtue and greatness; and if we read the memoirs of those heroes and statesmen which our own age and country have produced, we shall find an immense interval between their *first* beginnings and their present celebrity – witness the President of Pennsylvania, and our plenipotentiary at the court of London.[182] I feel a resentment against the member of Convention which I do not wish to conceal: I will hazard a prediction concerning the duration of his present popularity; in times of commotion, when the spirit of party carries every thing to an extreme, a man becomes more or less esteemed, in proportion to the zeal which he manifests in support of his faction; and men heretofore disregarded, during the first transports of a political phrensy, are very apt to become of some consequence, and obtain small delegations of trust and power; but the fever having once subsided, and the state restored to peace, they sink back to their former insignificance, let the prevalence of party take either an unfortunate or a favourable bias. Anarchy and confusion are in their natures very perishable, and when we are once more so happy, as to have a good understanding between the government and the people, the member of Convention will fall to the horizon of his forty years obscurity; like the feather in the wind, which in the height of the tempest, is carried to the clouds, as that abates, it comes nearer to the earth, and when the storm is entirely past, it gently descends to the surface; or to make an allusion more suitable to the nature of my object, like the seed planted by the prophet of Nineveh, which in six hours surprizingly matured to a perfect gourd, and in the lapse of as many more, became rotten and perished.[183]

'Teach me to feel another's woe' is a sentiment of beneficence worthy of the Deity, but in the mouth of the member of Convention, is uttered I fear, only with the vile insidious motive, to rouse the passions of unthinking men, and transfuse into their bosoms, the same spirit of discord, fanaticism, and revolt, which lies rankling in his own. Teach me to sympathize with, and to relieve every distressed object, as far as the compass of my abilities will enable me; teach me the principles of honour, honesty and good faith, and to know that every motive of national policy which is not founded upon the indelible sentiments of the human heart, will in the practice, produce both individual ruin and publick misery; and finally and lastly, teach me to admire a man, who by the mere dint of talents and industry, renders himself conspicuous among his fellow citizens – and when I contrast so amiable and worthy a character with that of the member of Convention, to feel an increasing respect for the one, and a proportional detestation and contempt for the other.

Go, unworthy member of Convention, go back with your 'portable representation of property', to your old business of administering emeticks, catharticks, and alternatives to your patients, as their respective infirmities may require; and leave to your betters and superiors in Convention the more difficult operation of reducing the gangrene, which threatens the dissolution of the body-politick.

COMMON SENSE

Uxbridge, October 15, 1786

The member of the convention who evoked Paine's contempt and published the piece to which he responded, might have been Hugh Williamson of North Carolina, a physician who was chosen by that state to attend the Annapolis Convention, but he arrived too late to participate in the proceedings. During the Revolutionary War, he had served as North Carolina's Physician and Surgeon General, and Paine's final paragraph identifies the subject of his article as a physician. Williamson was the only physician delegated to the Annapolis Convention; he also attended the following Constitutional Convention. On the other hand, the member might have been James McClurg, a physician of Virginia, or James McHenry of Maryland, who had trained as a physician, but did not practise the profession. Both attended the Constitutional Convention of 1787 at Philadelphia where the present federal Constitution was drafted, and the government of the United States of America established.

In the meantime, the protests of the farmers and soldiers had come to a head in February 1787 when over 1,000 rebels attempted to take the Springfield arsenal. The government prevented the attack, but not without loss of life. With the capture of most of the insurgents, the rebellion came to an end. The leaders were condemned to death, but later pardoned, and laws to ameliorate the rebels' conditions were enacted by the Massachusetts legislature.

20 MARCH 1787

With the unstable financial position of the several states, which had issued their own currency, it is clear from this letter to Thomas Willing that Paine's good friend Colonel Joseph Kirkbride was having as much trouble as any other citizen in changing a pound for a pound. The paper money used during and following the Revolutionary War had led to hyperinflation, and was virtually worthless against the British pound. The ratios by which it varied from state to state were from one-hundredth to one-thousandth. It probably embarrassed Kirkbride greatly to request his friend to make an effort on his behalf to enable him to meet his obligations.

March 20th, 1787

Dear Sir,

A very intimate friend of mine Col. Kirkbride, has a bond of Mr Richard Penn for about £1000. He has a present occasion for 400, for 6 or 7 month. His landed estate is in Pennsylvania. He called on me this morning and mentioned these with other circumstances to me, accompanied with a wish, that if it was convenient for me, whether I could accommodate him with that sum for that time. I acquainted him with the manner in which what money I had would be disposed of, which puts it out of my power to oblige him.[184]

My desire to serve him on any occasion induces me to mention this circumstance to you. I believe it is not regularly within the line of business done in the bank, but as he can deposit real security to a great deal more amount, it would give me much pleasure to be the means of promoting his convenience. I intended waiting on you this evening on this occasion, but as I cannot, I must defer it until the morning.

I am Dear Sir
Your obedient humble servant
Thomas Paine

The letter Paine wrote to Willing has not appeared in previous collections of Paine writings; it was sold to a private buyer in August 2007.[185]

20 NOVEMBER 1787

With the Revolution successfully completed in America, with credentials of fame as a writer, with a model bridge and with money in his pocket,[186] Paine set sail for Europe on 26 April 1787. Hoping to find a sponsor to construct his bridge, he went first to France, where he arrived during the early stages of the Revolution. There he wrote a political pamphlet, *Prospects on the Rubicon*, before crossing the Channel later in the year. In London, he moved in upper circles of Whig society, and was well known as a radical and the writer of *Common Sense*. As this letter of 20 November 1787 shows, he was *au fait* with the politics of France and England, where he wished to see change. Just two months earlier, from Thetford, Norfolk, he had written to the Marquess of Lansdowne, second Earl of Shelburne, expressing his regrets at not having met him in London; he wished to pass on the respects of a mutual friend, the Abbé Morellet as requested by the abbé on Paine's departure from France.[187] It was to the marquess, a man of no known political persuasion, that Paine had addressed his *Crisis Number VII* in response to a speech Lansdowne had made, which seemed to be a complete turnaround of the policy of the former Prime Minister, Lord Rockingham, whom he succeeded. Rockingham had been committed to an independent United States and Shelburne to negotiating a peace treaty.[188] Unfortunately, it has not been possible to transcribe the letter in full as it was sold to a private buyer in 1994. This extract, a response to Shelburne's reply to Paine's letter of September, was transcribed from the sale catalogue.[189] The letter began with Paine expressing hope of meeting the marquess before long and continued thus.

… Sincerely do I wish that this infamous business of perpetual wrangling between England & France might end. It would be called by a coarser name than I chuse … to express were a like case to happen between two individuals; and it is a curious paradox that enlightened Nations should have less Sense than enlightened individuals.

I most heartily wish that some great line of Politics worthy of an opposition might be struck out. Peace might be easily preferred were proper persons in the Management of Affairs. There are so many these in France who would very heartily concur in such a measure, and unless this be done, it appears, at least to me, that something worse than war will follow, for tho' France is not in a good condition for war, England is still worse.

I enclose your Lordship a Pamphlet which has just made its appearance ….

The enclosed pamphlet was *Prospects on the Rubicon*.

4 MAY 1788

Written from Paris, in the following letter to Lewis Morris, brother of Gouverneur Morris, Thomas Paine wrote chirpily of matters that had been occupying him since his arrival in Europe the previous year.[190] The tone of the letter is that of a jubilant man, pleased with his present circumstances, writing to an intimate friend. The piece was mentioned by David Freeman Hawke, but has never been published.[191] It is transcribed and edited from a copy of the original held by the American Philosophical Society.

Paris May 4th 1788

My dear Sir

It was with a great deal of pleasure that I received a letter from Jacob dated Morrisania November 1st informing me among other agreeable things that you were all well.

I was in London last October and November when the Ministry and the Nation were running mad legs to war with France on account of Holland, and I published a pamphlet to shew them their folly.[192] They abused me in the newspapers, said that I had a most unparalleled stock of impudence, but they never attempted to refute the arguments nor contradict the facts, and the event has proved that I was right.

I was happy at finding all my friends and relations hearty and well and rejoiced to see. My mother, good old woman, told me that she got an American newspaper during the war in which there was a proclamation of Congress for a fast day and that she kept it very strictly.

I am very anxious to return to America and see you all, but find I shall not be able to leave Europe till the latter end of the summer.

The gentleman who takes charge of this letter brings with him the opinion of the Academy of Sciences at Paris on my mode. It is under cover to Dr Franklin but I have left the seal open that he might show it to you, if you happen to meet with any body who reads French.

There is a prospect of the construction being adopted in this country for a bridge opposite the king's gardens at Paris, in which case, the bridge is to be made in America and sent to Paris ready to be put up.

The Marquis de la Fayette, Mr Jefferson and myself have had a conference with the Minister on the subject, and we are so far advanced, that M. Le Couteulse the banker has proposed to furnish all the money.

If I can succeed only in one contract in Europe it will very sufficiently answer my purpose and I shall be able to build the Schuylkill bridge myself.[193]

Jacob mentions everybody in his letter except Sally and everything except the willow trees. The trees I fear are all dead and that Sally has neglected them.

My family of Joe and Button I hope are doing well. Mr Constable has money of mine in his hands. Please to take a guinea of him and give to Joe.

I shall go to London next week to bring over the model to Paris. I sent it to London last summer after the Academy of Sciences had finished their report. It is at present in the care of Sir Joseph Banks, President of the Royal Society. The English newspapers have very ingeniously found out that the author of Common Sense is an *arch rebel*. However, they are disposed to give me credit for the ingenuity of the model.

> God bless you all
> Your Affectionate Friend and Humble Servant
> Thomas Paine

Negotiations for the building of a larger model of his bridge delayed any plans Paine had for returning to America. Had he done so, his life story would have read very differently. Despite words of praise, his bridge was never built on either side of the Atlantic.

A noticeable feature of this letter is mention or lack of mention by his correspondent, Jacob, of 'Sally' and 'My family of Joe and Button'. It would seem that Paine had asked Sally to care for the willow trees on his property at Bordentown; Joe, apparently, had worked for him and Button, Paine's horse, was probably in his care. In asking his friend to give a guinea to Joe, Paine was not referring to one of equal status to himself. It is highly likely that Joe had been, in earlier years, Paine's slave.[194]

Apart from not having been the abolitionist professed by Conway and others who followed, there is strong, circumstantial evidence suggesting that during 1775 and 1776 Paine owned slaves. His private arrangements have not been recorded, but it would have been unusual for a Philadelphian in his situation, and of his standing, not to have owned some.[195]

In an article printed in *American Literature*, Frank Smith tentatively and wrongly suggested that Paine had authored an unsigned poem which appeared under the title of 'The Dying Negro' in *The Pennsylvania Magazine* of January 1776.[196] It was not by Paine, but was published in London in 1773 with the full title *The Dying Negro, a Political Epistle, Supposed to be Written by a Black, (Who lately shot himself on board a vessel in the river Thames;) to his intended Wife*. It was written by

Thomas Day and John Bicknell. Later editions of the work are described as having added to the poem 'a Fragment of a letter on the slavery of the negroes, by Thomas Day'.[197]

A letter written by Thomas Day in 1776, in reply to a request for his 'sentiments upon the Slavery of the Negroes',[198] bears every indication of having been addressed to Paine. The letter did not name the addressee and was published, in part, at the request of friends to whom Day had shown his copy. They suggested 'that its publication might not be unattended with utility'.[199] Written in England, Day's 'Advertisement' stated:

> Should this essay ever reach America, it may, perhaps, displease those who have not learned to discern friends from flatterers, and to distinguish between the language of truth and calumny. Those, on the contrary, who are enlightened by a more extensive knowledge of human nature, may, perhaps, respect an Englishman, who, after daring to assert their cause through all the varied events of the late revolution, dares now with equal intrepidity assert the cause of truth and justice, and of that part of the human species whose wrongs are yet unredressed, and almost unpitied. Should it be asked why I rather publish a Fragment than a complete essay, I can only answer, that I respect truth so much, that I am not inclined to violate it even as an author; and that this Letter having been really written in the year 1776, and being still in the possession of the gentleman to whom it was sent, I do not choose to piece it with additions in the year 1784.[200]

The year of writing is significant. It was the year that *Common Sense* was published and revealed by Robert Bell to have been 'Written by an Englishman'.

The person who had sought Day's opinion 'professed an intention of restoring all his own [slaves] to liberty, could he be convinced that duty required the sacrifice'.[201] Not recognizing the handwriting, Day read the letter through before realizing, from the signature, that it came from one whom he had met with John Laurens.[202] As Day had never visited America,[203] his meeting with the addressee must have taken place in London. It has not been previously suggested that Paine met Laurens in England, but it is interesting to note that, in August 1774, at a time when Paine was in London, Laurens left Geneva, where he had been educated, to study law in England.[204] It is possible that the two met in the months prior to the former's departure for America, where they might have met again in 1777 on Laurens's return.

In his reply, Day stated his surprise at his opinion being sought by somebody 'of whom I have heard so advantageous a character'.[205] Waving aside pleasantries, Day addressed the inquirer as 'a member of that society which has now made a solemn appeal to Heaven, and taken up arms against the nation to which it owes its establishment',[206] and penned the letter in the language of the author known as 'Common Sense'. The year of publication of the letter is more significant than that of its writing. It did not appear in 1784 as the writer's 'Advertisement' suggests, but in 1793, after his death,[207] and, as will be seen, soon after Paine was forced to flee England. Day only considered publishing after carefully reflecting upon the suggestion of his friends, and proceeded 'because, whatever discredit it brings upon my head, it may contribute to establish the sincerity of my heart'.[208]

Day described the American revolutionaries as '[i]nglorious soldiers, yet seditious citizens; sordid merchants, and indolent usurpers'. He continued:

> [T]hese are the men whose clamours for liberty and independence are heard across the Atlantic ocean ... Let her [America] remember, that it is in Britain alone, that laws are equally favourable to liberty and humanity; that it is in Britain the sacred rights of nature have received their most awful ratification.[209]

It is obvious that these words were written prior to American Independence, and that the writer had probably noticed *Common Sense*. It seems apparent that Day, while not piecing the letter 'with additions at a later date', did add to the dedication of his publication. In his introduction, the editor of the posthumous publication added: 'May the true patriot he [Day] sketches, be found a useful touchstone applied to some of the questionable shapes of the precent [*sic*] crisis!'[210]

Despite his not wishing to 'piece it with additions'; Day's published letter bore phrases from, and language similar to, all of Paine's then published works. Phrases and words such as 'the general good', 'rights of nature', 'natural rights', 'tyrant', 'oppressor' and 'despotism', and suggestions of the natural equality of all men, appeared throughout the 27 printed pages. Of Englishmen using such terminology at the time, none answered the description of Day's addressee better than Paine, whose identity was less than thinly veiled. The addressee had professed to be guided by 'reason and morality', and had written of his 'country's cause'.[211]

A particular reason for Day's not wanting to 'piece his letter with additions' in the year 1784 might have been that it was the year of Anthony Benezet's death. Tributes were paid to him from around the world,[212] yet no public tribute came from the pen of Paine, who, in the next century, was to be credited with having published *African Slavery in America* in 1775. Surely, if Paine was a fellow abolitionist, he would have extended his sympathy during a year when his pen seems to have been laid aside; only three private letters are known to have been written by him, and nothing published, in 1784.[213]

PUBLISHED 13 FEBRUARY 1789

This item, signed 'Common Sense', comes as a surprise from the pen of the man who seemed, throughout his life, to have opposed the monarchical system of government. A comment on the times, it appears to be an exhortation to the Prince of Wales of his need to abandon his profligate way of life for something more closely resembling the moral standards of his father, the 'gracious' George III. At the time Paine wrote, the king was ill and frequently thought to be mad. The Prime Minister, William Pitt the Younger, had lost the king's support due, Paine suggests, to the king's illness, and the likelihood of the Prince of Wales becoming regent as proposed by the opposition, which the king supported. It was in Pitt's best interests to restrict the powers of the regent in order to maintain his own position. His ministry insisted that the prince had no right to rule as regent while his father lived. Such was the situation that Paine was certain there would be a change of ministry, but it did not happen,[214] and Pitt was not dismissed as surely would have happened had there been change. The exhortations of 'Common Sense', that follow, were in vain.

For the Times

Friends and Countrymen

There is no page in history marked with more danger than that which now threatens this kingdom. The administration of Mr Pitt has gone on with great success, and with his years he has encreased in wisdom – his conduct as a Minister, so early in life, has never been equalled, nor will ever be surpassed. How zealously has he supported their majesties in the worst of times; while opposition, among whom many have been raised to places of great honour and profit, forgetting him who raised them from nothing into consequence, would now dethrone the king, and ungratefully take from him all that sovereignty, which heretofore, as from the fountain of honour, watered one with military, and another with judicial, and a third with nobility, a fourth with a mitre; yet, no sooner is the sun set on our gracious king afflicted with a visitation from the Almighty, claiming the pity and prayers of all his loving subjects, than these time-serving sycophants join hand in hand in the most infernal measures that ever disgraced men so appointed.

On the other hand, behold our young minister, disregarding his own private interest and emolument, anxious only to secure an immortal name, as far as that belongs to truth, founded in the integrity of an honest man.

His measures have astonished all mankind; and his example is without an equal, either in public or private life. How would any father, if visited by sickness, approve of his heir at law, during such an indisposition, coming into full power, sell his timber, destroy his prospects, turn abroad his faithful and well tried servants? How would returning reason be amazed at the change; to see, in the place of honourable, moral, religious men, gamblers, destroyers, comedians, and spendthrifts appointed to take care of that property for another, which they had wasted themselves in riotous living? Let us think how fit those are, who have abused their own talents, to become counsellors and guardians of the state, defenders of the faith in a national capacity. *Defenders* of the faith in a national capacity, who, in private life, have neither faith nor religion? How dreadful is the prospect! If the man of the people, and the man of the stage, and their honourable associates and colleagues, should now succeed to the government of this country; having the ear of the prince, and the purse of this nation under their influence; whose morals, in private life, are baneful to society, and obnoxious to all that is good. Will the nation learn righteousness from such examples? Can confidence be placed in men, who say and unsay, change sides with every faction, and who are in politics, the true descendants of the Vicar of Bray;[215] from whose manners and politics *good Lord deliver us*!

Can the Ethiopian change his skin, or the leopard his spots? Then may the man of the people, and his *honest* colleagues learn to do well? Can the same fountain send forth bitter and sweet water? Then may the people reconcile contradictions in politics, and vile private example with public economy and virtue. It is very unfortunate that the prince, in early life, has associated himself with men more profligate than Falstaff and his colleagues, in the days of Henry V. And happy will it be, if like unto that wondrous prince, he should now banish them far from court, and continue under his protection and in his service, the faithful, wise, and unexampled ministers of his father, who have already given a pledge of their fidelity to him, in the perseverance of their duty to his gracious and much beloved parents. This conduct will reconcile all men, but those who are needy and desperate, to the interests of the prince, by which means he will become beloved and amiable in the eyes of all his father's truest and best subjects, being, in his regency, the terror of evil doers, and a praise and protection to them that do well; wherein the appointment of regent and the administration under him, will be a blessing to the country, consistent with the good of the nation as well as with

COMMON SENSE

The surprise of this coming from the pen of Paine, of course, lies in the fact that he then supported the monarchy, or at least the regency in the person of the Prince of Wales; his position made clear in a letter to Thomas Walker written just some days after the article in *The Times*.[216] The tenor of the letter confirms that the writer was the same individual who had signed himself 'Common Sense', a pseudonym no other would have adopted, regardless of admiration or scorn; 'Common Sense' was Thomas Paine on both sides of the Atlantic. Aware of the fact that his opinion differed from Walker's, Paine wrote:

... So far from Mr Pitt asserting and supporting the Rights of people, it appears to me taking them away; but as a man ought not to make an assertion without giving his reasons I will give you mine ...

The Regal Power is the majesty of the nation collected to a center, and residing in the Person exercising the Regal Power. The Right, therefore, of a Prince is a Right standing on the Right of the whole Nation. But Mr Pitt says it stands on the Right of Parliament ...

... And if the Regal Power, or the person exercising the Regal Power, either as King or Regent, instead of standing on the universal ground of the Nation be made the mere creature of Parliament, it is, in my humble opinion, equally inconsistent and unconstitutional as if Parliament was the mere creature of the Crown.

It is a common idea in all countries that to take Power from the Prince is to give liberty to the people, but Mr Pitt's conduct is almost the reverse of this. His is to take power from one part of the government to add it to another, for he has encreased the power of the Peers, not the Rights of the People.[217]

Paine was defending popularly based kingship. His article in *The Times* brought no response. Both it and a pamphlet of 1791, yet to be presented, were the issue of his letter to Thomas Walker.

PUBLISHED 18 MAY 1789

This poem, when first published in the *Federal Gazette, and Philadelphia Evening Post*, 18 May 1789, was said to have been 'written at a tea-table, on the author being asked what kind of woman he should prefer'. It is particularly striking because, contrary to the frequently expressed view of many commentators on Thomas Paine that he did not appear to be interested in women – one having recently written of his being a 'model ascetic' who lived an 'outwardly asexual existence'[218] – it reveals a healthily lusty, passionate man. Poetry was not Paine's strong point, but this piece says what it says loud and clear. Published when it was, it was possibly written in England or France, where Paine's coterie of friends included several such free spirits as the one he describes. It has the appearance of having been given to the editor of a paper by the one for whom it was written, or copied and passed on by an acquaintance, which suggests its having been first published in France. It is possible that the manuscript is still treasured in an unknown, private collection. Signed 'Common Sense', it was only tentatively offered as Paine's in 1955 on the grounds that he had, at the time of its appearance, left America for Europe and it was possible that another had adopted his pseudonym; that would seem unlikely. Just the two opening lines were then published for the first time since original publication.[219] There is now no way of knowing when or on which side of the Atlantic the poem was written unless, in the future, an unknown manuscript in private or forgotten papers should come to light.

Give me kind Heav'n – if this wide world has one –
    The girl that loves me for myself alone,
  Whose soul disdains the subterfuge of art,
    Attends to nature nor belies her heart;
  With dauntless freedom to the breast replies,
  And owns within the language of her eyes.
  Give me a girl that feels the mutual chain,
    Nor meanly triumphs in a lover's pain;
    Whose reason shakes off ev'ry yoke beside
  What nature forms, and gentlest love has ty'd;
    Whose feelings strongly rivetted to mine,
  Grow to each sense and round my bosom twine.
    Give me, – or kindly quench the tender fire
  That wakes the throbbing impulse of desire –
  Give me the girl whose eyes, with decent ease,
    Beam on mankind and unaffected please;

While, strickly faithful to the voice of love,
She scorns all passion but our own to prove.
But this deny'd, may Heav'n in pity give,
    With dull insensibility to live:
May cold indiff'rence guide each grovelling thought
    To senseless apathy 'till Nature's brought;
    And when my term of vegetation's o'er,
    May earth receive me to revive no more.

This verse hardly speaks of an 'asexual', 'model ascetic' who, in his own words, lived a life of 'senseless apathy' or 'vegetation'.

29 JUNE 1790

Between March and June 1790, Paine was in England overseeing plans for exhibiting a large model of his bridge in London. Although the extent of the model bridge was 90 feet, when taken apart it was small enough to be transported anywhere in England. During Paine's absences in France, it was stored, hidden among shavings, in the Walker brothers' workshop.[220] The model's building had been an expensive exercise, which ran its designer into debt. Having spent all his financial resources, he was forced to draw on his funds held in the United States of America by his friend Lewis Morris, through his brother, Gouverneur Morris, then serving in London as private agent to the British government. On 29 June 1790, Paine wrote to Gouverneur Morris:

Tuesday Morning

Dear Sir,

Being informed at your hotel that you were out of town for two or three days I leave this to meet you at your return. I find that I cannot well get thro' the expenses of erecting my bridge (which I expect to have complete at the time of the meeting of the new parliament) without drawing some of the monies in General Lewis Morris's hands. I shall be glad you would assist me in this negociation. I wish to draw £50 – in two drafts of £15 each and one of £20 – this I presume will not be inconvenient to him now, and the want of it will be a great inconvenience to me. As soon as you return I will wait on you on this subject.

Your Obedient Humble Servant
Thomas Paine[221]

Morris endorsed the letter 'London 29 June 1790 Thomas Payne. He wants money for a Bill on Lewis Morris'. Morris obliged on behalf of his brother.

PUBLISHED 26 APRIL 1791

This considerable publication was offered as a persuasive follow-up to *Rights of Man* and a prelude to *Rights of Man, Part the Second*, most particularly chapter 5.[222] The work addresses matters treated both more fully and simply within a wider context in the known publications, matters of crime and poverty. Figures quoted appear in both parts of *Rights of Man*. Beyond similarities to *Rights*, there are hints of Paine's opinions on religion as published later in *The Age of Reason*. Early in the pamphlet printed below, the writer identifies himself as 'Common Sense; that constant and faithful attendant on Human Reason ... who founds his hopes on the fitness of Time, or Occasion, which is said to be the most powerful, as well as the wisest counsellor of all'.

Tantalisingly, the following writing may relate to a short paragraph of a letter Thomas Paine wrote to William Short, American chargé d'affaires at the court of France, on 22 June 1790. With the letter, he enclosed a manuscript he wished to have published in France if Short and others thought fit. If the enclosure was to be published there, Paine requested that it be returned to him by safe hand, as he had no time to make a copy. He planned to publish his returned, original manuscript as a translation from the French translation of the original.[223] It might well have been the piece here offered for the first time as a work by Thomas Paine. A search and queries of the libraries and archives of France have not revealed the work in their catalogues, which suggests that it was not published there. Interestingly, in the following paragraph of his letter to Short, Paine wrote of the increase in production of grain since the revolution in the United States and how that fact alone was 'great encouragement to promote the principle of Revolution'.[224] The matter of grain products being mentioned in this piece implies with some certainty that it was the manuscript he sent to William Short and that it was complete in June 1790, but not published until the following year. There is no doubt that Paine's intention was 'to promote the principle of Revolution'.

It is difficult to understand why the pamphlet, indubitably by the well-known author, attracted little notice at the time – only one review has been located – and none since. It is not as if it was suppressed; suppression would have brought it to public attention, but it ran to a second print in the same year. The contents are identical. The text below is transcribed and edited from a book printed for James Ridgway, a publisher of reformist literature, of No. 1, York Street, St James Square, London, in 1791. The title page reads: *Reflections on the Present State of the British Nation by British Common Sense*. The second book, titled *British Common Sense; or, Reflections on the Present State of the British Nation, Recommending a Free, Uninfluenced Representation of the People, on the Ground of National Utility and National Necessity* was printed for W. Miller, Old Bond Street, London.[225] The shorter title was chosen for inclusion here as it names an author. The longer title does not.[226] It will be recalled that Robert Bell's print of *Common Sense* in 1776 bore the words 'Written by an Englishman' on the title page; under the circumstances, naming the author of this work might not be seen as unrelated as a clue to his identity as an outsider.

As already mentioned, it was well known in both America and Europe that the writer known as 'Common Sense' was in fact Thomas Paine. He revealed his real identity early in the American revolutionary war.[227] It is possible that he wrote this piece under his pseudonym due to his enormous pride in having written *Common Sense*; as mentioned earlier, he requested that the words 'Author of Common Sense' be engraved on his headstone.[228] They were.

The pamphlets, not reprinted since 1791, rebuke the commoners for giving up the exercise of their reason to priests and, beyond the king, to the regent. The writer calls upon all to use their own reason. He reassures his readers that use of their reason does not mean a stirring up of dissension or, worse, bloodshed and revolution. Just as he had in *Common Sense*, Paine invokes his readers to consider the effect the results of their lack of reason will have on posterity. He proposes to promote 'universal concord ... which alone can prevent ... the rage and resentment of a whole people against their government' such as had been recently witnessed in France. He points out the difficulties which will be faced by industry and commerce due to the changed situation of France; he writes glowingly of the success, as it appeared to him at that stage, of the French Revolution; and appeals to the 'Godlike Reason' of his readers to take action to save their country from a certain 'state of misery, ruin, and despair'. Paine urged the citizens to demand their rights of representation, voting at short, fixed periods.[229] Just as in *Rights of Man*, his words were designed to stir the minds of ordinary people, the commonalty, to thinking about their money bags in relation to the high taxes they were required to pay. Paine considers the state of the poor and shows that they are less well off than farm animals. He points out the excessive amounts of money spent, or wasted, on such characters, money extorted from the community under the name of taxes, to employ, imprison or transport them across the globe. He points the finger of blame at the police, and that he refers to as the 'Poor System'. He writes of prevention being preferable to and more a deterrent of crime than punishment, and draws on the reader's conscience in not standing up against the 'crime' of punishment by the government, which Paine saw as perpetuating crime and poverty. He takes his readers back to Saxon and Norman times, when the commonalty was able to choose its own magistracy, and reminds them that the Crown usurped that privilege. He suggests a means of returning to that system which is again to be administered by the common people.

As in all his works, Paine demonstrates his awareness of the need to hold the attention of his readers; in this booklet of 125 pages, he reserves those things that he thought might be found dull or digressional for an appendix, while treating the subject matter fully in the body of the piece. The appendix explains the origins of the Poor Laws, the legal complications of providing for the poor, and the origins and present state of the English government.

He comments on the effects of the Industrial Revolution on farm labourers and takes into account its ongoing nature. He observes the plight of returned servicemen who, unable to subsist by other means, are compelled to 'steal or starve'. For those of his readers who perceive his words and warnings to be true, in not protesting to their government and seeking reform, Paine calls their patriotism into question. As in *Common Sense* and *Rights of Man* he implores his readers to consider posterity.

Throughout, he reminds his readers of his pseudonym of 'Common Sense', only on the title page and final page expanding it to 'British Common Sense'. For the most part, he writes as an outsider, using the words 'you' and 'your' in addressing his readers, less frequently employing 'we', 'our' or 'us', although he does address 'My fellow citizens'.

The language used here is more formal than that of *Rights of Man*. This is not the persuasive, easily read language of *Rights*; it is the sort of language that ordinary but educated readers, disinclined towards reform, would probably have discarded as the impossible imaginings of a solution to a problem inherent to then so-called civilized society since its beginnings. The words had none of the conviction of the soon to be published *Rights of Man, Part the Second*, which was immediately recognized as seditious by both laymen and the authorities. Nevertheless, readers conversant with Paine's works will recognize familiar phrases, of which he was obviously proud.

Paine was well aware that his plans could never come to fruition without reform of government, a matter he kept back for bolder treatment in *Rights of Man, Part the Second*, although he makes it clear that urgent action needs to be taken. He writes with certainty of forthcoming revolution in Britain, and advises the king and landed gentry that if they would only recognize the needs of their country, they would find greatness and the respect of the common people, unlike the King of France, whom he calls a 'detested vagabond'. He offers a plan for hasty and complete reform of government.

To this piece, Paine added three footnotes. One to his page 81 is to be found here, marked, as by Paine, with an asterisk. The second, to his page 86, and the third, to his page 124, are marked with two and three asterisks respectively. The notes are to be found at the end of Paine's text, which follows.

Reflections on the Present State of the British Nation

In this country, where corruption has so completely subdued and strongly fettered human reason, the attempt of one or more obscure individuals to again erect the standard of forlorn reason, and take the field against her seemingly irresistible vanquisher, may appear desperate presumption, bordering upon insanity.

But I, for one, esteem it base and dastardly to despair of the commonweal. Indeed, why should I or others despair! Since the world began, nay, almost in our own day, we have beheld human reason in a situation still more forlorn; more completely subdued, bound in stronger fetters, by an enemy of still more mighty power. And we now see that once omnipotent, haughty, and cruel oppressor prostrate at the feet of reason; and that through the means of individuals, till then obscure.[230]

Who is there amongst you so ignorant or uninformed, that does not, at this day, look back with disdain and contempt, on that supine slothful credulity of men, which suffered a few religious jugglers, by means of gross trick and fiction, to fetter their reason, to insult and abuse their understanding, to rob them of their property, and to trample upon their privileges as men.

Yet, with the same supine slothful credulity, you now suffer a few state jugglers to fetter your reason, to insult and abuse your understanding, to rob you of your property, and to trample upon your privileges as men, in a degree far more oppressive and injurious to your interest, by means of tricks and fiction still more gross and worse disguised; and there in a manner less excusable and more disgraceful to you.

For these religious jugglers effected their deceptions by means of a celestial engine; the nature and properties of which were above the comprehension of human reason. The ignorant laity were humbly conscious that they knew nothing of what was going on in heaven; whereas the deluding clergy pretended to a perfect knowledge of those matters, through divine revelation, exclusively understood by them, the chosen ministers of heaven, acting under its express commission, specially delegated to them; and in particular to one of them, who was appointed by God his vice-regent in these matters on earth;[231] with farther power to open or shut the gates of heaven to whomsoever he pleased. It was therefore highly excusable in men, consciously ignorant, to superstitiously surrender the implicit guidance of their reason, in matters evidently above the reach of that reason, to those supposed unerring guides, and all powerful disposers of their future eternal interest.

But what excuse can you plead for having surrendered the exercise of your reason, and yielded up the guidance thereof, in a degree not less passively superstitious, to men who have not the shadow of claim to divine mission; who can plead no right to authority or power over you, save what they derive from your own gift; which they hold only by your own consent, and subject to your own controul: who can pretend to no supernatural or exclusive knowledge of the matters which they so mysteriously conceal from you? These matters being your own temporal concerns, and of a nature so completely within the comprehension of human reason, that every one of you is, by nature, equally qualified to judge of and distinguish on them, as any one of these who assume the present mysterious management of them. By the rules of reason as well as of nature, every one of you has an equal right as they to judge on those concerns. And every one of you is now called upon by the very first law of nature, to exercise that right of judging on those your own concerns; seeing that each of you has an equal risk, and consequently an equal interest in the stake; namely, your *all*; Be that *all* comparatively great, or comparatively little.

And let not any one of you believe, or suffer others to persuade you, that these truths are here mentioned for the purpose of opposing or impeding the due authority of government, to serve the purpose of party, or to stir up dissention. Reason is not the foe, she is the surest friend and most zealous supporter of good government and due subordination. She disdains party or cabal of every description; and she abhors dissention. For she attempts nothing by bodily force or compulsion. The mind is her subject, on the understanding, and not the passions of which, she works by soft persuasion and clear conviction, producing unanimity of sentiment amongst men, and a general concurrence of their will. To effect this she requires nothing more than a candid and attentive hearing. If men will vouchsafe the hearing to Reason, her power is irresistible. Folly, with her train of tyrants and slaves, immediately flies before her, and vanishes from the face of the earth; but, as her voice is still and gentle, and the voice of Folly is loud, boisterous, and imperious, it is extremely difficult for Reason to obtain the hearing from men.

To obtain for reason this candid and attentive hearing from you, my fellow citizens, is the present purpose of an individual but little known; stiling himself *Common Sense*; that constant and faithful attendant on human reason. He is perfectly aware of the seeming impossibility to shake the throne of Folly; so strongly established on long habit and custom; supported by the whole wealth of an opulent nation, profusely lavished on the purposes of general corruption; and watchfully guarded by an innumerable host of seduced and deluded mercenaries. But he founds his hopes, and strong hopes of success, on the fitness of *Time*, of *Occasion*, which is said to be the most powerful, as well as the wisest counsellor of all.

It had long been, and ever was till of very late, the confirmed opinion of all men, in the least acquainted with your national concerns, that a continuation of the same management must, in a short space of time, produce national insolvency. And your language then was, '*We hope it will last our time*'. A mean spirited and dastardly trust, yet it was your only trust.

But astonishing as it now doth appear to Common Sense, and incredible as it would, but for woeful feeling, appear to posterity, such has been the late influence of corruption on your understanding, that, without any change in your situation for the better, but on the contrary, much for the worse, your present language is, 'We are very well as we are, we do not wish to be better'. And your conduct corresponds with your language. Revelling in profound security, in mirth and in jollity; acting precisely the thoughtless spendthrift bankrupt, who exceeds his former degree of extravagance and expensive debauch, at the time when his commission is about issuing.

Could you possibly exhibit more striking instances to the effect, than in your late wanton armament, and your present Indian war?[232] And which are here termed your acts, because by your concurrence therein you have rendered yourselves accessories after the fact; and thereby become disqualified for ever after to sit as judges on those, or indeed on any other act of your government wherein you shall so concur; be it ever so pernicious to your interest.

At any rate, crimination of your government for past misdeeds, irritation, or dissention, is far from being the object of this present address. Prevention of future evils is its only aim.

Instead of discord or sedition, it is hereby proposed to promote universal concord; an unanimous concurrence of this whole community in adopting that measure, which alone can prevent the most dreadful and fatal of all seditions; even the desperate rage and resentment of a whole people against their government, upon discovering that they have been abused, deceived, and ruined: and which must unavoidably and speedily prove the case, unless the measure herein after pointed out shall be adopted.

For the moment it shall be discovered that the national resources fall short of answering the present enormous yearly expenditure, that moment popular delusion vanishes, and desperate rage succeeds in its place; and it is not in the power of despotism itself, with all its cunning contrivances, to long procrastinate that day of dreadful reckoning.

For, besides the wasteful profusion and abuse of your government, causes altogether sufficient to this effect in themselves, there has lately arisen another cause, which will greatly accelerate that said dreadful event; and which, as being a foreign cause, beyond the reach or influence of your government, will force it, as well as you, to *feel*, in defiance of corruption, deception, slothful credulity, or national infatuation.

The cause here alluded to, is the late reform of the wasteful profusion and oppressive abuses of their government in France. A country so situated, with respect to yours, in a variety of circumstances, besides that of contiguity, that no alteration whatever, for the better or worse, can happen in the one, that will not in a great degree affect the situation of the other country.

It shall hereafter be set forth at large, in what manner and to what degree, the present reform of government abuses in France, when it shall come to operate on the manufactures and commerce of that country, will affect the present flattering state of your manufactures and commerce; which is the principal source from whence you derive the means to support your present enormous expenditure.

In this introductory part it shall suffice to observe, that so soon as the manufactures and commerce of France shall come to feel the alleviation of one half part of their former taxes; and when they shall farther feel the benign and active influence of a mild, just, and attentive government, instead of the haughty oppression, and contemptuous discouragement of their late despotic government, and both which alterations they will strongly feel in a very little space of time; then, and at that time, will the manufactures and commerce of Britain woefully feel the ruinous pressure of their present burdens, in case the same shall be continued.

First, and at all events, and that very speedily, in a total deprivation of the French market for these manufactures, which Britain has enjoyed for some years past, almost entire; particularly through the late confusions in France. And the loss of that market will be felt here severely.[233]

Second, in a loss of the market for these manufactures in other foreign countries; from which under such a great difference of circumstances, Britain will soon be cut off by France.

And finally, in the loss of our own market, or home consumption; as France has lately experienced.

And suffer not yourselves to be lulled into ruinous security, by the mean unmanly expectation, that this late necessary reform of government abuses in France; this first rational and effectual effort of a people, to vindicate the dignity of human nature, to rescue men from that ignominious state of abject slavery, and cruel oppression, under which they have been ever held, by the unnatural force of feudal tyranny, will or can be defeated, or even retarded. These expectations are not more mean and unmanly than they are false and groundless; suggested and inculcated upon you, by pernicious parasitical sophisters, and other retainers to or dependents upon tyranny and corruption;

whose base minds being totally void of that generous spirit, that principle, and sentiment, which first animated the people in France to undertake this glorious enterprize, they cannot conceive or believe that such a spirit exists in human nature. And thereupon, they persuade themselves, and endeavour to persuade you, that this undertaking of the French people differs nothing from the rash ebullition of an English mob, suddenly excited, and as suddenly quelled. And, in this persuasion, they daily labour to impose upon your credulity forged facts, and vain predictions of counter revolutions, which exist only in their own wicked hearts, and crazed imaginations.

To enlarge on this subject here would interfere with our intended purpose. Thus much however it is necessary to add, that the lapse of two years has furnished the proof of *actual* facts, in contradiction to these *forged* facts and vain predictions, sufficing to convince all of you, the credulous as well as the incredulous, that the same spirit, which first animated the people of France to this glorious undertaking, still animates them, with a zeal increased by increase of rational knowledge, to prosecute that undertaking to a complete, perfect, and a firm perpetual establishment. And farther, that they do so prosecute it with profound wisdom, and great skill, daily improving by experience; and at the same time with astonishing temper, moderation, and magnanimity.

And, from these premises, you may assuredly conclude, that it is altogether beyond your power, (even if you were so basely disposed) that it is infinitely beyond the power of those few desperate and despicable retainers to despotism in that country; that it is beyond the power of all the surrounding despots, with their mercenary bands, united; nay, that it is beyond the power of all these, combined, to shake the strong basis, or even to retard the complete and firm establishment of that rationally modelled government in France; supported, as it is, by the souls as well as the bodies of twenty millions of people, enlightened and guided by pure human reason.

And, from the same premises, you may draw this farther assured conclusion, that so soon as the wise and just regulations, which have been framed by their present government, shall be carried into full execution and practice, and which is now nearly the case, they will infallibly produce all those effects on the commerce and manufactures of France, operating in the manner that hath been mentioned, a subversion of your manufactures and commerce.

But it is altogether in your power to prevent this subversion of your manufactures and commerce, by means that are perfectly honourable, and easily practicable. Relieve them from the burden and effects of all such taxes as are unnecessary, and from those wanton abuses of power, by which they are at present intolerably oppressed. This relief being granted in time, and before your manufactures and commerce shall come to feel the effects that have been mentioned, will place them, in other respects, nearly upon a footing with those of France; and will even preserve to them the advantage they at present possess, in superiority of skill, and priority of establishment. But if you shall delay that relief, until oppression in the one country and encouragement in the other, shall have drawn your manufacturers, together with the skill in manufacture, from you, relief will then come too late. Manufacture and also commerce will then be departed from you. And, once gone, they never will return.

And thus much it appeared necessary to premise, respecting the imminently dangerous situation of your manufactures and commerce; in order to thereby arouse your attention, and obtain from you a hearing for Reason, on the subject of your other national concerns; which, notwithstanding they are not so immediately affected by that said foreign cause, as are your manufactures and commerce, yet are they otherwise in a situation so truly dangerous, that unless an effectual remedy shall be speedily applied, this nation must soon be plunged into a state of misery, ruin, and despair.

And, if your national concerns are actually and truly in such an imminently dangerous situation (and that they are in such a situation Common Sense undertakes to prove), and if there be within your reach and power the means to prevent this imminent ruin (as Common Sense likewise undertakes to prove), shall not Reason prevail on you to apply those means?

To what end or use did he who made you with such large discourse, looking before and after, bestow upon you that capability, and Godlike Reason? Was it for the purpose of qualifying you, either aggregately or severally, to be more ingeniously and usefully subservient to the will and purposes of one or more beings of your own species, who hold no interest in common with you, or who at least have separated their share from the common stock? Or was not this Godlike faculty bestowed upon you for the purpose of enabling you to distinguish between good and evil; to preserve yourselves from danger; and to promote your own welfare and true happiness, either as a community, or as individuals of that community?

And think not these questions impertinent or absurd! Your conduct warrants them. Nay, and if they were to be answered ingenuously, according to that conduct, the answer would be little for your credit. What a falling off is here! What a shameful defection from the standard of Godlike Reason, to that of the beastlike tyrant, Folly! Yet it is not too late; the day of grace is not yet past; nor the door to salvation shut. But little time is there to be lost.

Rouse then, my fellow citizens! Rouse up your reason from that disgraceful *deliquium*, into which it hath been thrown by base, accursed Corruption that lewd procuress of the tyrant Folly; that fell hag and sorceress; which, like the fabulous Circe, hath by her wicked charms and incantations transformed you into beasts, the passive drudges of her cruel employer! Hearken to the voice of Godlike Reason; and immediately obey her call, to rescue and save yourselves, with your posterity, from impending ruin, by employing the means that alone can save you; by applying that remedy which alone can prevent your almost desperate disease from proceeding to an absolute mortification!

Nor is this remedy a mystery, confined within the knowledge or power of a select few – it is obvious to every eye, and readily within your own power. Acquire that voice, that power, and share in your legislative government which, according to reason, nature, and the due order of things, inherently appertains to you, and which self-preservation now calls loudly upon you to exercise: by means of a real actual representation of yourselves; according to the only true, genuine, and natural sense, or signification of that thing, *Representation*; which is, that the persons, who are to represent you in your legislature, shall be chosen to that office by the free voices of all and every one of you who are to be represented; *and by none other*. And that these representatives, when so chosen and appointed, shall not possess the power or opportunity to convert the trust committed by you to them, into a personal right of their own; but shall execute that trust under the full controul of you their constituents, *and under no other controul or authority*; by means of a perpetual obligation to recur frequently to your judgement of their conduct, by fresh elections, at short fixed periods.

Such a representation of yourselves can alone save and secure you and your posterity from ruin; and such a representation will do that effectually. For, reform of every one abuse in your government will flow as naturally from such a representation, as water flows from the full fountain. Whereas a fallacious, fictitious, or nominal representation never will reform one single evil or abuse; but, on the contrary, will only serve to countenance and abet the *actual* government, in perpetuating and aggravating every present evil and abuse.

But it hath been undertaken to first convince you that your national concerns are at present in such a situation as to indispensably require the immediate application of this remedy.

And, to that end, it is proposed to place before your eyes a view of those concerns, principally respecting the present state of your finances, and the manner in which they are administered. And also respecting the present state of your police; and the manner of administering your municipal government.

And, in this intended view of your financial administration, you will perceive such an unjustifiable, profuse waste of national treasure on those establishments that may be termed necessary to government; and, what is worse, on establishments that shall appear to be not barely unnecessary, but highly pernicious to the commonweal. Nay, you will perceive the national wealth squandered in a manner so wantonly profuse, on purposes where even the personal ambition or avarice of government do not appear to be rationally concerned, as would induce the inspector to conclude, that the parties concerned in causing this waste did really consider national wealth, or affluence, to be the greatest human evil; which it was their duty, or otherwise their interest, to prevent by all possible means, and to get rid of as soon as possible. And, when you shall perceive all the various sums that are yearly drawn from this community, for these several purposes, collected into one total sum, that total sum will be found so astonishingly enormous, as will convince the most inconsiderate, that the present wasteful expenditure of its government cannot be long supported by the resources of this state – even if they were to remain in their present flourishing situation – whereas, there is not a truth more certain, or more obvious than this, that these resources must speedily feel a mighty diminution.

And, in proof of these assertions, it is farther intended to point out how, and by what means, many millions of the present expenditure may be yearly saved to this community.

And, when you shall come to view the present state of your police, and the administration of your municipal government, you will perceive that government administered in such a manner, as if they who are invested with the power of administering it, considered it their duty, or at least their interest, to promote purposes, directly opposite to those purposes for which they are vested by the community with such power.

You will perceive your whole labouring commonalty wilfully and intentionally debauched and seduced from industry. Not barely permitted, but tempted and invited by the peculiar nature of that government, and the practice of those who administer it, to be idle, dissolute, extravagant, negligent of their families, disorderly, and disobedient to all rightful authority. You will perceive above one third part of that labouring commonalty existing in unspeakable misery; wallowing in filth, squalor, and beastly slavish ignorance; placed by the management of your government, in a state of absolute idleness, and total uselessness to this state; nay, converted, by the practice of that government, into an intolerable burden, an insufferable nuisance, and desperate destructive enemy to the honest, the peaceable, and industrious part of the community.

Whilst, on the other hand, you will perceive this peaceable and industrious part of the community loaded, by that government, with such a burden of taxes, yearly paid by them, for the express purpose of protecting and securing them from those very evils and abuses, as greatly exceeds the whole sums paid yearly, for the like purposes, by all the other communities on earth together.

And here likewise, in order to convince you that it is practicable to remedy and prevent all this, the special ways and means shall be pointed out, whereby that yearly waste of public treasure on these municipal purposes may be saved to the community; and, at the same time, these present evils and abuses be converted into future national benefits and advantages.

Here then, my fellow citizens, doth Common Sense address himself at your tribunal, the unfee'd advocate of Human Reason; to prove the truth of all the several charges he has here laid. And farther to prove that all the several enormities, evils, and abuses so charged, are within the power of remedy. All that he desires, in return for his pains, is a fair and candid hearing from you.

And here again Common Sense disclaims all intention to criminate your present government for past misdeeds, to irritate, or to inflame. And this repeated protestation he makes, for the purpose of counteracting that artifice, which state jugglers have of late revived with such success, to prevent your granting the hearing to reason, on the subject of your national concerns.

For, even as religious jugglers did formerly prevail on mankind to reject with horror every attempt to undeceive them in religious matters, by branding all such attempts with the general epithet of '*Schismatical opposition to Holy Church*' – '*Damnable Heresy*'; and, by that artifice, held the minds of men, for so many ages, in dark ignorance, and blind slavish superstition. Even so have state jugglers of late revived that very artifice, with equal success, by branding every attempt to undeceive you in your national matters, with the general appellation of '*Seditious Opposition to Government*'. Neither do they want their court of inquisition to secure that success.

A View of the Municipal Government in England

Intending to lay before you a view of your national concerns, principally respecting the present state of your finances, and of your police, there occurred a doubt which of those two objects held the best claim to your first attention. But, for obvious reasons, it was judged proper to first consider the present state of your police, or the administration of your municipal government, as it affects the morals, the conduct, and the state or situation of the several individuals, or classes of individuals composing this community, as well as that of the whole community at large.

And, for our present purpose, it will suffice to divide that community into only two classes. The first, to comprehend all those above the degree of servility. The second, to consist of the labouring commonalty.

On the morals, the conduct, and situation of that first class, a respectful silence shall here be observed. It is the second class that becomes the subject of our present observation.

And the second class shall be again subdivided into two parts. The first, to comprehend all those of the commonalty who actually do labour, and maintain themselves and their families by industry. The second, to contain all those who, having no honest means of subsisting but by labour, yet do not labour, but are idle. Though, in fact, there is a middling sort betwixt these two; and a numerous sort they are, but all these shall be reckoned in with the first, or industrious part.

On that first, or actually labouring part of the commonalty, it shall here suffice to observe that, however disorderly, dissolute, insolent, and disobedient to due authority they may be, it is owing entirely to the natural goodness of their own disposition, or to the force of parental education, and not in the slightest degree to the attention or care of your government, that they are so good; or properly, that they are not much worse.

But, when we come to consider the case of that other part of our commonalty who, having no honest means to subsist but by their labour, are either through slothfulness, viciousness, or the want of opportunity, idle and unemployed, what a scene presents itself to our view! A scene so truly horrid, so exceedingly degrading and disgraceful to human nature, and at the same time so totally repugnant to all the principles of good or just government, as never yet disgraced any other country, or any other age. And this, whether we consider the number and the situation of those wretched poor, or whether we consider the relative situation of the other part of this community.

For, respecting the number of those idle or unemployed poor, if we shall take into the reckoning all those who exist in absolute idleness, by parish charity and vagrant beggary, by robbing and thieving, and by other vicious courses, we shall find that they exceed in number one third part of our whole labouring commonalty.

And, if we shall take the trouble to consider the situation of that part of those idle poor who subsist by parish charity and vagrant beggary, we shall find it to be, not only beneath the rank of human beings, but greatly beneath the rank of those beasts that are useful to men. For these wretches, being entirely useless to every one valuable purpose in nature, are not of the slightest account, consideration, or consequence, either to others, or to themselves. Excluded from the taste of every thing like rational independence, or free agency, and consequently excluded from every ray of comfort or satisfaction in life, they crawl about, like unheeded vermin, in the streets, and in the fields, in a state of inconceivable ignorance, profligacy, and lewdness. Or otherwise, immured within the precincts of a parish workhouse, they exist in beastly squalor and filth, in slavish miserable dependence on charity, extorted from those who wish the whole of them extinguished.

And now let Common Sense call for your judgement, my fellow citizens, whether the above truly described situation is such as befits rational beings!

Yet the state of this begging part is far less deplorable, than is that of those others who subsist by robbing and thieving. This class of beings hath of late become amazingly numerous indeed, as consisting of the whole progeny of numberless vicious parents; who through the nature and practice of our government are permitted, indeed encouraged, to rear their entire offspring in their own wicked courses. And these are reinforced by multitudes of others, better educated, who have been led or driven to that course of life, by perhaps some one single act of irregularity, committed through unavoidable temporary distress, or possibly through the inconsiderate levity of youth, to which the present annual state lotteries are no slight inducement. For having, by such single act of irregularity, incurred reproach or the loss of good character, they thereby become disqualified for and excluded from all private employ, because, in every situation of that nature, there exists a degree of trust or confidence. And, being thus cut off from all opportunity of earning a subsistence in private employ, there exists not at present any possible means whereby they can earn a subsistence through labour, or honest employ of any kind. Of course all these unhappy beings become unavoidably reduced to this horrid alternative, either to steal whereon to subsist life, or otherwise to starve, a death, of all deaths, the most repugnant to human feeling. And therefore they put forth their hand, and steal.

The moment they have committed one single act of theft they are, from thenceforth, chained down for life to subsist by thieving, and are irretrievably consigned to the gallows. They are for ever cut off from the paths of men, and are placed in the state of prowling wolves, to subsist by ravage and depredation, living in perpetual horror, and hourly dread of detection. For, like wolves, a price is set upon their heads. And, when detected, they are hanged up like wolves, or transported to the farthest corners of the earth. Otherwise they are inhumanly punished for years, in jails, and in Justicia gallies[234] and, when let loose, are under the unavoidable necessity of again returning to steal, or starve, on which terms, liberty, or going at large, which to all other beings on earth is the most desirable of blessings, becomes to these human beings alone the most dreadful of all curses. And more especially if, after such confinement, there shall remain in them the slightest ray of rational reflection, or one latent spark of human virtue.

And here again permit Common Sense to call for your judgement, whether it is fit, or becoming even uncivilized human nature, that such a number of your fellow citizens should be irremediably placed in this horrid situation. More particularly if you shall consider, that many of these may be youths of ingenuous disposition, of generous sentiment, of extensive natural abilities, and of liberal education, who, if any possible means had been held forth of earning an honest subsistence, or if any the slightest regard were paid to these matters by your government, would have returned to the paths of honesty, would have become useful, perhaps an ornament to society. Is it fit, I say, that these, or any of these should be irretrievably placed in this horrid situation, which hath been here truly described, provided there are any possible means to prevent or remedy it? And that there are such means, not only effectual, but easily practicable, Common Sense hath undertaken to prove incontestably.

But first we have to consider the relative situation of the orderly, honest, and industrious part of the community, as it stands affected by this conduct of their government. Through such total inattention of government, together with such accession of genius as hath been mentioned to the society of thieves, the practice of thieving hath, of late years, become elevated, in this country, to the dignity of a learned profession. They have their regular seminaries, where novices are instructed in the whole mystery of thieving, from the first elements, to the highest degree of professional skill, where students undergo honorary probation, respecting their ingenuity and dexterity of practice; their craft and steadiness to evade or resist the inquisition of the law; and their intrepidity and firmness in dying hard. Where, in their dreadful orgies, they are sworn to desperate secrecy, and are steeled against the feelings of fear and compunction, by repeated exhibitions of the whole process of events to which the profession is subject, from detection, to trial at the bar, to confinement in the cells, to the gallows, and finally to interment. But it was reserved for this country, and this present age, to produce those nouvelle monsters of human nature, the house-burners, who lay waste a whole neighbourhood for the purpose of plundering the wretched inhabitants.

It is difficult to conceive, but altogether impossible to describe, the danger, the dread, and the loss to which the honest and industrious part of this community is subjected by the existence of such numerous, desperate, and skilful bands of professed ruffians. But what aggravates the case of this community is, that (as hath been before observed) it contributes more money to its government, for securing the persons and property of the people from the danger of thieves, and the importunity of vagrant beggars, than is paid for these purposes, by all the other communities on earth together.

For, in the first place, the community in England and Wales exclusively is subjected, by the authority of their government, to the payment of a tax, peculiar to this community alone, termed *poor rates*; which is levied by half-yearly payments, to the amount of four millions sterling yearly, for the expressly declared purpose, of maintaining and providing employ for all their idle or unemployed poor.

In the second place, this same community pays in the way of county rates, and other various taxes, charges, and contributions for protecting them from thieves and felons, for detecting, confining, and convicting those felons; for hanging them and punishing them, in jails, in houses of correction, and in Justicia gallies; and for that unnatural whim of transporting them to Botany Bay, a sum that may be estimated at more than one million yearly.[235]

To this reckoning we must add that which is extorted from the honest and industrious part of this community, by the importunity of vagrant beggars, together with what is pettily pilfered and wasted by those beggars, who are permitted, notwithstanding the aforesaid enormous poor rate provision, to infest our fields, our highways, our streets, and our houses, in a degree beyond what is seen in any other country, where no such settled provision is made for the poor. And this may be estimated at one million yearly.

And finally we must subjoin the value of what is robbed and plundered from the honest and industrious part of this community, or otherwise destroyed and wasted, by the various operations of highway robbers, footpads, thieves, pickpockets, swindlers, burglars or housebreakers, and above all by that modern sect of house-burners and barn-burners. And which together may be estimated at one more million yearly.

So that, when the whole expence incurred, shall be added to the loss sustained, by the honest and industrious part of this community, for and on account of, or by and through the means of the idle and unemployed part of the labouring commonalty, it will all together be found to exceed the sum of seven millions sterling. A sum far exceeding the whole revenue that is paid by any other state in Europe, France alone excepted, for every expence of its national government. And which exceeds three times over the whole revenue that was paid by this state, for the whole expence of its government in the reign of Charles the Second; being little more than a century ago.

It is impossible that you can have so blindly or passively yielded up the use of your reason to the will of your government, as to shut your eyes against such gross and wanton abuse, when laid before your view; or to shut your ears against Common Sense, proffering to point out the certain and easy means or method whereby this enormous yearly waste of seven millions sterling may be saved to the community; whereby you may be completely secured from those dangers, dreads, and losses to which you are at present hourly subjected; and whereby such a number of your fellow citizens may be rescued and relieved from their present wretched noxious situation, and be converted into useful subjects of the state.

In searching out the true remedy of any evil, it is necessary to trace out the true primary cause of that evil, from its visible or apparent effects, through its various intermediate or secondary causes. Thus the present idleness or non-employment of those noxious poor appears to be the immediate cause of the evils sustained from them by the other part of the community. And it shall be shown how this idleness, with those consequent evils and abuses, including that enormous yearly waste of seven millions, are to be traced up, in the next stage, to the malversation of your government. First, in the matter of your police. And second, in the matter of your Poor System.

The *general* charge against the nature and state of your police is, that your government has adapted and applies it solely to the purpose of *punishing*, and in no degree that of *preventing* the commission of crimes. Whereas it is evident that punishment, as it cannot precede but only follow the commission of crimes, so cannot it possibly prevent or remedy those evils that unavoidably attend such commission. And as to that pretended effect of punishment to prevent the commission of crimes, by deterring the surviving criminals through sight or example of those punishments, your long woeful experience has sufficiently proved this self-evident fact, that *punishment*, whether exemplary or personal, never hath, never will, nor ever can, deter or reclaim one single criminal, so long as they shall all continue to be so situated as that they must of necessity either *steal* or *starve*, inasmuch as the dread or even the suffering of punishment, however repeated or severe, cannot subdue the rage of hunger. Nor can a momentary death be compared with the long protracted pangs of starving. It is indeed a truth notorious, that the frequency of executions serves merely to harden the surviving criminals.

Punishment is the tyrannical and odious part of a government's duty, which a rational and equitable government will ever studiously shun, by carefully removing from before the people every stumbling block, and every temptation to the commission of crimes, whether through the facility of committing them, or through ignorance, levity, or distress. But a government that employs punishments as the only means to prevent the commission of crimes, is altogether tyrannical. And, under such a government, the frequency of crimes and punishments will ever increase, in proportion as the degree of tyranny increases.

But if indeed it actually shall or may be within the power of a government to provide for every unemployed person in that state which it governs, the ready means of subsisting by the honest earnings of labour, then the execution of every one individual who shall have been forced, through the want of such means, upon the commission of crimes deserving that punishment, or who when willing to repent, has through the same want been forced to persist, must appear in the eye of that *Being* who made all men, and before whom all men are equal, a wanton murder committed by that government. And however innocent of this the people of that state may consider themselves individually, yet as a community, possessing the natural and rational right, together with full power to restrain their own government from doing wrong and to enforce its doing right, it must stand an indelible reproach on their national character, if they shall passively suffer their government to persist in so cruelly tyrannizing over the persons and wantonly sacrificing the lives of their fellow citizens.

The means whereby that cruel and disgraceful frequency of punishments in this country may be prevented, by preventing the frequency of crimes, will more properly come into consideration, after we shall have examined the nature and present state of your Poor System, as will appear.

This Poor System, as hath been said, is peculiar to the community of England and Wales; for it exists in no one other community. And it will appear, when examined, to be the most viciously absurd system that could possibly be contrived by any government; as being productive of numberless and grievous evils, but of no one good to that community wherein it exists. For, on the one hand, it is cruelly oppressive and perfectly useless to the wealthy and industrious part of this community, who are compelled by their government to support it. And, on the other hand, it is equally useless and highly pernicious to that other part of the community, the labouring commonalty; for whose benefit it is pretended to have been instituted.

But, notwithstanding these be facts self-evident and universally known, yet as nothing less than the most forcible conviction can suffice to rid the minds of men from prejudices which, however absurd and erroneous, have been deeply impressed thereon by long habit, and never considered custom,[236] it becomes here absolutely necessary to thoroughly investigate the nature of this Poor System. To trace its origin, with the motives, views, and causes that induced your government to first institute it. To examine the mischievous principle of the several regulations which it prescribes. And to point out the many grievous evils which it causes at present to this community: and which are increasing every day.

But as these remarks on the origin of this Poor System, with the motives of government for first instituting it, might appear to some prolix and tedious, they shall be stated apart in an appendix.

Yet, however iniquitous the first institution of this Poor System was, and however injurious in its nature to the commonweal, the evils it caused at the first were altogether trivial and inconsiderable, when compared with the mischiefs it causes at this day. *Then* it was merely the serpent's egg. But hatched as it hath been and fostered, for near two centuries,[237] by the viciousness of the government and the passive negligence of the people, it hath grown up to acquire in these present times the fabulous properties of the *Lernean Hydra*.[238] Every attempt that hath been made to strike off one of its many venomous heads having only served to produce two more in its stead, until they have so multiplied that only its utter extinction can relieve this community from its all-destroying powers.

For that statute, the 43 Eliz. which was then devised and intended merely as a temporary provision for such of the labouring commonalty as happened to be, at that new and extraordinary juncture, idle, unemployed, and dangerous to government, hath been converted, in process of times, into a system to debauch the whole labouring commonalty of this country, and to seduce them from industry.[239] For what argument or stimulation to labour and industry doth or can there exist in the minds of these labouring poor, saving alone the fear or apprehension of future want and distress to themselves and their families? Withdraw that fear, and you thereby withdraw from the minds of the labouring commonalty the sole stimulation to, not only labour and industry, but to frugality, sobriety, care of their families, and every degree of due subordination. And this Poor System doth, at present, not only withdraw that sole stimulation to all these virtues, but it holds forth to the labouring poor a tempting lure to all the opposite vices. The sense and knowledge that their respective parishes are compelled, by law, to provide all necessaries for themselves and their families, whenever they shall chuse to demand it; or, in their own phrase, 'That the parish is bound to find them', is in itself sufficient to debauch the mind and vitiate the morals of any labouring commonalty on earth. And that our labouring commonalty are not, through this cause alone (was there none other) still more vicious than we find them, is owing merely to a peculiar rectitude of their own natural disposition.

But it would be difficult for any government to contrive a measure more wantonly wicked, or more mischievously and unnecessarily pernicious to the good of the people, than is that regulation of this Poor System which compels each several parish (and in still more mischievous subdivision each town and vill within a parish) to distinctly maintain all its own respective poor. For thereby all these several parishes, towns, and vills, are perpetually involved in feuds, disputes, and expensive lawsuits betwixt themselves. And the community at large is thereby subjected to the enormous expence of at least one million sterling yearly paid by it, for this one purpose, and for no other individual purpose on earth, than to determine, by these troublesome, expensive lawsuits, whether this one individual or the other of these numberless parish paupers, who must at any rate be one and all of them maintained at the expence of the community, shall be so maintained in this one particular parish, or in some one other parish.

The particular and curious process of this Parish and Poor settlement regulation shall also, to avoid prolixity, be stated in the appendix.

We have next to consider that other regulation of this Poor System which respects the manner of maintaining and employing those parish poor. It is ordered by law that two or more overseers, for each parish, town, or vill, shall be annually appointed under the hand and seal of two or more justices of the peace, for the purpose of providing meat, drink, cloathing, lodging, and all other necessaries for all the poor and needy within such parish, town, or vill, with full power in those overseers to assess each parishioner in a proportionate share of whatever expence shall be deemed requisite for so maintaining those poor. And, upon non-payment, to distrain for the same.

And, by way of recompence to the parish for this expence, it is enacted that the said poor shall be set to work by *those overseers*, on flax, hemp, wool, thread, iron, and other wares and stuff; and that each parish shall be entitled to all the benefit of this Poor work. And the overseers are ordered to provide a convenient stock of these said wares and stuff. And for the purchasing this convenient stock, those overseers are farther vested with a like power to assess all the parishioners in a sufficient sum of money.

But it was soon discovered by the parishes, that this intended recompence for their expence turned out to be an addition to that expence, of nearly so much money as was the first cost of those said wares and stuff. For they found themselves charged in a high price for that first cost; and, when these raw materials had passed through the hands of their workhouse manufacturers, they found the value of those manufactures to be almost nothing. And, for this reason, all the several parishes have long abandoned the pursuit of that intended recompence from parish workhouse labour on wares and stuff. Excepting it may be a very few of these parishes; where the numbers, the opulence, or the indolence of the parishioners render them indifferent to that addition of expence which is caused to them by the whim of a few consequential individuals, who chuse to amuse themselves with experiments at the expence of others.

For it is now about seventy years, namely, in the 9th George, since the parishes obtained a statute to legally release them from that *compulsory working clause* in the 43d Elizabeth, and for enabling each parish to contract with any person or persons for the provision and maintenance of its respective poor, at so much a head. And accordingly this mode of contracting for the maintenance of their poor has now become general. The labour of these poor being ever thrown into the bargain; as a value perfectly understood by both the parties contracting.

The nature of this parish maintenance may be guessed at. But the conjecture of those who do not know it will fall short of the reality. It is a common saying, that 'Beggars must not be Chusers'. The true force of that saying is no where so fully felt as in a parish workhouse. In truth these paupers feel their poverty to be a crime grievously punishable. No criminal confined for the purpose of punishment feels that punishment more severely than the pauper feels his. The only difference is, that the pauper has the choice of liberating himself. And of this choice they commonly avail themselves, soon after they have tasted the nature of parish workhouse discipline. They quit their confinement; either upon furlough, in collusion with the contractor, who continues to receive the parish allowance for these temporary absentees; or otherwise they totally desert the workhouse. But their minds having been once habituated to idleness, very few, if any of them, ever return to labour and industry. In both these cases they commonly first try their chance in vagrant beggary; and thus load the community in a double capacity. If they fail in that profession, they commonly betake themselves to pilfering and stealing, at the risk of the gallows or transportation, rather than remain in the parish workhouse.

It may appear unnecessary, perhaps tiresome, to farther demonstrate the natural impossibility of employing the idle poor to any sort of public benefit, on manufacturing these said wares and stuff in parish workhouses. Nevertheless as it actually happens that there still exist in this country certain well meaning individuals who, not being convinced of that self-evident truth confirmed by the experience of the several parishes for above a century past, are ever contriving and proposing schemes for amending and continuing the practice of this pernicious Poor law, in direct counteraction of the immutable laws of Nature and Reason, it may be proper, for the satisfaction of such individuals, to state the following supposed case. As thus,

Supposing it might be possible to employ the idle poor on manufacturing these said materials in workhouses to some good purpose. Nay even supposing it possible that all these materials could be manufactured by those idle poor, under their annual overseers, in equal perfection and equally cheap as they are manufactured at present by the industrious skilful workmen employed under the direction of ingenious master manufacturers, what would be the consequence in even that case? Or where would be the benefit resulting therefrom to the community? The market for those manufactures, both home and foreign, is limited; and is already fully supplied by the private manufacturers. Of course these workhouse manufactures must come in as a glut to the market; and so must either remain unsold and useless; or otherwise, if sold abroad, or consumed at home even for the use of those parish poor themselves, they must operate a diminution of the private manufacturing market; and thereby diminish in a proportionate degree the present employ of the industriously disposed private workmen; and so force them into the parish workhouse. And thus *Circum Circa*.

The industrious, ingenious, skilful, and highly deserving master manufacturers in Manchester, in Birmingham, in Leeds, in Norwich, in Halifax, and in all the manufacturing towns and counties, feel already in a variety of shapes, and in an intolerable degree, the pernicious effects of this Poor System, on their workmen, and on their own industry. It is high time to relieve them from these intolerable grievances, instead of aggravating them by attempting moral impossibilities.

And thus, my fellow citizens, you have placed before your view, at least, a true sketch of the nature, and also some few of the pernicious effects of your Poor System. It may be added that all these evils have of very late amazingly increased, and are daily increasing. It may therefore be presumed you will conclude they ought to be diminished; or, if possible, remedied. And, on this presumption we proceed to the proposed remedy.

It must appear from the preceding sketch that, exclusive of this wantonly wicked parish regulation, the most essential and productive vices in this Poor System are, first, the mode which it prescribes for employing the idle poor on work that is perfectly useless and unprofitable to the community. And, second, the manner of providing for and maintaining those idle poor in workhouses under the despotic authority and arbitrary will of overseers and contractors, instead of placing them in the capacity of earning an honest independent subsistence, by means of useful labour and industry. Indeed this second mentioned abuse is an unavoidable consequence or effect of the first. Because, if the work or pretended work upon which these poor are employed is altogether useless and of no value to the community, they can have no right or claim to the wages of useful industry. And so *vice versa*, on the part of the community. At any rate these two abuses are so complicated and jumbled together, that they cannot be separated either in their existence or in the remedy. In fact this whole Poor System evidently appears to be a jumble of gross, unnatural absurdities, contrived solely for the ease, the convenience, and the despotic purposes of government.

But the nature and tendency of the leading vices and abuses in this Poor System having been thus pointed out and ascertained, the nature of the remedy to these abuses will naturally suggest itself to every mind. Being simply this: Devise or find out some species or mode of employing all the present idle, unemployed poor on work that shall, in the first place, be useful, valuable, and beneficial to the community. And which shall, in the second place, be freely open and readily accessible or attainable by all and every one of those idle poor, without question or difficulty of any kind, but immediately on their applying for it.

For it must here be kept in view that, under the description of idle, unemployed poor, is comprehended not only the present useless parish paupers, but all those others who subsist at present in idleness, by vagrant begging, by thieving, and other vicious courses.

It will farther occur that this supposed work must necessarily be of a nature that requires no previous practical skill or knowledge; but merely bodily labour; so as that each and every one of those idle poor, who is not actually lame or impotent, shall be capable of being usefully employed on it.

And, so much being premised, it naturally follows that, the present idle poor, when they shall be thus employed on work useful, valuable, and beneficial to the community, will become entitled, according to reason and the right order of things, to wages that shall be adequate and sufficient to provide them the necessaries of life. And upon the same principles the community is warranted and ought to pay them such wages.

There is not in nature a truth more certain or more self-evident than this, that in a country extensive, rich in manufacture and commerce, as Britain is, there cannot possibly exist a want, but that on the contrary there must be a superabundance of ways and means to usefully employ all the present inhabitants. And a great many more. No! the want of useful employ is not the cause that above one third part of our labouring commonalty exist in their present unnaturally wretched and noxious state; crawling about like useless unheeded vermin; or otherwise savagely preying upon their fellow citizens; who in return hang them up like dogs; or transport them by hundreds to starve in the most distant corners of the earth. Whilst the community is, through this wantonly wicked and unnaturally tyrannical whim, of Botany Bay transportation, subjected to the expence of paying yearly the enormous sum of about one hundred pounds sterling for each wretch thus cruelly punished. Besides an equal sum for each of those numerous unoffending citizens who, in consequence of this absurd whim, are equally transported and equally punished.

However, amongst the many branching paths of honest industry that will afterwards open and become accessible to our present idle poor, the wide highway of agriculture, or the breaking in and cultivating our present barren and waste lands, at the public expence, appears to be the fittest means for first breaking in those idle poor to labour, and initiating them to industry. This cultivation likewise appears to be, in every one other respect and property, exactly that species of employ which hath been herein before described and required, for this desired purpose, of setting on work all our present idle and unemployed poor.

For, in the first place, this breaking in those barren and waste lands is a species of employ highly useful and beneficial to the community. There are in this island many hundred thousand acres of land, equal in measurement to two fifth parts of its whole superficies, which at present lay in a state almost equally lost and useless to the community as if they did not exist; or were covered by the ocean; and which, in the present disposition of the private owners, will remain for ever in that useless state, unless the community shall undertake to cultivate them at its own proper expence. And, of these so many hundred thousand acres, there is not one single acre, of accessibly level surface, that may not be rendered productive to some one purpose. Be that surface bare rock, barren sand, dead clay, gravel, marsh, or bog. All these will yield to the power of human art, labour, and industry. Nor is there a single acre of these present useless lands that, when thus properly broke in and improved, will not prove a clear gain to the state, or accession of domestic territory, equal in value to thirty pounds sterling; according to the present rate or value of properly improved lands in this country. Exclusive of many other benefits that will accrue to this state from such undertaking.

For public utility or convenience is not the sole argument for breaking in and cultivating those present barren and useless lands. The still stronger argument of public necessity calls loudly for such an undertaking. For that the lands at present cultivated barely produce, in even a plentiful year, sufficient to supply the necessities of the poor inhabitants; and at the same time to feed the luxuries of the rich, who will ever be first served. But, in a year of scarcity, this state has, in these later times, been necessitated to purchase grain from other states, to the amount of £300,000. Such has been the late incredible increase of luxury in this country; which ever, till within these twenty years last past, used to export every year about £300,000 sterling worth of grain.

Nay, besides that want of necessary food, this state is at present totally dependent on the will or caprice of other states, for a production of the earth which is so indispensably necessary to the very being of her navigation, warlike as well as commercial, that neither the one nor the other can exist without it: and which is, at the same time, of a quality so bulky, that she rarely possesses above one year's store of it; that is, hemp. And for that one production, when obtained on even these terms, this state pays yearly large sums of hard money to foreigners, possibly to enemies. Surely there is as little policy as there is of charity in this, to pay such large sums of money yearly to those who will probably employ that money against the state, instead of paying it in wages to our own unemployed poor, for cultivating this important production in our own soil; which is perfectly adapted to produce it.

But, besides grain and hemp, there is flax, tobacco, and many other productions of the earth, which this state purchases from other states, at a great yearly expence; and which can be cultivated at home with great success.

In the second place, this breaking in and cultivating those present barren and useless lands, for the public benefit, at public expence, is a species of employ that will be open, readily attainable and accessible, without question or difficulty of any kind, by all and every one of our present idle, unemployed poor, of every description; in the manner that shall be pointed out in the sequel.

This is also a species of employ that demands no previous practical skill or knowledge; and on which, through that reason, each and every one of those idle, unemployed poor would be qualified to work usefully, provided he is not lame or impotent.

And thus, by a public undertaking of this nature, you may throw open a wide and all-receiving gate; through which the whole and every one of the present idle, unemployed, and noxious poor may enter; and earn, by their labour, the means of subsisting honestly, in a state of rational, useful independence.

Nevertheless your holding forth the means of employ will not, alone and of itself, suffice to accomplish the reform of those many evils and abuses that are at present caused by the idle, noxious poor. For it cannot be expected that those of them who have been long habituated to vicious idleness, will at once or of their own accord betake themselves to painful labour, even when held forth to them. And, therefore, at the same time that you throw open this gate to labour and industry, it will be absolutely necessary to closely shut up every possible access to their subsisting in idleness, by begging, thieving, or other vicious courses; so as that, finding themselves effectually precluded from the possibility of subsisting otherwise than by labour, they shall be forced to submit, and voluntarily betake themselves to it.

To effect this will demand, and especially at the first, the vigorous exertion and watchful attention of a police, formed upon a very different principle from that which exists at present. And this necessarily recalls us to the more particular consideration of your present police, or municipal system.

It hath been said in general that the nature and form of your present police is adapted and applied solely to the purpose of punishing, and not in the least to that of preventing the commission of crimes and abuses. And the reason of this is, that your government, possessing a power altogether unlimited and uncontrouled by the people, did, in the formation of your present existing police, consult only its own interest and despotic purposes, without regarding the good or welfare of the people. And herein the conduct of your government was still less excusable, than even in the matter of your Poor System. For this reason in particular, that the people did, at one time, actually possess the privilege of chusing their own municipal magistrates, by the consent of the Crown itself. And so continued in possession during several centuries, under the Saxon government, and also after the Norman conquest, until the I Ed 3 when the infamous Mortimer, discovering that this privilege allowed to the people could be of some use to the Crown, forcibly wrested it from them.[240] As will appear from a retrospect to the origin of this municipal system. And, to which end, and likewise for other good purposes, it will be necessary to take a slight glance at the origin of your government in general, so far as it relates to the institution of that municipal system. But, in order to avoid digression, this too shall be placed in the appendix.

Soon after that privilege of the people had been wrested from them by the Crown, the stile of these municipal magistrates was changed from *Conservators of the Peace*, to that of *The King's Justices of the Peace*. And, notwithstanding the Crown is the only one part of the community that holds no interest or concern in the administration of this office, as not being in the least liable to be affected by its good or ill management, yet, ever since that said usurpation of the people's right by Mortimer, the Crown alone hath possessed the whole exclusive power to nominate, appoint, commission, superintend, and direct the magistrates who execute that office.

Whilst the people, who are so deeply interested, whose peace, safety, order, well-being and happiness as a community, depend altogether on the due action of this municipal magistracy, have not the slightest voice, either in chusing men fit for that office, or in afterwards superintending, directing, or controuling their conduct. The people can neither punish nor reward these magistrates. Of course they can neither prevent their doing wrong, nor compel them to do right. These *King's* justices of the peace are all volunteers in office; they owe no duty of any kind to the people, and they perform as little for them. And, in consequence, the use or virtue of this important municipal magistracy is as completely lost to the people as if it did not exist.

Where these justices may be said to act at all, as in this enormous capital, it is merely for the purpose of inculcating a slavish, servile dread and awe of the regal authority; by bringing malefactors to punishment, in the name of the king, for crimes committed against their fellow citizens. In which capacity these Westminster justices are very aptly termed *Thief Catchers*. Though, even in this part of their office, they are collusively permitted to sacrifice the good of the community to their own gain. For they are suffered to protect those malefactors so long as they can afford to pay for that protection. So soon as this ability to pay ceases, the justice then executes his office; by apprehending and convicting the malefactors, as offenders against the royal dignity. And, for each capital conviction, these justices are enabled, by the authority of government, to draw from the community a reward of forty pounds.

In the other part of their office, these justices still serve themselves at the expence of the community, in a variety of shapes; and particularly by encouraging insolence, discord, and strife, amongst the ignorant and lower class of the people; in order to sell their warrants for bringing the parties before them. And, in this branch of their office, they are very properly denominated *Trading Justices*.

But, as to preventing the commission of crimes and abuses, or preserving the peace and good order of the community, or the enforcing a due observance of the laws, with industry, morality, decency, and a proper subordination amongst the lower class of the people, which is the sole end and purpose of this municipal magistracy: to all these said purposes it may be truly said, that 'in these our days there is no judge in Israel; but every man doth that which seemeth good in his own eye',[241] provided he does not trespass against the sacred majesty of the Crown. So he be an obedient subject to the king, it matters not what sort of a citizen he is.

From this slight but true description of the present state of your municipal magistracy, the true cause of its present inefficacy must occur to the mind of every one. Neither can it be at all difficult to discover the means or method to remedy that inefficacy; together with all those disorders, evils, and abuses, which flow from that said inefficacy.

Nevertheless, as that necessary reform of your municipal government cannot be looked for, until such time as you, opening your eyes to your present general situation, shall acquire an actual, real, free and uninfluenced representation of yourselves in your legislature; and as such a representation, when formed, will stand in no need of direction or advice as to the mode of reforming this and every other present abuse of your government, therefore the following description of the plain and easy means or method whereby your municipal government may be rendered truly effectual to the *Salus Populi*, which is not only the *Suprema Lex*, but the sole end and use of all government, is here stated, merely for the purpose of convincing and satisfying one and all of you, that the present inefficacy of your municipal government, with those consequent disorders, evils, and abuses, are not caused by unavoidable necessity; but that, on the contrary, all these evils can be easily, readily, and effectually remedied, so soon and whensoever you shall be pleased to adopt that naturally right and absolutely necessary step; which will speedily remedy this and every one other abuse; but, without which, no one abuse ever will be reformed.

For whereas, at present, every man who wishes to stick that feather in his cap, or to make a gainful job of it, is immediately on application appointed to this important municipal office by the simple *Dedimus Potestatem* of the king; without the slightest regard had to his qualification for that office, in respect either of honour and integrity, or of ability and skill. And whereas all these men, when so vested, considering themselves as volunteers, bound by no tye of duty or obligation, act in that office merely as they please, when they please, or not at all if they please; whereby this mighty important magistracy is become altogether titular or a job, and perfectly nugatory, in fact noxious to the community. Now it is morally certain and clearly manifest, that all these several causes of this present inefficacy would be completely remedied and removed, by the simple act of vesting the direction, superintendence, and controul of this their own municipal magistracy in the people; who are alone entitled to this power upon all the principles of nature, of reason, and the due order of things; and who alone are qualified to properly exercise that power.

For, in the first place, the people, in their different local situations, are alone competent to know, and consequently to chuse from amongst themselves, men that are duly qualified in the aforesaid respects to properly execute this important office. And their own interest would lead them, when uninfluenced by the Crown or its corrupt dependents, to elect only such men.

In the second place, the people alone possess the power, and inclination through interest, to compel these magistrates, when chosen, to duly discharge their duty; through the only natural and truly effectual means of *Rewards and Punishments*, in the following manner; which nearly corresponds with that mode for reforming this municipal magistracy, which was proposed by the ingenious and learned *Lambard*, who lived in the reign of James the First, and grievously complains of the numerous and unsuitable appointments to that office, with the consequent abuses, even in his day.[242] Though that abuse was then merely trifling, when compared with the present.

Let each county be divided, for this particular purpose, by a standing act of the legislature, into five or six districts or sections, less or more, as may seem proper. And let this mighty city of Westminster be likewise divided into a proper number of districts. Let the people, in each of these several districts, be assembled by the sheriff of the county, at a certain place, annually on a fixed day; then to chuse, for their own district, one justice of the peace; a man of respectable character; who may be willing, from public-spirited motives, to execute that office without fee or reward. And let these same people also then chuse, for their own district, one other justice; a person of good ability, well skilled in the functions of that office, and of good repute; who shall agree to reside at a particular place in that district; and shall not practice in any other profession; but shall dedicate his whole time and attention to the duties of that charge; and who shall, in compensation for his time and trouble, receive a salary from the people that shall be adequate to the importance and utility of the office.

And so, in each of the several districts throughout the whole country, and in this great city of Westminster, let two justices of the peace be chosen annually by the people: one of these justices to be honorary, and the other stipendiary. All these justices, when thus chosen annually by the people, may, if thought proper, be returned to the Crown; and from thence receive a commission for executing their office. Or the legislature may, by other fixed means, empower them to act.

Upon this principle, of *annual* elections by the people in the several districts, there appears to be no need for penal or compulsory clauses; which will be ever found nugatory to the purpose of enforcing the good conduct of those magistrates. For the sense that these, who are to be his electors in the ensuing year, are the witnesses of his present conduct, will ever act upon the justice, and particularly the stipendiary justice, as a sufficiently powerful impulse to his doing right, and would equally restrain him from doing wrong. Though, after some time, these elections might, if found proper, be made biennial.

And thus you perceive that, by means of this one simply natural, rational, and just act, of assigning (properly restoring) to the people their right to annually chuse their own municipal magistrates, in the manner here described, this magistracy may be rendered completely effectual to the purpose of *preventing* the commission of crimes, and of enforcing a due observance of the laws, which at present are a mere tinkling cymbal. Whereby the peace, the safety, and good order of the community would be re-established, and regularly preserved. And by no other means can this important object be possibly attained.

In particular, such an effectual municipal magistracy could easily and speedily ferret out every one idle person, from their present means of subsisting by thieving, vagrant begging, and other vicious courses.

But here we are necessarily recalled to a more circumstantial consideration of the ways and means whereby these present idle, noxious, and perhaps at first refractory poor, when they shall be thus ferreted out of their idle recesses, may be compelled to accept of that employ, which is here proposed to be proffered them.

To effect this purpose, the legislature may, in the first place, establish in each county a proper committee; to consist of all those newly-modelled justices of the peace in that county, for the time being, by virtue of their office; and of so many more public-spirited respectable persons as may seem proper.

Under the immediate direction of this committee, it would be necessary to appoint a county treasury; properly empowered to collect and receive, from every parish within the said county, the several sums that were last assessed on it, for parish rates, county rates, and other municipal taxes. For it is possible that, in the first year of this proposed undertaking, all these sums may be wanted. Possibly more may be required in that first year; which in such case may be proportionately assessable by the committee. The books of this treasury, together with minutes of the committee, to be laid open at the end of every month, for the inspection of such as contribute to the expence.

Each of these county committees may also be empowered to survey and fix upon such part or parts of the barren or waste lands, within that respective county, as may be the most proper to first set the idle poor at work upon. As also to ascertain the value that shall be paid by the public, to the private proprietors of those lands. That value to be liquidated, as in other cases, by means the least burthensome to the public. And if, in any one or more counties, there shall not be a sufficiency of barren or waste lands to employ all its idle poor, then this superabundance of poor may be turned over to the nearest county that shall abound in barren lands. And such an allowance in money to be made, by the county turning over its idle poor, to the county receiving them, as to the legislature shall seem meet and just.

Farther, these county committees may be empowered to provide all necessary implements of husbandry. As also beasts of draught; which may properly be oxen; because these will be the least expensive to the public; in fact no expence at all, besides their temporary keep. And, in like manner, to provide skilful, careful, and active bailiffs, and superintendants of the work; with other necessary officers; and every thing besides that may be requisite for immediately setting the idle poor on work. Such as ready markets for accommodating them with provisions and other necessaries. As also houses, or habitations; which may be constructed of wood, and removable; either at the public expence; or otherwise by contract with private undertakers; upon the allowance of sixpence a-week for each labourer, to be deducted from their wages.

Every thing being thus prepared for immediately setting the idle poor on work, notice may be given in each parish church, and in other the most public manner, that every idle or unemployed person within that county, whether parish pauper or other, provided they are not lame or impotent, shall repair, by a fixed day, to the place appointed by the county committee; there to be set on work, and to receive daily wages for their labour.

It may be presumed that, by the day so fixed, the parish workhouses will be greatly disburdened of their paupers. And also, that every one of the present vagrant beggars, with the greater part of the other idle, noxious poor, will, upon their being informed of the methods intended for completely cutting off their former means of subsisting, voluntarily repair to the place appointed.

But as it may be also presumed that some of the hardened sinners will require coercion, it would, on that account, be necessary that, immediately before issuing the aforesaid public notice, the two justices of each district, attended by proper persons in every parish within such district, should visit every one house or dwelling within these respective parishes; and strictly examine and record the name of every individual living or lodging in each house, together with the nature of his employ, or means of subsisting. And to every one of those who shall not appear to be properly employed, a ticket or order may be given, to be delivered by him to the clerk of the public work in that county, who should again make a daily return to the justices, of every person presenting such tickets; as also of all such as may have deserted the work.

At the outset of such undertaking it would be necessary that the justices should repeat their visits in the manner aforesaid, every week, though specially to suspected houses. But, after two or three months, the necessity of those frequent visits would cease. For, by that time, the most artful of those offenders would be traced out, and the most obstinate of them subdued, by the following mode of treatment, in a proper house of correction.

Let the refractory offender be confined in a dark cell, secluded from all conversation or communication with any one, saving his keeper alone. For it is the society of others, wicked as themselves, that supports the obdurate minds of these unfeeling wretches, and renders them callous to shame and punishment. Let him be there fed as sparingly as may be consistent with existence. And, if thought necessary, hard labour may be added, with severe correction on failure of his task.

Such discipline would, in the space of a fortnight, subdue the most hardened offender. So as that he would, immediately on his being liberated, thankfully accept of the employ offered him. And, for his whole life after, he would be properly cautious of incurring the necessity for returning to the cell of discipline. Which he would be sensible must inevitably follow his again transgressing.

It is clearly manifest, as well as morally certain, that a due application of the means here mentioned would, in the space of a very few months, completely suppress thieving and robbing; and cleanly root them out of this country.

As to vagrant begging, that would totally vanish and disappear on the very day that the aforesaid public notice of general employ should be promulgated. Seeing that, exclusive of the active exertion of a proper municipal magistracy, there would be no person found weak enough to give charity, when there could exist no shadow of plea for begging. And the moment that weak minded charity shall cease, vagrant begging will also cease.

Though, in order to more securely guard these well-disposed bestowers of charity against their own weakness, a pecuniary mulct may be imposed on every person convicted of giving charity to a vagrant beggar, after the day fixed. And this is suggested from an example in the Austrian Netherlands, where vagrant begging prevailed some years ago to an amazing degree, (though on far more excusable plea than here), and was in one day completely suppressed; as it still remains. Notwithstanding these Netherlanders possessed none of those means for employing their idle poor, which abound in this country. For they had not a yard of waste land to cultivate; they had no poor's rate or other fund ready prepared for paying wages to their idle poor; and they had next to no manufacture or commerce, yet abounding in population to an excess. And, from their precedent, certain of the foregoing hints are borrowed.

As to the actually lame or impotent poor, these might still be maintained at the public expence. But such would not be found very numerous. The whole of them in each county might be placed under the direction of the county committee; and be maintained in two or more of the present parish workhouses; on terms far more comfortable to them, and infinitely less expensive to the public, than at present. Allowing very liberally, the sum of five hundred thousand pounds would more than suffice to comfortably maintain all the actually lame and impotent poor in England and Wales, even in the first year of this proposed undertaking. But this expence would diminish every year after the first, by means that shall be shown.

And in order to still more fully convince you of the perfect rationality, the ready practicability, and great utility of this proposed public undertaking, we shall venture to offer, not an exact calculation, but a rational conjecture at the expence that would be caused to the public by such an undertaking; together with a state of those funds that are ready provided in this country for defraying such expence. And we shall farther present a sketch of the several benefits and advantages that would accrue to the public from such a measure.

The only material expence that would be caused to the public by such undertaking, would consist in the wages to be paid to the public labourers. It would be unnecessary, and also imprudent, to pay these labourers more wages than would suffice to purchase them the necessaries of life. And as they would feed in messes, sixpence a day would suffice for that purpose, provided they should be lodged at the public expence, otherwise seven pence, as one penny a day would be deducted therefrom for the contractor, in the manner mentioned.

Thus the wages of each labourer would cost the public three shillings and sixpence a week. And suppose four hundred thousand labourers should, at the first outset of such undertaking, be set on work in England and Wales, the wages of these, at the aforesaid rate, would cost the public three millions six hundred and forty thousand pounds for that first year. And farther supposing that the cost of implements, the keep of bullocks, and other charges, should amount to three hundred and forty thousand pounds more, the whole expence to the public on this proposed undertaking would be four millions, for even that first and far most expensive year.

And if to this we shall add the five hundred thousand pounds before assigned for the maintenance of all the lame and impotent poor, then the whole expence that would be caused to the public, by thus setting on useful work all the present idle, noxious able-bodied poor in England and Wales, and also for maintaining all the actually lame and impotent poor, would amount to four millions five hundred thousand pounds for that said first year. As for the consideration to be paid the private proprietors of the barren and waste lands, that would not be a ready money expence.

And to furnish or answer this said expence of four millions five hundred thousand pounds, there exists ready in this state, first, the present poor's rate tax, amounting yearly to four millions. And next there are those various sums paid at present by this community for protecting them from thieves and rogues, for detecting, convicting, hanging, punishing, and transporting malefactors; together with the value of what is at present stole, robbed, plundered, and wasted by those malefactors; and farther, what is extorted, pilfered, and wasted by vagrant beggars; amounting together, as hath been shewn, to above three millions. And all which said various sums would, by this proposed measure, be saved to the community.

These two collected funds, making together the sum of seven millions, at present drawn annually from this community and wasted without any sort of return, would here stand forth as a fund ready provided and prepared to furnish the expence required for this proposed mighty national undertaking; without calling upon the people for one shilling of new or additional contribution on that account. And so this hitherto vicious abuse of her government would hereby be suddenly converted into an advantage particular to this state, that she alone of all states on earth stands possessed of a fund ready prepared for immediately setting on foot such a mighty national undertaking, without subjecting the people to any new tax: whereas any one of these other states, undertaking such an important national improvement, must necessarily burden the people with new and heavy taxes to furnish the expence of it. At the same time it is proper to observe that, unless this state shall be prevailed on to apply that said present wasted fund of seven millions to the purpose of such a national undertaking, she is in that particular worse situated than any one other state, by all the difference of seven millions sterling, at present annually wasted by her government.

Nay it appears, from the preceding statement, that, after defraying every necessary charge of that first and most expensive year, there would still remain, out of the said fund of seven millions, a surplus or saving to the community of one million and a half. And this large saving of expence to the community would be the first pecuniary fruits of that proposed measure.

And neither are we to reckon or consider the four millions, that have been here allotted for the expence of that first year, to be for ever lost without any return to the community, in like manner as the said seven millions are expended at present. No! The community would receive, for these four millions, the same sort of returns, though perhaps not in an equal degree, as the farmer receives for his money expended on labourers' wages, on working cattle, and implements of husbandry.

It may not perhaps be greatly necessary to condescend upon the degree of farming returns that the public might receive from this first year's expence. Nevertheless we may, for the sake of farther illustration, venture the following guess at an estimate of these returns.

And, considering the process of first breaking in barren lands to be exceeding difficult, tedious, and laborious, as consisting in the removing, changing, and mixing one species of soil with its opposite, or perhaps fetching soil altogether from a distance, we shall allot the labour of four persons, for a whole year, to properly break in one acre of barren land, and bring it to an improved state of cultivation. At this rate, 400,000 labourers, being the number to which wages have been assigned for the first year, would in that year duly improve 100,000 acres of barren land. Which, when so improved would create a clear accession or addition of so much *domestic territory, that is not liable to be lost or wrested from the state*. And which, at the present value of improved lands in this country, would, in money, be equal to three millions sterling.

These newly-improved lands the public could either farm out, on their own account, or otherwise they might be sold to private purchasers: for of such purchasers there would be no want for those lands, when once brought into a proper state of cultivation.

Though at the same time it may be proper to remark, that it is vain to expect that these barren lands ever will or can be broke in by means of private undertakers, at their own expence, even if they were to get those lands for nothing. First, because of the very great first cost, and the inferior and slow returns for that first cost. And next, because of a still weighty impediment: that private undertakers cannot, in like manner as the public, have the command of various and opposite soils, without which it is not possible to break in barren lands. Sundry other obstructions there are to private undertakings of this nature, forming together a moral impossibility of ever breaking in the present barren lands of this country, otherwise than by a public undertaking.

But the said 100,000 acres, so supposed to be improved in the first year, might at any rate be subjected to the two following conditions. First, that they should for ever remain divided into farms of fifty acres each. And second, that they should, where possible, be cultivated with hemp and flax. Though this new accession yearly to the present stock of cultivated lands would naturally induce the farmers of other lands better adapted, to cultivate these articles. Or, if these farmers could not be induced otherwise, bounties might at the first be applied.

Each of these fifty-acre farms, being arable land, would require two men to cultivate it. And thus the 100,000 acres, so improved in the first year, would furnish in the succeeding year a newly-acquired field, that did not exist before, to employ and maintain 4000 peasants, with their families. And this new field of employ, extending every year, would serve to re-establish in this country a strong, robust peasantry. Which, though they be in the day of danger the only sure bulwark of defence, have in this country become nearly extinct. Our labouring commonalty having, through the nature of our government, been converted into debauched, enervated artisans or manufacturers, and the effeminate, useless trappings of luxury, or otherwise into thieves, beggars, or parish paupers. Moreover, this yearly accession of new employ on those improved lands, would every year diminish the original number of those public labourers; and of course would every year diminish the public expence on that undertaking.

Though when once the present idle, noxious poor should be fairly initiated into industry on this proposed public undertaking, as at a school, and should be properly kept at hard labour by active bailiffs, they would soon find out for themselves a variety of means to subsist by easier labour. And, provided those means should be honest, it matters little to the community what they are. If they shall be honest, they must needs be useful. And a proper municipal magistracy will effectually prevent their subsisting by dishonest means.

For instance, in these Austrian Netherlands,[243] which are a pattern of agricultural industry, numbers of men and women earn a subsistence, by collecting off the streets and highways all matter fit for manure, which they carry to their respective heaps, and sell it to the farmer, whereby the earth hath every thing restored that ever it produced, to the great benefit of that country. And by useful means of this nature might many thousands earn an honest subsistence in this country. And thereby the number of public labourers would gradually diminish every year after the first.

So as that, within a very few years after commencing this proposed public undertaking, public expence on that account would totally cease. At least the original argument of public necessity would cease. The state would have a free choice whether, upon the ground of public utility and convenience, that undertaking should be continued in any degree, and to what degree.

And as soon as that should be the case, then could this community congratulate itself upon being completely delivered, in every sense, shape, and respect, from the heavy burden of seven millions sterling, at present drawn from them every year by means of their government and wasted.

But, at all times, a public undertaking of this nature would be highly eligible, for the purpose of furnishing an asylum, or the means of honest subsistence, to those hitherto cruelly treated citizens who, upon every rumour of our frequent wars, have been dragged from their families, and often from a comfortable employ, into the military service of the state. And, the moment that necessity for their service has ceased, government hath uniformly and without remorse dismissed them, on the cruel terms of that aforesaid alternative, *to steal or starve.* Such base ingratitude, and cruel, unfeeling tyranny, so diametrically opposite to the true national character of the English people, furnishes in itself a sufficient proof of the voice or share that these people hold at present in their own government.

Moreover a just, a humane, and equitable government would assuredly consider it a duty to provide some honest means of employ and subsistence for those numerous females who subsist at present by means not less vicious, and if possible still more disgraceful to human nature, than do the noxious males. A municipal magistracy, such as hath been here described, could speedily drive these females out of the present vicious and noxious means of subsisting. But what is then to become of them? Must they be left to starve? That would be inconsistent with the principles of a just and equitable government. Or must they be maintained in idleness, at a great public expence, in Magdalen and penitentiary houses erected in every parish?[244] That would not be the conduct of a wise government. But an equitable and wise government would first find out useful employment for them, and then it would force them into that employ, of which there is no want in this country, easily within the power of an honest government.

For instance, the linen that is worn by the inhabitants of this country is purchased from other states, at a vast expence of hard money. We certainly can come at the flax by the same means as these other states do. We may, upon the plan of this proposed undertaking, rear it at home, without interfering with the other wants of the inhabitants. Why then should such multitudes of females be permitted to subsist in vicious, noxious idleness, when they can be put in the way of earning an honest subsistence, by means so beneficial to the state as would be the fabricating this linen?

But if this state could once cultivate within itself a quantity of hemp and flax, sufficing or nearly sufficing for its own wants, the very dressing, or preparing these productions for fabrication, would furnish employ for multitudes of those idle females, as well as for many of the lame poor in the county workhouses. And this would diminish the public expence of maintaining those lame and impotent poor.

Application of the Preceding

And thus hath Common Sense presented you a view of national benefits accruing from a reform of your present municipal government. You are not, however, to consider this as a full enumeration of all those benefits. And still less are you to suppose that the methods here proposed for effecting those national improvements are held forth by the proposer as a regularly digested plan. No! He is perfectly aware that the plans of individuals will not be necessary to an assembly of legislating representatives chosen in the manner, and acting upon the principles that have been herein before described. And he is also sensible, that until such an assembly shall be formed, no reform of government abuses, or plans for national benefit, will ever be undertaken.

But the aim and intent of the preceding full statement is to convince and satisfy you, first, that your municipal government is at present extremely vicious, and absolutely requires immediate reform; second, that such a reform is not only practicable but easy; and third, that this reform, when effected, will be productive of mighty national benefit.

And this conviction, being presumed, is applied as an argument for your adopting that said *sine qua non* measure, which alone can procure all these national benefits. And assuredly an acquisition of even these benefits, herein before described, is a sufficient argument for your adopting that measure, if none other were to be expected from it.

But the benefits here described are held forth, merely as a specimen or muster of other more mighty savings of national wealth, benefits, and advantages, which must accrue from that same measure, operating in reform of the present numerous and destructively wasteful abuses in your legislative, your executive, and financial government, if indeed it can be properly said that there exists here at present any distinction betwixt the administration of these three different branches of government. When the benefits accruing from this last mentioned reform shall be described, then the argument for adopting that said measure, on the principle of national utility, must appear irresistible.

Yet still there is the argument of national necessity, infinitely more urgent for this reform than is that of national utility. For that, *otherwise*, ruin to yourselves and your posterity must inevitably overtake you, and that speedily. A yearly public expenditure by your government, far exceeding the utmost capacity of your present resources, and that expenditure increasing every year, through fresh debts contracted against you by your government. And on the other hand, an evident moral certainty that, in the short space of two years, probably in much less time, these your present resources will suffer a mighty diminution. What effect must or can ensue from these evidently existing causes, but national insolvency, misery, and ruin?[245]

Your case can admit of no delay, and assuredly it requires no deliberation. For it is impossible that thinking beings, if indeed they can be brought to think at all before direful necessity forces them to feel, should hesitate for a moment in the choice, whether they shall, for the gratification of one or more undeserving individuals, incur certain ruin to themselves and posterity;

or whether they shall prevent that ruin, by adopting a measure that is otherwise in itself just, right, honourable, and useful.

Look round and examine whether there exists in nature any medium or alternative, any other means to save you from ruin. Here is not the slightest ground to rely on your old stand by, *the Chapter of Accidents*. And woeful experience for many years past, and for every year as it passes, forbids you to trust for one moment longer to the wisdom or goodness of your government – as little can you trust to its power. For that power, irresistible as it appears to you, because unresisted by you, is confined within the four seas. Across your narrow channel it is despicable imbecility. It cannot influence or controul one single decree of the French National Assembly. Nor can it retard the effect of those decrees for an hour. And it is the effect of those decrees that urges and presses you from without, even more than the wasteful abuses of your government press you within. As your manufactures will speedily experience. And first, as hath been shewn, in a total deprivation of the French market for these manufactures, which you have for some years past wholly engrossed, but which you must soon lose, because the wise and active regulations of the National Assembly will, in a very short time, enable France to supply herself with these manufactures.

And when the loss of that one important market shall have thrown a multitude of your manufacturers into idleness and the want of employ, do you imagine that these manufacturers will remain with you to starve, or that they will put up with your parish workhouse fare, when they shall come to understand that, at the short distance of three hours sail, they can find comfortable employ, affluence, and respect, with the enjoyment of every right and privilege that appertains to man? The prejudice for the *natale solum* will indeed do much, and will prevail on men to bear much. But, in bearing, there is a *ne plus*. And, when your manufacturers shall have transported your present skill in manufacture, the difference in the price of labour will do the rest.

But emigration, once begun, will not be confined to the manufacturer. The merchant is to the manufacturer what the shadow is to the substance. Nay, to the thinking man of independent fortune, there are certain things dearer than even the *natale solum*. If the enjoyment of his natural rights as a man will not or cannot come to him at home, he will go abroad to enjoy his natural rights, especially when that is to be found so near.

And, when emigration shall have thinned the land, how shall that part of the people which remains support a burden that was too weighty for the united strength of the whole? Actual inability to pay must unavoidably produce actual insolvency.

Nay it is possible that, even before this actual inability shall arrive, the people, tired out with endless imposition of fresh taxes by their government, may open their eyes to the gross abuse that has been so long practiced on them, and resolutely reject these fresh impositions.

Who can without horror look forward to the consequences that must ensue from the desperate rage of an abused, aroused, and incensed people, on either of these events befalling. And that either the one or other of those events must take place soon is most certain, unless you shall prevent it, by putting a speedy stop to the present wasteful ruinous abuses. You have a recent example of this very nature before your eyes. But you have no reason to expect that a reform, effected by sudden violence, will be so calmly conducted here, or so easily concluded, as it was in that country.[246] There is a mighty difference betwixt the two cases, in a variety of circumstances, and particularly in the degree of abuse committed, and offence given to the people, by existing characters.

The man, who perceives the horizon already darkening with the thick black clouds charged with this mighty storm, must be void of feeling for his country, if he shall not arouse the sleeping crew who, in perfect security, are driving on the public bark with every sail out to certain destruction. In such a situation as ours actually is at this present, there is no time for hesitating or delay. The attempt to delay a reform of abuse is equally mischievous and pernicious as an attempt to prevent it. Not only on account of the many other evils that must attend a violent and hasty reform, but also because it will, by that time, come too late for preventing the subversion of your manufactures and commerce. These must, through such convulsion, be totally driven from you, if indeed they shall not have previously forsaken you. And, when you shall have once lost them, you will never recover them.

When Common Sense looks round, he cannot discover one individual or class of individuals, possessing any thing like property, real or personal, in this country, who can possibly have either interest or inclination to obstruct or even retard a reform of the present abuses. It cannot be the interest of that class stiling themselves statesmen who, in and out of office, have hitherto monopolized to themselves the first rank in that basely servile and wicked employ of deceiving abusing, and plundering you. These days of delusion and plunder are now nearly past; the day of dreadful reckoning approaches fast. And woe be to those of them who shall, on that day, be caught in this wicked employ! Let these behold their brother of France, wandering abroad a despised, detested vagabond, bearing about on his devoted head the curses of a whole nation, in hourly dread of deserved vengeance. And possibly by that time they may not find one remaining despotic court to protect them. On the other hand, Common Sense will venture to prognosticate that he of this class, who shall now stand forward the real honest friend of the people, will soon find himself truly great and respected. It cannot be for the interest of men possessing landed estates in this country to obstruct a reform of those abuses which, if continued, must subvert our manufactures and commerce. These will surely advert to the consequences resulting to them from such subversion. That, in the first place, it will sink near half the present value of their estates, by depreciating the yearly value of their produce. And that, in the next place, it will greatly enhance the present yearly charge or outgoings from these so depreciated estates, by throwing upon them that burden of taxes, which is at present supported by our yet flourishing manufactures and commerce. Upon this consideration, even these of them who at present receive the wages of corruption, will find they are engaged in a bargain or transaction so very disadvantageous to them that, for every shilling they shall so receive, from this time forward, until the day that reform, (if compulsatory) shall completely suppress corruption, they will have lost a pound in the value of their estates. Besides the infamy and reproach that must attach to all these who shall have continued till that period to receive such wages, for assisting to betray and ruin their country. For all such receiving will then be deemed wages of that nature, whether taken under the colour of salary for a useless sinecure place and post, or as a downright pension, or in the way of an honorary title. Can these, who accept wages in any shape for such base service, imagine that they shall be held noble or respected, because they bear titles, or expend largely? No! It is such conduct that defeats and undoes honorary titles, rendering the bearers not simply despicable, but odious, and unsufferable under a well-regulated constitution.

And least of all is it the interest of the monied men, or public creditors, to obstruct or delay a reform of the present abuses. As they will perceive from the following true statement of their case, which it becomes necessary to lay before them; because great pains have been taken, and with astonishing success, to deceive the judgement of that powerful and active part of the community, respecting their true interest.

At the time when the government of this country first took upon it to borrow money for its own purposes, on the credit of the people or nation, it so happened, that at the same time there existed a competition for the Crown, betwixt the king who then wore it, and the other who had then lately lost it. And this competition has subsisted ever from that time till of very late, betwixt the heirs or successors of those two original competitors, the people having been so long divided in their opinion about the respective right or title of the said competitors.[247] But those of the people who had lent their money on that public security, adhered unanimously and zealously to him who was in the possession, for this reason, and upon this principle or opinion that, so long as he who had been the borrower should hold possession of the Crown, their security for payment was good, and that, on the other hand, if he who was the Pretender should acquire the Crown, their security was gone.*

This said opinion of the public creditors, that their security for payment rested on the person or the will of him who wore or might wear the Crown, became extended and confirmed by a long continued habit of thinking, and hath proved a most convenient foundation for the ministers of corruption in these latter times, whereon to establish their doctrine of passive obedience and non-resistance to the will of the Crown or government. And so successful have their endeavours proved that, at this day, if government should say, '*eat straw*', the public creditors would eat straw, and would study to prevail on all others to eat it with them. Lest, by opposing the will or deranging the measures of government, whatever these measures may be, they should shake their own security for payment.

And, so long as the public creditors shall entertain this opinion, the bare mentioning a reform of government abuses, will fill their minds with horror. But a slight attention to the following considerations will clearly convince these public creditors, that a voluntary or optional reform of the present abuses, instead of shaking or disturbing their security, will convert that which is at present an ideal or imaginary security into a really substantial and perpetual security. And farther that, unless they shall unanimously concur in such a reform, they will very soon have neither substance nor shadow of security for payment.

For, on the one hand, supposing that such a voluntary reform should not take place, but that the body of people, passively submitting to the will of government, shall suffer matters to go on as they now do, still the people's submitting will not alter the actual nature of their situation, nor can it alter, prevent, or retard the effect that existing causes must, by the immutable order of nature, operate on human affairs. And therefore their so submitting, though it must prevent a voluntary or optional reform, yet is it more than probable that it will not long prevent an extorted and violent reform, produced through either the one or other of those two events before mentioned; that is, either by an actual inability in the people to furnish the calls of government, or otherwise by a want of will in at least a part of the people to longer answer the perpetually-increasing demands of government. And, amongst the other consequences ensuing from either of those events, a sudden stop to the payment of your interest must be one.

Nay, even supposing that the people should for ever submit to the will of government, without once attempting to remedy themselves, yet cannot government, with that unresisted power, draw from the people that which the decay of manufacture and commerce, emigration, with other causes, will have disabled the people to pay. It is a trite saying, that *'Where it is not, there the king must lose his due'*. And, when the king or government shall fail of receiving their full claim or due from the people, then must some of the claimants fail of receiving their due from government.

Now you are sensible that government is the common paymaster of your annual interest, as well as of its own wants or expences, out of the monies which it draws from the people for those common purposes. And you are further sensible that government, being this common paymaster, will be careful to pay its own wants first; as also, that, in the event of public deficiency and consequent discontent, the ordinary wants of government must be greatly enhanced by the extraordinary necessity of supporting itself by its wonted means. And therefore you are or may be assured that, whensoever any deficiency in the receipts of government shall happen, from whatever cause that may be, all such deficiency in the government receipts must fall upon you, and produce a proportionate deduction from the full payment of your yearly interest.

This you will admit to be a fair state of your present security for payment, so far as it respects the good faith or disposition of your present paymaster, government, to pay you.

And, on the other hand, supposing an unanimous concurrence of the people, including the public creditors, in reforming or putting a stop to the present ruinous abuses of government, through the before-mentioned natural, rational, and easy means of an actual, real, and true legislative representation of themselves. Nor mark the alteration that such a reform will create in the state of your security for payment, so far as that respects the good faith of your paymaster. Instead of relying totally, as at present, on the sole faith of a government so situated as that it will (because it can and soon must) stop the payment of your yearly interest, you would, in the case of such a reform, obtain the faith or security of the whole nation; firmly and irrevocably pledged to you, through an assembly of representatives, returned by the free, uninfluenced choice of the whole body of people, acting under the sole authority and controul of the people, and therefore speaking the true sense and voice of the people. A faith or security that would dure so long as the nation itself should dure: and which would be ever respected, in preference to even its own wants.**

But, besides the *good faith* of your paymaster, there is to you another consideration, still more important, which is the *ability* of your actual debtor to pay you. Now you are sensible that the nation is your actual and only debtor, having been constituted such by its government. For that *this government, notwithstanding it has constituted itself your only paymaster*, will not pay you a shilling out of its own separate purse, however well filled that separate purse may be, and richly stored out of the national purse. Therefore you have alone to consider the present and future ability of the nation to continue your payment.

And, in order to ascertain the difference betwixt the degree of national ability to pay the public creditors under a continuation of the present management, and that degree of ability which the nation would possess in case of such a reform, we have only to take a slight glance at the sum total of that yearly pecuniary expence which the nation is subjected to at present by her government, and to compare that sum with the amount of national expence which, in the case of reform could and would suffice yearly.

The first part of the present *ordinary* national expence, is the sum that *government* admits to be received by it yearly from the nation net into *His Majesty's Exchequer*, being about seventeen millions sterling. Of which sum *government* expends about seven millions yearly on what it terms the necessary expences of government: and the residue goes to pay the yearly interest of the national debt. But on extraordinary occasions, that is, when *government* chuses to engage the nation in a war, then that above-mentioned sum of seventeen millions has been greatly more than doubled, every year, during the time that *government* has thought fit to continue such war.

But, besides this sum so admitted to be received net into *His Majesty's Exchequer*, there are very large sums drawn yearly out of the nation's purse by *government* and its officers; and which sums, though actually paid by the nation, cannot be ascertained; because a great part of them are not (indeed cannot be) brought to any account; but are sunk invisibly in the present extravagant and oppressive mode of collecting the public revenue; in enormous fees, perquisites, and emoluments of *government* offices; and in a variety of other shapes. But all these sums, though paid in this invisible and unascertained manner, affect the national commerce and manufacture, and consequently the national purse, equally as doth the above-mentioned sum admitted to be received net into *His Majesty's Exchequer*. And this said unascertained national expence may, upon a moderate computation, be estimated at four millions sterling yearly, in ordinary times. On the aforesaid extraordinary occasions this expence is proportionally increased.

And, to these sums, we must add that other sum which, as hath been shown, is drawn yearly out of the nation's purse, to the amount of seven millions sterling, through the present management of the municipal government.

So that the whole amount of the present national expence, or of the sums that are drawn yearly out of the nation's purse by means of its government, may be reckoned about twenty-eight millions sterling, in ordinary times.

Whereas, on the supposition of a reform, there would be saved to the nation, out of this present expence, first, that whole sum of seven millions so drawn and wasted by the present municipal management, but which, in the case of a reform, would be completely saved to the community, by the methods that have been pointed out. And, second, there might be saved out of the present expenditure on the said wasteful oppressive mode of collecting the revenue, on unnecessary posts, places, pensions, fees or emoluments of office, and other purposes of government, which are not simply unnecessary, but pernicious and destructive to the national welfare, a sum equal to, at least, four millions sterling. And these two sums, making together eleven millions, being so saved to the nation, would reduce the present national expenditure of twenty eight millions, to seventeen millions yearly.

It would be an insult on the understanding of the public creditors to doubt their readily perceiving that the national ability of regularly continuing the payment of their interest would be wonderfully extended and confirmed by such a reduction of the yearly national expenditure, from twenty-eight millions, to seventeen millions.

Another important consideration, on this head of future national ability to pay the public creditors their interest, is that a parliamentary reform, such as hath been proposed, would prevent all future accumulation of the national debt, by putting an effectual stop to those ruinously expensive wars, in which the nation hath been hitherto perpetually engaged by her present government.

And a slight attention to these several considerations will clearly convince the public creditors that their particular interest is more deeply concerned in promoting a reform of the present government abuses, than is that of any one other part of the community.

Respecting the military part of this community, it happens fortunately that our soldiers are all citizens, and none of them foreign mercenaries. And, notwithstanding these have been hitherto taught to look only at that hand through which their pay passes to them, yet will they readily reflect that not a shilling of this pay comes from the paymaster, but entirely from their country. And, upon such reflection they will, instead of obstructing, zealously concur in promoting a measure that will rescue themselves from tyrannical oppression, and their country from ruin and misery.

As to the remaining part of the community, who feel all the evils of insupportable taxes and intolerable oppression, without even tasting the wages of corruption, who pay all to and receive nothing from the present government, these will readily and unanimously concur in promoting this necessary reform, which will relieve them from such a burthen of taxes.

Who are there then in this community that can have either interest or inclination to obstruct a reform of abuse? There can exist no such beings, saving a few who, possessing no property real or personal in this country, subsist entirely by the wages of corruption, paid them for the base service of deluding and deceiving their fellow citizens, by their pamphlets, their public speeches, and private declamations. These are the vile vermin bred in the putrid sores of a corrupted body politic; and these will indeed exert themselves to prevent a reform, because, when that corruption on which they feed shall be purged away by reform, they must lose their existence. But these will soon be deprived of their present capacity to do mischief. The first ray of reason darting on the mind of the people will discover the loathsome quality of these vermin; and they will then be abhorred and shunned.

And, as it is thus manifestly the interest of the whole people (those few vermin excepted) to promote a reform of the present ruinous abuses, it might be naturally concluded that the whole people would concur in adopting it. And so they would, if they did perceive or understand their own real interest.

But there are in this state those who consider the power of governing to be no power, unless upon the terms of *Sic volo, sic jubeo*, without limitation or restraint. And these, being conscious that the duration of their present unlimited power depends entirely upon the voice or consent of the people, and consequently that the people will, upon discovering their own true interest, immediately put an end to that grossly-abused unlimited power, they employ the before-mentioned vermin, with every base means of corruption and falsehood, to hold the people in ignorance, to delude, deceive and mislead them respecting their own real interest.

The aim and object of this publication is to undeceive the people on that head. And it is equally the interest and duty of every individual in this community, as of Common Sense, to exert himself in endeavouring to counteract and defeat these wicked delusive schemes and contrivances for perpetuating that unlimited power of governing; the gross and shameless abuse of which hath brought the national interest into the present ruinous situation; and which, if not speedily arrested, will completely accomplish that ruin.

The *vox populi* can readily, speedily, and easily, without disturbance, opposition, or confusion, effect this complete and only efficacious parliamentary reform. For who shall dare to oppose the *vox populi* which, when either unanimous or nearly unanimous, is as irresistible by man, as the voice of God. And it is from the *vox populi* alone that such a parliamentary reform is to be expected.

For only the most extreme folly and weakness can expect that such a parliamentary reform will ever come from those who at present possess a voice or share in the powers that are. Mere passiveness, or an acquiescence in such a reform, is the utmost that can be looked for from them, and even that should be considered a sort of patriotic sacrifice. But it would be madness to expect that they should themselves be the sacrificing priests, or that they should by their own vote deprive themselves of a property which either they, or their patrons under whom they hold it, have purchased for valuable consideration. Whether the purchase has been made *bona fide* or *male fide* could never stand an argument with them, they being the only judges; the only object in their view must be that a valuable consideration had been paid by them or their patrons for a purchase which they were then called upon to yield up by their own vote. At any rate you may rest assured that, if you shall wait for a parliamentary reform, until it shall come to you through the act or vote of these who at present hold a voice or share in the powers that are, you must wait until your present government can draw no more money out of you.

Still less ground of expectation have you from any of these would-be ministers or statesmen who, when out of office, promise you parliamentary reforms and every thing else you can ask for, but who, when through your help they have got into office, find things very well as they are, and do not wish them to be better.

But it must appear to uncorrupted human reason (that is, to the reason of every man who exists without the vortex of our government corruption) the most astonishing of all monstrous absurdities, that the people of Great Britain should apply to or depend upon any man, or any set of men, for obtaining that which is their own, by natural and inherent right, which is not barely useful, but indispensably necessary to them, and which is so completely and easily within their own power, that the moment they shall will it should be so, it must be so. If the truth of this is doubted by you, my fellow-citizens, or by any part of you, or by any one individual besides, a very little more time will prove the fact to your woeful experience. For, in case you shall not now voluntarily exert yourselves, with the spirit of men, or rational beings, direful necessity will soon force you to feel, feeling will force you to exert yourselves, and that exertion will incontestably convince you and all mankind that it ever was easily within your power, at any and at all times, to arrest and reform the oppression and abuse of your government which, by that time, will have ruined you.

It must be the fervent prayer of every Briton, who sees and feels for his country, that this dear-bought experience may be prevented by a timely exertion of the people. Seeing that, besides the confusion, distraction, and outrages that must attend a reform effected by popular rage and resentment, which never yet did things well, reform will then come too late. It will be like 'Shutting the door after the steed is stolen'. For your reason, in defiance of government corruption, must convince each and all of you that France, being now nearly lightened of her former oppressive weight, and completely released from all her clogs and fetters, will speedily recover the ground you had gained on her, in the race for manufacturing and commercial wealth, during the time she had stopped to knock off these fetters. She will then easily pass and distance you, loaded as you are with your present intolerable burden, and impeded by galling fetters. And, having once possessed herself of the rich prize, she will never afford you the opportunity of again contesting it with her.

But prayers to Heaven will not effect this necessary reform. We have no right to expect a miraculous interposition of Heaven to effect that which can be effected so easily by the natural and ordinary causes it has instituted; even by a slight exertion of that reason, which Heaven has bestowed upon men, for the purpose of enabling them to distinguish the difference between truth and falsehood, between good and evil; and to guide them in chusing between those two opposites.

And, as it is the duty of every man who sees, to lead or direct his neighbour who is blind; so is it the duty of every individual in this community, who sees and perceives what is so necessary for the good of the whole, to undeceive and instruct his deluded or less enlightened neighbour; to the end that the whole people may speedily and unanimously concur to effect that which, through such unanimity, will be accomplished with perfect ease, with complete good order, and calm, deliberate consideration. For it is the want of unanimity alone, caused by government deception and corruption, that can occasion the smallest delay, confusion, or opposition to this *ultimately unavoidable* parliamentary reform.

And let not any one, the lowest individual in this community, suffer himself to be deluded into sluggish inaction, on this pressing occasion, either by the deceitful representations of others, or of his own indolence, 'That he is of too little consequence to meddle in these great matters', and 'What can one poor individual do?' Every one individual is an integral part of this whole community: that whole is composed of individuals. The lowest has his *all* at stake; the greatest can have no more. The *all* of the lowest is of equal value to him, as his *all* can be to the greatest. And therefore in a question that so imminently concerns the common good and safety, of not only the whole present generation, but of all future generations, the lowest individual holds equal right to a voice on that question, as doth the greatest. It is equally the interest and equally the duty of that lowest to exert his right, and his individual voice will tell for as much on such a question, as will the voice of the greatest.

These are not levelling principles. They are the principles of eternal reason. They are eternal truths. And, notwithstanding the rule, 'That truth is not to be spoken at all times', yet, on an occasion of such urgent necessity, when *Ruin* stares the nation in the face, and will certainly and speedily seize her unless the truth shall be told, it becomes a crime in any and every one citizen, who can serve the common cause by speaking the truth, to hold his peace. When once we shall have secured ourselves from *Ruin*, then may we, in safety, return to ceremony, and to the etiquette of distinction, rank, and title. But, upon this great question, all affectation of distinction is absurd nonsense and folly; nay it is an outrage and offence against human reason, as well as the common good.

On this head, Common Sense has only to again inculcate on you, my fellow-citizens, that all half or compromised parliamentary reforms will turn out mere delusion. And that all partial reforms of abuse (as all such reforms undertaken, or pretended to be undertaken under the present management, will turn out to be) are mere delusion, calculated to continue the present unlimited power of completing your ruin. The first, the last, and the only thing you have to do, and the only thing that can save you from ruin, is to speedily and unanimously concur in adopting a full and complete parliamentary reform, grounded on the principles of representation that have been here described. That representation being once established, will, *under your own controul*, honestly, faithfully, and completely do all the rest for you.

Conclusion

And thus hath Common Sense laid before you such arguments for your speedily adopting a complete parliamentary reform, as arise from the consideration of national utility and of national necessity.

Another argument to the same effect is, the consideration of national dignity, or the dignity of human nature concerned in you aggregately and individually, as beings endowed with reason, and, as such, holding a natural right to be treated, by those who govern you, with due respect to your understanding and to your feelings as men. Whether you are and have been governed with that due respect, the world and yourselves can judge. For this is a subject of too great delicacy to be enlarged on by Common Sense with moderation, and at the same time with truth.

But there still remains one other argument, for your speedily adopting this measure, which, with rationally reflecting beings, ought to act more forcibly than even all the others. This is a consideration of the situation in which you will place your posterity, through your now neglecting to adopt it. You have irrevocably bound your posterity to the payment of near ten millions sterling yearly, for the interest of a debt contracted mostly by the present generation, a great part of it indeed in the present reign. An unnaturally cruel legacy for parents to bequeath their children! But, in the case that you shall suffer yourselves, and consequently your children, to be despoiled of those manufactures and commerce, which have hitherto alone enabled you to support that burden, you will treat these your children with greater cruelty than Pharaoh is said to have treated the Israelites, by compelling them to make brick without straw.[248] And yet this is the situation in which you will irretrievably place your posterity, if you shall now neglect to adopt that necessary reform.

Whereas, by speedily and unanimously concurring in that measure, you will not only secure those manufactures and commerce to yourselves and your posterity, but by so greatly diminishing your present national expenditure, through the same measure, you will be enabled to considerably diminish that heavy burden of debt, even in your own generation. And you will farther be enabled, under the same measure, but not otherwise, to create a richly valuable accession of domestic territory, by means of that public undertaking which hath been here proposed and described, for cultivating your present useless barren lands. Besides that, by the same public undertaking you will rid yourselves and your posterity of those numberless thieves and beggars, which, under your present form of government, have ever been a ruinous nuisance to this community. There are many other important national benefits, that would result to you and your posterity from that reform, too tedious to recapitulate.

Above all things you will, by adopting that measure, procure for yourselves, and leave to your posterity, that which your fathers did not leave to you, *a rational and free constitution*, that will ever completely protect and secure you, with your posterity, from the rapacity and oppression of government. And, by procuring for them such a constitution, you will atone for the injury you have done, in burthening them with that enormous debt.

But if you shall now slight the voice of Reason soliciting you to save yourselves and your posterity from ruin; and shall persist in the same supine, passive, and servile submission, to feed the rapacity and ambition of your government with the whole resources accruing from your manufactures and commerce; thereby enabling it to harass yourselves and disturb the whole world around with perpetual wars; then the sooner that you and your government shall be despoiled of these so perniciously applied resources, the better it will be for all the rest of mankind; nay the better it will be for yourselves.

Appendix

The Origin of the English Poor System – and the Motives of Government for first instituting that System

It is universally known that this English Poor System was first instituted towards the latter end of Queen Elizabeth's reign. For that the statute the 43 Eliz., is the first that enacts and prescribes a public provision for the idle, unemployed poor, with particular regulations for that provision. And this said statute has ever since continued to be the fundamental regulating law of the English Poor System. All the numerous subsequent statutes on that head having been merely auxiliary, or explanatory of the said 43 Eliz.

And we must observe here, *in limine*, that this necessity for so many aiding and explaining statutes, together with the contradictory, perplexed expression of those statutes, producing daily clashing in opinion between the several justices of the peace, who administer this same Poor System; and between those justices of the peace and the judges in the Court of King's Bench, to whom all such differences are ultimately referred; nay the contradictory opinions that have been delivered by different judges of that same Court, upon cases in this system exactly similar in every one circumstance, furnish the most convincing general proof, that the principle of this said system must be somehow altogether faulty and absurd.

The reason assigned by government for first instituting this Poor System, by that statute 43 Eliz. is, that the idle, unemployed poor had, towards that period, become very numerous, discontented, and likely to prove troublesome and dangerous to government. And this was indeed the true reason for then acting that said Poor Law.

But the cause that is at this day assigned and universally received why the poor became thus idle, unemployed, numerous, and dangerous to government at that period, is not the true cause. But, on the contrary, is a gross mistake, which it becomes necessary to here correct and rectify.

For the cause so assigned and received at present is, the dissolution of the monasteries in England. As if those dissolved monasteries had, ever till the 43 Eliz. maintained all the idle, unemployed poor in England. Whereas the truth is, that these monasteries had been dissolved near to seventy years before the 43 Eliz. And we hear nothing of this discontented and dangerous poor existing, till at most the 38 Eliz.

But we clearly understand, from the practice of those numerous monasteries which still exist at this day in other countries, that the only maintenance or relief ever afforded to the poor in England by those dissolved monasteries, must have consisted in an optional distribution, by each monastery, of that broken meat and offals which ever exist in large societies, to the lame and impotent poor in its respective neighbourhood. But the lame and impotent were not the poor which, about that period, appeared dangerous to government. And, at any rate, the withdrawing that monastic relief, being such as is described, could not have thrown a numerous discontented poor upon the public. Though, this same monastic relief, whatever it was, having been withdrawn about seventy years before the 43 Eliz. we must upon that and every possible consideration necessarily conclude that the dissolution of the monasteries in England was not the cause that the idle, unemployed poor had towards the 43 Eliz. become so very numerous, discontented, and dangerous to government, as to occasion that necessity of enacting this said poor provision law. And therefore we must find another cause for it.

The true and real cause that the idle, unemployed poor, or labouring commonalty, had become so numerous and dangerous to government towards the 43 Eliz. was the following innovation in the disposition and conduct of the English nation, which had taken place towards that period. Ever till about that time the English had attended solely to agriculture and the improvements of their lands. They had so totally neglected navigation and commerce, and also manufacture, that they employed the Easterlings to transport even their raw wool to the continent, where it was manufactured. But the rich discoveries then lately made by Spain in the new world, inspired the English, as well as other nations, with a desire to share in those discoveries. And the war that broke out with Spain, early in Queen Elizabeth's reign, had compelled the English to apply, in their own defence, to navigation. This spirit was farther promoted, by the opportunity presented through that war, of intercepting those riches of Spain in their passage from America to Europe. And the success of those first adventurers so encouraged others that, by the middle of this reign, the rage for discovery, naval enterprize, and commerce had completely seized the English nation, and entirely changed their former disposition and conduct.

Agriculture became at once totally neglected. The nobles, and men of large estates, pledged their lands for money to engage in those naval adventures. Of course the cultivation of their estates, and particularly the breaking in of their waste lands, was altogether intermitted and laid aside.

This sudden and general intermission of agriculture necessarily threw into idleness and the want of employ multitudes of the labouring commonalty, who till then had, by their earnings in that species of employ, maintained themselves and their families. And this deprivation of their wonted employ and subsistence was the true cause that such numbers of the labouring commonalty became, about this period, idle, unemployed, and discontented. And these, being able-bodied men, appeared dangerous to government.

Despotic governments which can, without feeling or remorse, plunge their subjects, whom they consider and treat as their slaves, or indeed as their cattle, into all the horrors of foreign wars, and send them abroad to be slaughtered by thousands, for the most trivial cause, perhaps for no cause, are all over feeling at the appearance of domestic insurrection, disturbance, or bloodshed. Because this, like the mutiny on board a ship, brings danger and trouble home to their own persons.

Therefore, as soon as that discontent of a numerous strong bodied poor presented to Queen Elizabeth's government the appearance of danger from a cause, which, if not removed, threatened to increase, that government determined to completely secure itself from this danger, by for ever removing the cause thereof.

And assuredly that said statute, the 43 Eliz. was a device the most completely effectual that could be contrived, for perfectly securing the then government against danger, and even against trouble or inconvenience.

For the arbitrary despotic regulations of that statute, compelling each parish distinctly to provide meat, drink, cloathing, lodging, and all other necessaries, for every one idle person within that parish, who should chuse to apply it, completely cut off all cause of discontent, and consequently of danger to government, from the then idle, unemployed poor. More especially as these idle poor were restrained, by this parish regulation, from wandering about, or assembling in bodies.

But this government, which was thus curiously attentive to the security of its own despotic power, and even its ease and convenience, sacrificed without remorse the most important interests of the people to these considerations. For, by this parish work-house regulation, all these unemployed poor were placed in a state of absolute uselessness, totally lost to the state. And, whilst the wealthy and industrious part of the community received no kind of return for the expence that was cause to them by this regulation, these unemployed poor, instead of receiving any benefit or comfort from that expence, felt themselves thereby stripped of all that little self consequence, that pleasing consciousness of rational dignity, which the contemplation of reciprocal utility furnishes to the mind of the lowest individual in society, who feels himself capable of being thus useful. They soon found themselves degraded to a state of useless, despicable, and slavish dependence on extorted charity.

Whereas if, instead of thus absurdly converting those unemployed agricultors into useless slavish manufacturers of flax, hemp, thread, wool, iron, and other wares and stuff, in parish work-houses, under the tyranny of overseers annually changed, the then government had ordered that all those unemployed labourers should have been again restored to their wonted situation and employ, by setting them to cultivate, for the benefit of the public, those waste and barren lands, that had then lately been deserted by the private owners, for wages to be paid them, out of those very monies which that statute compelled the public to pay for maintaining those same poor in absolute idleness; then, and in that case, would the public have received a return, that would have been nearly adequate to their expence; and the unemployed discontented poor would have been replaced in a state of useful, comfortable independence. But such a measure would have clashed with the ease, the convenience, and the despotic purposes of government.

But notwithstanding the wealthy part of the community, accustomed to the yoke, and equally afraid as government of popular disturbance, did passively submit to the absurd, tyrannical, and oppressive regulations of this said statute, the unemployed poor did not so tamely acquiesce in their part of it. These soon expressed their dissatisfaction. And, in a little time after, namely about the beginning of the next reign, they broke out into open insurrection in two counties, under Reynolds, surnamed Captain Pouch. And imagining that the then new undertaking of enclosing lands had contributed to the loss of their wonted employ, they vented their indignation on those enclosures. They were indeed soon overpowered by government, supported by all the wealthy.[249] But this insurrection, with the declarations of the insurgents, furnishes a clear concurring proof, that the cause herein before assigned, was the real and actual cause of that great increase and dangerous discontent of the idle, unemployed poor, towards the 43 Eliz. As also that these same idle, unemployed poor were far from being satisfied with the nature of that provision made for them by this said statute.

And such was the origin of this your Poor System. And such were the views and motives of your government for first instituting it.

The process of the Parish Provision, and Poors'
Settlement Regulation

This is the process of that parish regulation. The idly disposed person, who means to throw himself a burden upon the parish, makes oath before the nearest justice of the peace, that he is poor, or impotent, or not able to provide for himself and his family; that he belongs to such parish; and that he had been refused relief by the overseers thereof. And thereupon this said justice is compelled, by the law, to summon before him these overseers, to show cause why they have refused the demanded relief. And as the overseers cannot, in this stage of the business, traverse the pauper's oath, they are immediately compelled, by an order of the same justice, to maintain and provide for that pauper and his family, till otherwise ordered according to law.

The only remedy of this parish is to examine the pauper's right to settlement there; and whether he may not, according to the law, have a better right to settlement in some other parish. And as the vestry clerk is commonly the oracle on these examinations, and being himself a dabbler in the law, is keen for the management of a parish lawsuit, it would be strange if, amongst the many contradictory statutes on parish settlements, he could not find out some flaw in the pauper's title to settlement in that parish, and his better title to settlement in some other parish. Upon this discovery immediate application is made by those overseers to two justices of the peace, for an examination of the pauper's title before them. And it is rarely difficult to obtain, from those two justices, an adjudication of the pauper's better right to settlement in the other parish, together with an order for delivering over this pauper and his family to the overseers of that said other parish who by virtue of the same order are obliged to receive and maintain him, till otherwise ordered according to law.

The legal remedy of this other parish is by appeal against the order of removal, before the justices of the county at their next quarter sessions. Of which appeal notice being usually given to the removing parish, the two contending parishes appear before the quarter sessions, by their counsel learned in the law. And, which ever way the appeal goes, a case is seldom refused by the justices, if required by the losing parish. Which case carries the cause before the justices of the King's Bench at Westminster. Where this important, inexplicable and unintelligible cause is argued by two or more of the most eminent counsel at the bar, for each parish, fee'd at an enormous expence.

It most commonly happens that the order of quarter sessions is quashed by the Court of King's Bench. So that this pauper and his family may be removed backward and forward, from one extremity of the kingdom to the other, at a prodigious expence to these contending parishes. And when the bill of charges, for litigating this single pauper's right of settlement, consisting of the charges in removing, the overseer's personal charge, and the attorney's bill of costs for himself and agent, with counsels' fees at the quarter sessions, and Court of King's Bench, shall be delivered in, the whole charge to each parish may exceed one hundred and fifty pounds.

Nay possibly the dispute about that one pauper's settlement may not terminate here. For the losing parish may afterwards discover that some third parish is more legally subject to the pauper's settlement. In which case exactly such another process may be renewed.

Such are the effects of this parish provision and poors' settlement regulation. And, amongst other considerations, this one naturally suggests itself. That if the maintaining one single pauper is held such a grievance that, for the bare chance of escaping it, two parishes shall chuse each to incur the expence of one hundred and fifty pounds, the maintaining so many thousand of these paupers must needs be to the community a most insufferable grievance.

The Origin and present State of the English Government

The Saxons, our progenitors, who first landed in Britain, were all soldiers, engaged in a military enterprize, first to assist, then to attack the former inhabitants, and wrest from them their possessions. It required about one hundred and seventy years to accomplish this enterprize. And, during all that time, the only government of these Saxons was necessarily of a nature merely military. Because, not only the success of the enterprize, but the safety of all these who formed that community depended upon a strict observance of military discipline, which consists in a perfect subordination, or prompt passive obedience of the soldiers to the authority of their officers, and of these officers to the general or commander in chief. And, of course, the general possessed, during that whole time, all and every possible power of government, in a degree that was altogether unlimited, not only in such matters as were merely military, but in every matter of distributive justice. All the other Saxons who afterwards landed in this island, whether they came under distinct and independent chiefs, or whether it was to join any of the former chiefs, were all, through the same cause, governed upon the same principles that have been here mentioned. Consequently the original government of the British Saxons was altogether military. And it would seem that, through the very same cause, all the governments on this earth have been originally founded on the very same principles.

Afterwards when, upon the subjugation of the former inhabitants, military enterprize in some sort ceased amongst the Saxons, and thereupon their situation became in some degree altered from that of soldiers to citizens, the form of government to which they had so long habituated, underwent little or no change, saving in the name or appellation of the different ranks or classes. The commanders in chief, who had before been kings as well as generals, now assumed the title of kings only, still retaining however all the original power that had been exercised by the generals. The great officers were called barons, and still formed the great council to the king, as they had formerly been to the general. And the soldiers became villains [villeins], equally subordinate to the authority of the king and barons, as they had formerly been to that of the general and officers.

Nevertheless this despotic military government held so much regard to the good of the people, that it indulged them in holding their public popular assemblies of various kinds. Where they were allowed to deliberate and propose regulations for their own good order, in every thing relating to their mutual intercourse, and for preserving the peace amongst themselves, but in nothing that related to the public or general government. That was solely directed by the king, assisted by his aforesaid great council of the barons. In particular for the purpose of promoting and preserving the peace and good order of the people, they were permitted, by a writ from the king to chuse from amongst themselves certain municipal magistrates, termed conservators of the peace, who, being thus chosen by the people, and returned to the king, received his commission, to act with full power, in keeping the peace, executing the laws, preventing the commission of crimes, and maintaining good order. And it is said that, under this magistracy, the public good order was maintained in an excellent manner.

Thus matters were conducted under the Saxon government, and the Norman conquest, though it was far from adding to the privileges of the people, yet made no alteration in that municipal magistracy.

It was in the year 1327, commonly called the first of Edward the Third, though then no king, that this privilege of chusing their own conservators of the peace was first wrested from the people, and seized by the Crown, on the following occasion. Young Edward, then a minor, returning from France, with his vicious mother, and her paramour Mortimer, imprisoned his father Edward the Second, and, meaning to formally depose him, Mortimer assembled a parliament packed for that purpose. But apprehending opposition from the people, whose minds began to waver, and particularly from those conservators of the peace, then acting under the commission of Edward the Second, this Mortimer, who entering the house of parliament with a band of armed ruffians could threaten the members with instant death if they should oppose his will, took upon him to dismiss, in the name of parliament, all the conservators of the peace and, without allowing to the people their wonted privilege of chusing new conservators, he himself appointed certain of his own partizans to that office.

And in this manner were the people despoiled of that privilege, which they had enjoyed for so many centuries, to chuse their own conservators of the peace. The barons, who felt no inconvenience from this usurpation of the Crown, gave themselves no concern about it: and the people, accustomed to the subordination of villains [villeins], seem to have silently acquiesced.

What hath been here said, respecting the original government of the British or Anglo Saxons, relates entirely to your present municipal government. It may be proper however to add, that this account of the Saxon government differs a little from that account given by certain learned and ingenious Whigs who, in their controversies with the Tories, finding nothing in our present system of government like to a free constitution, looked back for such a constitution under the Saxon system of government. Their disquisitions are collected by Mr Millar, the learned professor of Glasgow, who after endeavouring to torture the Saxon word *Wittes*, and the Latin words *Procuratores, et magnus concursus populi*, at their Wittenagemotes, into something that could carry the resemblance of a free constitution, is forced to conclude 'That the Anglo Saxon government was not calculated to secure the liberty and the natural rights of mankind'.[250]

But if these ingenious Whigs meant, by their disquisitions, to discover a precedent under the Saxon system, whereon to found a right in the British people to a free constitution, they bestowed their pains to very little purpose. The truth is that they, with the majority of mankind, make no distinction betwixt *precedent* and *rule*, whereas there are no two things in nature more different. Precedents are founded on and drawn from the practice or opinions of *men*, which are fallible, subject to error, and in fact oftener wrong than right. Rule is founded on *Nature, Eternal Reason, and the due Order of Things*, which are infallible, subject to no error, consequently never wrong. And therefore, in any case where there exists an applicable *rule* so founded on Nature and Reason, for men to look about for a *precedent* to guide that case, is folly; to substitute precedent instead of that rule (when they differ) is error; but to oppose precedents against that rule, can only be the wicked act of designing men, basely disposed to promote some evil and unjust purpose.

In the formation of human government there does exist a guiding rule, founded on Nature, Eternal Reason, and the due Order of Things, which has been ever known to, and ever admitted by all civilized mankind, in all ages, though never carried into practice till of very late. This universally-known and admitted rule in human government is the *salus populi*, the good of the people governed, and that rule is, and ever ought to be, the only guide in the formation of all governments. It is also the ever-standing measure and standard, whereby all governments, that are already formed and do exist, should be frequently and carefully examined and tried. And whenever it shall be found that the existing government varies or differs from this standard, that difference should immediately be corrected, so as that the whole government should be rendered completely conformable to this said standard.

The next point is, who are to be the triers or examiners of government. And, at any rate, that cannot be the existing government itself, or the persons concerned in the administration thereof, because that government, or the administration of it, is the very subject that is to be tried. The people governed are alone competent, and alone entitled by Nature, by Reason, and the due Order of Things, to examine the present state of their government, and the conduct of those who administer it; first, because the power of governing is originally derived from the people, who on that account are paramount to government; and second, because the good of the people being the ultimate and only end of government, they alone are qualified to judge whether that end is accomplished by the present government. And this act of so examining the state of their government is not only a right inherent in the people, but it is a duty they owe to themselves, to the dignity of human nature in general, and to their own reason in particular. Also that duty of so examining becomes incumbent on the people, at least once in every generation, because, notwithstanding a government may have been originally formed according to that before-mentioned standard of the *Salus Populi*, and may also have been long conducted so, yet that same government may, through the conduct of those who then administer it, have become suddenly or of late extremely vicious and noxious to the people. And to say that, in such a case, the people have not a right to stop this noxious administration, and to rectify and restore their government to the foregoing standard, is to contradict the surest principles of Right Reason, of Nature, and of Eternal Justice. It is affirming that the people were made for the service of the existing government, be it ever so vicious, instead of all governments being made for the people. It is affirming that the Creator exists for the service of its creature. And that is, in religion, impious blasphemy;

in human government, it is the absurd nonsense of tyranny and despotism, by whatever sophistry it may be disguised. And this right of the people to correct recent faults or errors of government, extends equally to faults or errors of long standing. So soon as these faults shall be discovered, the generation that discovers them has a right to correct and remedy them; without regarding the antiquity or long standing of the error; and without regarding the precedent of the last or any number of generations, which may have been erroneous; but regarding alone that infallible standard of human government, the *Salus Populi*.

But, besides the duty that every generation of the people owe to themselves, they owe it as a duty to their children of the next generation, whose natural guardians they are, to examine the present state and conduct of their government, and to rectify what is amiss in it, by the foregoing standard.

But the curious and laborious disquisitions of those ingenious Whigs into the form of the Saxon government was nugatory, for this farther reason: that the Saxon system, whatever it was, had been swallowed up by the Norman Conquest; which established the *Feudal System*; whereby the Conqueror became the sovereign lord and king of the English people; vested with unlimited power over every right or thing which they had acquired or possessed from *Fortune*, and also every right which they possessed or held from *Nature*. And that power continued thus unlimited for two reigns. Henry the First, and Stephen, each bribed the barons to support them against competitors, by a charter, granting back, as a favour to these barons the use and exercise of some few natural rights.[251] But the people still remained villains [villeins], the divided property of the king and barons. However, in the course of that long struggle between the tyrant John and the barons, the people had become of such consequence, as to be admitted by the barons, into a participation of the few natural rights, which were yielded back, in the charter extorted from that tyrant. And which charter is, on that account, called *Magna Charta*.[252]

The great wealth acquired by the people, through commerce, during the reigns of Elizabeth and of the Stuarts, roused in them a spirit to contend with their sovereign lords the kings, for certain other natural rights. And these contests ended in what is termed the *Glorious Revolution*.[253] On which occasion the people bargained with the new king, to relinquish these few contested rights; and, in exchange, they unwarily granted him a power, the extent and consequences of which they little understood or foresaw. They granted him a power to dip into their purse, by borrowing money on their credit.

This was the most advantageous bargain that ever a sovereign made with the people. For these sovereigns, having once obtained a power over the public purse, they found occasion to dip into it so often and so deep, by virtue of their prerogative to engage the nation at pleasure in war, that in process of time they have got the whole wealth of the nation into their power and management. And this power over the whole national wealth has established, by virtue of their own *gold*, a sovereign power over the people, that surpasses the sovereign power of the feudal system established by *steel* or *iron*, in a degree proportionably great, as the value of this first-mentioned metal exceeds that of the latter. For besides that this present power is inconceivably more extensive, it is perfectly secured from all those former disputes with barons and parliaments about natural rights. The mighty Lion now stalks majestic before, alone, and unopposed, his former troublesome opponents now sneaking after, as fawning jackals, for their share of that common prey, the timid, helpless herd.

The term *King* is now become obsolete, and changed for a certain mystical term, *the Crown*. And the material crown has become endowed with a talismanic power, to immediately transform the person who puts it on, in defiance of Nature, into a being super-human, possessing almost every attribute of the Deity.***

And thus we perceive that the Saxon system changed our generals into kings. The Norman system changed our king into our sovereign lord the king. And the Revolution system has changed our sovereign lord the king into a deity.

* This principle or opinion of the public creditors, that the validity of a security, which had been granted to them by the government, rested entirely upon the continued possession of the Crown by that king or his heirs who had been the borrowers, and that the pretender's acquiring the Crown would defeat this government security, clearly denotes and marks an actual and real, though tacit, perhaps insensible conviction inherent in the minds of the people, that their real government, by whatever name or names it may be termed, is nothing other than the Crown; that the person who wears the Crown is, to all intents and purposes, the government; or, in other words, that his will is the measure of government. And so manifest was that aforesaid opinion of the public creditors respecting their security, that the reigning king soon discovered and effectually availed himself of it, by industriously increasing the public debt, together with the number of public creditors, as the certain means of securing to himself the possession of the Crown against his competitor. And this was indeed no bad policy in the Crown. But it is a melancholy consideration to the people of this country that, about a century ago, a few men, assuming to themselves the name and authority of the whole nation, though assembled without even the wonted formality of popular

election (such as it is), should have vested the person on whom they had bestowed the Crown, and his successors, with absolute power or means to borrow whatever money they pleased on the credit of the nation; and at the same time made it the natural interest of that person and his successors to contract as much debt as they could against the nation. A slight attention to these circumstances will partly account for the present immensity of the national debt, as also for the astonishing alacrity of the British government to engage the nation in war. Though, besides the above, all governments possessing unlimited power of making war, have numberless inducements to be perpetually engaged in war; because, in that situation, the government draws the whole profit, whilst the people bear all the loss.

** When the pecuniary distresses of France compelled their government to assemble the Notables, which afterwards produced the National Assembly, the stop that had been then put to the payment of the public creditors would have been continued perpetual, had it not been for the reform of the government abuses effected by that Assembly. Whereas these public creditors have now obtained a security, in which the whole nation has joined. And, through that reform of abuses, the nation hath become enabled to not only pay the interest regularly to the public creditors, also to *really and bona fide* discharge a part of the principal debt. Whilst, at the same time, the people are relieved from the burden of various taxes, that were the most oppressive to them, and the most injurious to manufacture and commerce.

*** Our King is *eternal*; for he never dies. He is *infallible and all-wise*; for he can do no wrong. He is the *fountain of justice*; the *fountain of mercy*; the *fountain of honour*; we derive our lands and all our good things from him alone, &c. Whilst, in truth, his only real attribute approaching the Divinity is that of irresistible power over the people of Great Britain, acquired and maintained by their own gold. All these other divine attributes spring from the adulation of a people, who can despise and abhor the very same adulation paid by the Romans to their *Divus Tiberius* and *Divus Claudius*.

FINIS

Paine's remedy for poverty, a problem that has persisted to the present day, was one of idealism; its viability was never put to the test. In suggesting that the unemployed and indigent be set to work for wages, he offered the plans that would be required to put his scheme into action. However, as mentioned in the final section of the piece, he was aware of the improbability of such a scheme ever being undertaken.

PUBLISHED 1791

The following pamphlet, printed for the author and sold by J. Bew, of 18 Paternoster-Row and J. Debrett of Piccadilly, London, is undated. However, it is catalogued at the British Library as having been published in 1791; its contents confirm the year, but just when it was published in 1791 remains a mystery. Written in a somewhat rambling and confused style, much of the early part of the pamphlet requires some patience on the part of the reader as it appears abstruse, but the matter becomes clear as the work continues. It is an account of events in Britain's recent political past, particularly the instability of government and per-ception of weakness on the part of George III during the 1780s. It is a denuncia-tion of poor government and its waste of public monies, and a commentary on Pitt the Younger's government. As it draws to a close, the pamphlet hints at the possibility of revolution if the king does not enforce the constitution for the good of himself and his subjects. It can be seen as a warning to the king of his need to act in order to gain the confidence of his subjects and his Parliament.

At this point, the reader is referred back to the article for *The Times* published on 13 February 1789. An extract of a letter from Thomas Paine to Thomas Walker was given with it. Those familiar with Paine's anti-monarchical writings surely nurture doubts that the earlier and following pieces were by him. Difficult as it may be for many, those doubts must be dispelled; the phraseology, the wording, and the sentiments were first expressed in the letter to Walker.

A Letter from Common Sense *Addressed to the King and People*

Sire,

However dangerous it may seem (considering the present temper of Parliament), to address Your Majesty with salutary advice, or with a duti-ful and tender affection for your crown and dignity, *yet, if ever, this must be the awful moment to awaken the feelings of a generous people in the cause of an injured sovereign. That moment indeed must be highly perilous to the consti-tution,* when party has grown into faction, and cabal into sedition; when old prejudices are hypocritically revived under the distinction of Whig and Tory; when the temper and resolves of Parliament are edged with an enven-omed spirit, nearly similar to that which prevailed during the blushing aera of Charles I, when licentiousness reigned uncontrouled, *and wild specula-tions on liberty were insidiously held forth to allure the multitude;* until royalty was sapped by slow degrees, and the frame of our glorious constitution blown up by an usurper and tyrant.[254]

It is your peculiar misfortune, Sire, in which your people are equally involved, to have party and faction for a series of years, uniformly opposed to your wisest counsels. It came in every questionable shape. If you took it to your royal breast and confidence, in order to conciliate the ferment in the state, it stung you – and endeavoured to diminish your lustre and power; if you dismissed it, the hideous roar was heard, and insatiable in its desires, the monster Ambition, hydra-headed stalked along, and involved in its vortex every wholesome measure, proposed for the good of society. To illustrate the cause of those evils, and to fix the prejudiced mind upon a fair basis of reason, shall be the subject of the following epistle.

To the People

Sirs,

In the history of nations, empires, and kings, we shall not find a situation similar, or so singularly unfortunate as ours. Blessed with all the advantages of a form of government the most perfect under heaven; an empire that had been the most extensive and glorious, a sovereign the most attached to the rectitude and spirit of the constitution, the moral duties, public virtue, a tender and delicate exercise of prerogative, and, as a private citizen, an honour and an ornament to society; yet nearly since his accession to the throne, though possessed of all those great requisites of legislation, and of the human mind – though without one infringement on the laws, his life has been imbittered, and his kingdoms convulsed by party and design.

When we come to consider that it is not in the constitution we find those defects; that it is not in sovereignty; that it is not in defective laws; but that all those mischiefs of popular insanity, and petulant clamour, have originated in two men insignificant in the state, we must look at each other, and wonder how the imbecility of our senses gave way to the patriotic imposition; which, alas! Sirs, has long been the garb, the subtlety of every political apostate, and which is exercised so judiciously as to deceive both the eye and ear. Prolix, Sirs, it would be to depict the characters of the multitude of those gentlemen who have risen by popular support into power, and who have exercised that power like the tyrant's rod against the spirit of the constitution: however, from Mr Wilkes we may trace the first source of this pestilential stream in the period recited. The sober public drank deep of the infectious waters, and reeled in democratic intoxication to beset the throne; yet his ambition was not too great; a turtle and a bottle of Burgundy the summit of his desires – peace be with him; he has nested in a downy bed, and passes away life in festive irony at the multitude of his former followers![255]

The second opposition we find supported by Mr Fox, an opposition of a more daring spirit, the life of democracy, and the plague of kings.[256] In this opposition, if I may be allowed to follow the allusion of a noble Lord, (whose ironical simile does honour to his profound respect and grateful attachment to his sovereign for twelve years' favours) the scarecrow faction came in every questionable shape of unrelenting horror; not as the ghost of poor Hamlet, for he was a well-deserving prince. Forbid it, Heaven, that the spectre of the constitution should ever appear in such a questionable shape, and relate the foul deeds of her prison house, with the baneful draughts of democratic poison administered to her vitals!

Once Britons were endued with sound reason, liberal sentiments, great and animated souls, a reverence and admiration for their sovereigns, and a love for the constitution; a good man was sure of protection – the knave despised; and surely if ever such a moment was, the present calls aloud for redress, as we see all the bright virtues that constitute the good man combined in majesty; a majesty standing forth in support of his people; a majesty insulted by every unconstitutional epithet that can disgrace even the name of hypocrisy: but alas, Sirs, I fear that day of British glory is lost and absorbed in faction and misrule: dissipation has poisoned the springs of virtue, corruption has followed, and took its sanctuary in boroughs, to the manifest destruction of the constitution.[257]

By comparative views all things are best seen. Let us turn our eyes around, and behold the different powers of Europe in their various situations – the Emperor journeying through his empire diffusing salutary laws, reforms, benefits and commerce;[258] the King of Prussia, like a setting sun, viewing the conquests which he made; the Empress of Russia introducing the arts and sciences, agriculture and commerce; view the Bourbon Monarch idolized by his people, pulling down the British Lion, and bidding fair for the dominion of the ocean; Spain, Denmark, Sweden growing formidable, their people happy, their monarchs great. Behold England! her councils torn and distracted – the son opposed to father, brother against brother; her funds in a deadly consumption, pining away by atoms, her sovereign tottering before a factious hurricane, his pursuits of glory impeded, his resolves insulted, his rights scoffed and denied, and a fire of sedition formed in the bowels of the constitution, to consume the remnants of an expiring empire. The vengeance of Heaven cannot be more manifest against a deluded people, nor the idolatry of those who believed in false oracles more manifest. However, to close this account of the power of Europe, who are the unfortunate? Poland and England. The first distracted by her senate, the latter by her parliaments. Poland rent as poor Peter's garb, one skirt to Russia, a skirt to Prussia, and a third to the Emperor:[259] England similar, a large skirt to America, Ireland hanging by a thread, and the East Indies attempted to be purloined;[260] and held I am to affirm, if the ambitious minister had got that sweet morsel within his jaws, all the powers of England would not wrest it from him.[261] If my positions be fairly stated, and I believe few will deny those facts, where shall we find the cause of our misfortunes? It is acknowledged the constitution is good, and the laws are salutary; therefore we shall find the disease in faction and party, and have the consolation of being told, that all our present national grievances, political disturbances, loss of public credit, uproar and confusion, originate in the grand question, Whether Lord North and the Right Honourable Secretary shall rule this country by aristocratic laws, or whether the sovereign shall preserve the constitution inviolable, and exercise his prerogative agreeable to Magna Charta, and the subsequent laws grafted on that noble charter of rights.[262] However, under this lamentable picture of England (fatal only by its factions) we find a boast of freedom, the first and most godlike principle granted to man. On this principle, credulous and unsuspecting in its elevated nature, the designing man has oftentimes laid hold, and seduced Britons to the verge of destruction in support of their delusive liberties. Eloquence to us is a charm as captivating as the tinkling of bells to the bee, which we gather around and indiscriminately follow, to set fire to London – nay, to burn the world.[263] Thus freedom sometimes over-shoots its mark, and grows too luxuriant for the moderate capacity to exercise: therefore, whoever the man who disturbs public society with this species of popular phrenzy, administers inflammatories to the mind for some latent self-purpose, and destruction to society for some private attainment.

In all oppositions, Sirs, since the Revolution, there has been some object, or some phantom of object, in the discussion of which the minds of men differed. I shall not deny but Mr Wilkes's opposition had some good features, and that we stand indebted to him for the suppression of general warrants.[264] In the present opposition there is not a shadow of national concern. 'Tis not a question to carry on a glorious war, which our forefathers were accustomed to discuss: 'tis not a question for an honourable peace: it is an object of ambition daring beyond precedent, and petulant beyond faction; as its point clearly leads to aristocracy, and its *brat* an experiment to cajole the people with its seemingly innocent features, into a violation of the dearest rights of society. Had this babe got the East-Indies as a play thing, Heaven only knows how far its mature ambition would have reached.[265] Petted in his infancy with the sweet plum of charters, others might appear as delicious, and the little play-thing *necessity* a rattle to hold in his hand, with the inscription 'Precedent, precedent, Mr Fox's East-India Bill, to the total annihilation of funds, corporate bodies, &c.', until step by step, the infant would ascend to a situation better imagined than described. How oft has the innocent babe been rocked by the Noble Lord, whilst the Right Honourable Secretary poured eloquent orations on his promising features?

Though it be unnecessary to illustrate to many of you (yet to some it may be beneficial) that the constitution of this country is formed of three parts, each part possessing distinct rights, yet so blended in each other, that they must co-operate, and in essence and spirit form but one legislature. When any of those parts infringe upon the other, the constitution is violated. Therefore [it is] the duty of Common Sense, as the guardian of the people, to watch the encroachment, and to regulate the equipoise of each part agreeable to the maxims of the glorious constitution. Under the same authority exists our charters, those grants, those invaluable rights, comprehending almost every thing that is dear to man: comprehending the bond of mutual allegiance between the sovereign and people, which are not to be violated by unhallowed hands, nor the midnight whims of speculative ambition.

From example the best inferences are drawn. Should the Lord Chancellor bring in a bill, similar to the East-India Bill, under the plea of necessity, to place the West India trade under a Board of Directors chosen from the Lords, with a power to nominate governors and commanders for the islands without the participation or controul of the other two branches of the legislature, would not the Right Honourable Secretaries shake the Senate House with the thunder of declamation?[266] Would not the black man of portentous countenance be impeached, and the murder of the constitution placed at his door?[267] How loud would fond prerogative echo in the house, and the insulted rights of the nation? *O tempora mutantur!* I acknowledge it is debasing the great luminary's name which I speak of, to combine him in such an idea, being the father of justice, and rock of the constitution: However, thus we should soon find the three branches of the legislature, with independent rights and claims warring with each other, until some tyrant or usurper would come forth, swallow the fish, and leave the shells to the disputants.

In this delicate situation, Sirs, there is one grand view which ought to direct us, where our prejudices and passions should be laid aside; and that is, to enquire what the object, the merits and demerits, the claims, the utility to popular protection those gentlemen have, who are candidates for administration. The fruitful vineyard, no matter who cultivates it, is more beneficial to society than all the harangues of St. Stephen with a barren vintage: hear him, hear him – Heaven how he speaks! whilst the unfortunate public are trembling under a load of taxes, and the deliberation of their expediency impeded by faction and ambition. In this admonition, Sirs, to your feelings, I must advert to that glorious period of the immortal Chatham, when our cups overflowed with prosperity, and our nation with honour:[268] the fortunate shepherd's son well deserves the care of the flock; for though the partial cause of good or bad fortune stands undefined, we all know there is such an overruling power.

Shall I ask and solve what parliament is at this day? Is it a parliament of virtue? Is it a parliament of the people – with which I consider borough representatives have no more to do, than a new piece to merit which derives its existence from the plaudits of some hirelings engaged to support it? Is it not party against party, who shall bring most votes into the house, who the most interest in venal boroughs, and elections? Is not the plain question, whether parliament, in its present shape, shall be omnipotent, and form a cabinet; or, whether, the king shall nominate his servants, and exercise his prerogative? Unfortunate and insulted prince, who is denied the private rights of man, of friendship, of counsel – to smile, to frown; but solely to commit himself to the management of a minister who never gave him one specific proof of his political abilities; who, perhaps is not the most wise in the adjustment of his own affairs; who perhaps is inimical to prerogative, and friendly to aristocratic principles! Shall majesty, in such a situation, sequester his own understanding, and blindly submit to every encroachment on the constitution? Shan't he call upon his constitutional advisers, on the luminaries of the law, and those he can confide in, to take their opinion, the better to decide with justice, and act with the uprightness and glory of a monarch! No, says the minister; I am responsible, as the king can do no wrong by the spirit of the constitution; yet many a man lost his inheritance by the connivance of his agent, without doing any other wrong than intrusting his fortune to his care.[269] Another sophist will say, the king can dismiss his servants, and nominate others. So usually spoke the constitution; but the language of the majority of the Commons now say, they are not agreeable to us, and we shall vote them out again. Good Heaven! wherein then consists the use of the king's nomination? Is he not by this vote made a cypher removeable at the pleasure of the Commons, to place as a blank at the head of the column, or as a figure of importance, as best suits the players of the game? In this situation, had not sovereignty better surrender its rights, than become the shadow of royalty, without power; an image only to be bowed to, under an obsequious ridicule of scarecrow majesty? What is the language to his ministers by Mr Fox? Nay, that if they had done a million of virtuous deeds for the good of society, that still he would oppose them; therefore, it is not the salutary measure, it is not the good of community, which is the object; it is the man, the party who are to take the lead in administration. Thus are laid the seeds of corruption, and ministers drove to the necessity of buying, jobbing and bargaining, to engage men to their just duty. A peep into the expenditure of the missing millions of the treasury, I am fanciful would best explain this problem, and of those warm attachments which are now the basis of opposition.

However, to give my readers a proper chain to lead them to the arcana of this political finesse, and a just description of those gentlemen who formed administration for some years past; which I find the more necessary, from the false statement Mr Fox made of the political virtues of his noble friend; of his obedience to the sense of parliament; of his motives for resignation, and of that love which he possesses for the spirit of the constitution.

For this purpose, I must begin at that period shortly antecedent to Lord North's resignation. In that period, Sirs, you will find a display of political policy beyond the fathom of the human mind. That most unpropitious minister, finding the despoliation of his own counsels and administration – finding the empire severed, America lost – finding all the sovereign powers of Europe leagued against him – finding the revenue exhausted, the country impoverished, and even to his own fruitful invention, further aids of taxation impracticable, by a feint he gave way to the Rockingham opposition, whose powers he might have withstood at that time, as well as at any other period of his administration. Those were the laurels, those the advantages of that great and glorious minister, those his titles to the protection of the people. However, the noble lord had a more extensive and comprehensive view in his resignation: a peace he saw was necessary, which he dare not meet on the unfortunate ground that one could be obtained on; therefore to others he yielded the important business, to rebuild the fragments of an empire with a peace cement, to prop the tottering constitution, to provide ways and means for unfunded millions, and the labour and hazard of negociation he submitted to other hands. In this great mass of political business, his lordship naturally supposed there might be some room for cavil, therefore laid his train, in order to spring his mine at a future day, and with an obsequious bow, in the magnitude of dissimulation, took his leave of administration. Now began Lord Rockingham's administration, which was not let live a moment beyond the act of signing the preliminary articles; and now began that infamous coalition of men, more obnoxious to each other than the history of simulation can equal.[270] However, those two great apostates, sacrificing private piques for the general welfare (under the masque of a democratical ambition), at the period when no one national interest was in danger; at the period when the constitution began to renovate; at the moment when harmony only was wanting to give strength and efficacy to our councils. The roll being called over by the noble lord and his Right Honourable Friend, and finding their forces adequate, the thunder of declamation was once more begun, the peace was considered inadequate to our relative situation, and little short of an impeachment threatened against the minister; the nation was ruined; the times big with mischiefs; men must be altered, or all was undone; the taxes were obnoxious ones, and every oblique censure flung at the boy of the Exchequer.[271] The Cabinet thus beset, the king menaced, and a boast made of not leaving him a friend or favourite, the reins of government were seized, when the old jockies once more mounted to direct the course. Here I beg leave to relate an anecdote of a Barbary pirate, whose crew, on going to founder, fired signals of distress, which were humanely attended to by some pilots, who stopped the leaks, and prevented the crazy ship from sinking: however, she was no sooner in smooth water, and safe, than the virtuous crew flung the pilots overboard, and hoisted their sails before a fresh breeze in pursuit of a rich prize, which they had nearly taken, when, at the instant, the former leaks burst open, to the manifest disappointment of the crew, and to the general joy of society. Thus expired Lord Shelburne's administration, whose Cabinet, if we view in the collective or in the individual body must fill our minds with admiration and respect, as such a combination of men, profound in the knowledge of the constitution finances, and our relative situation, scarcely can be equalled in the annals of England: eulogium or panegyric cannot add to their importance. The constituents may naturally ask Common Sense, how came a cabinet of such descriptive greatness to be dismissed, or lose the confidence of the king and Parliament? I shall tell them; they made a peace upon the best terms that human invention could do. They met the cries, petitions, and voice of the people, who were labouring under the pressure of taxes, laid on by a rapacious and unfeeling minister, to carry on a war conducted without fortitude or enterprize; a war, as heterogeneous in its system as Whig and Tory; admirals fighting our fleets, and generals leading our armies to battle, inimical to our conquest, and original design. However, those were accommodating features of the great minister, the better to trim and temporize with party, until our captured armies were led in triumph by a feeble enemy, and our fleets disgraced by an inferior force. To liberate the people from these misfortunes were the sins of Lord Shelburne's administration, who no sooner laid the foundation stone for peace, than the mine was sprung by the old engineer, and the whole Cabinet blown up, which opened the first door to the democratic principles of this day. However, let us now examine what are the salutary fruits of this virtuous coalition, and for that purpose call on the most sanguine supporters (nay, even on the most fraudulent and partial contractors) of Lord North's administration, to shew me one proof of his magnanimity, wisdom, fortitude in council, great and enlarged conceptions of state, or any other political virtue beneficial to society; like *Pharaoh*, the rod turned into a serpent in his hand, and his touch became baneful to every salutary measure.[272] I am ready to acknowledge his lordship's great paternal affections and family regards, whose friends at one period occupied little short of fifty thousand pounds a year; nor shall I deny his lordship the great powers of eloquence, and of administering persuasive arguments to the dubious mind; much less shall I deny his wonderful abilities in *bon mots*, which were usually administered to the House as sugar-plums, to reconcile our misfortunes. Many and many a million those witticisms cost the nation, whilst those of the facetious Joe are sold in pennyworths in folio.[273]

However, now began the second political aera of those ministers, and the first of the glorious coalition, whose first object was to build an administration on a broad bottom, in which the Right Honourable Secretary shewed no less a noble display of generous adherence to former friends, than wisdom in their adoption; as the minister must be short-lived indeed, who has not private affections, as well as the rectitude, nay, the ability of his talents to support him. I am far from wishing to throw either an invidious or an oblique reflection on those gentlemen who composed Mr Fox's administration; they have acted agreeably with the dictates of gratitude and sincerity; their necessities, or, perhaps, some more powerful stimulative, made them enlist under a chief, whose great abilities they looked up to, as an adventurer of political fortune: their sagacity could not direct them better, nor the hand of munificence reward them more amply; for whoever the minister or popular man be, who attends sacredly to his promise, to his friendships, he will find himself, if not the first in the scale of administration, at least able to preponderate it in favour of a more popular claimant. There is a secret charm, a content and serenity of mind in pursuing the fortune of a leader, who rewards with munificence, and cherishes with cordiality. In the traits of Mr Fox's character, we find all those features; and verily I believe all his towering ambition originated more for the aggrandizement of his followers, than from any self-gratification: yet, though this be a generous principle, it is a dangerous one; as flatterers often urge on a chief to inroads upon society, from the hope of plunder, with very little consideration for the rectitude of the measure, or, perhaps, for the future good name of their commander. It is the maxim of many writers to defame the characters of those they write against: for my part, I acknowledge the highest admiration for Mr Fox's private character and admirable abilities, which in any other station than that of a politician would do honour to the human mind; yet I acknowledge that I consider him the greatest political evil this country ever beheld; as in the executive power, he is like an irresistible tide, which overflows the bank, and bears down every opposition: his ideas are too enlarged, and his conceptions too warm, which as wax, takes the first impression from the seal, though the head should be reversed. In opposition he possesses a fortitude of mind, a strength of reason, a versatility of hypothesis, and a power of eloquence, so as to entangle the subject and object in a world of declamation. Such powers are always danger-ous in an executive state, as they are not temperately active, or moderately passive. Would I could see Mr Fox in any other department of the legisla-ture, where the boundaries would be sufficiently marked out and limited to oppose the copiousness of an all towering imagination! However, in order to build this broad-bottomed administration, the select and unfortunate asso-ciates of the Right Honourable Secretary's former adventures, were placed in the first posts of emolument and honour, whilst the secondary stations of the state were filled with the convivial, the *bon mot*, and the *bon vivant*. To give the whole an appearance of importance, a head was chosen (though of amiable heart and disposition) of such a pliant and docile nature, as to bear impressions, and as paste to be shaped and formed as best suited the artist's hand. Thus the whole machinery of state was put into motion, by touching a certain spring, whilst the Treasury was turned into a comedy, and to Secretaries of State playing the part of Maskwell to each in the Double Dealer.[274] The fond and loving *cara sposas* thus deeply trenched in constitu-tion, the outposts of administration were equally well fortified by their confi-dential friends, who stood as faithful centinels to guard against the approach of an enemy; whilst the noble Lord and the Right Honourable Secretary were indulging in their visionary naps, and seeing kingdoms to come. How loud the beautiful and sublime on the appearance of a foe, with an inexhausti-ble respiration fascinating the ear of the audience with well turned periods, and legendary tales, until the eyes closed with the sapience of his declama-tion, and forgot the purport of the day: Next came Thalia,[275] decorated with tropes and figures in her laughable gesticulation, and nice critical satire, to set the house in a smile (who killed Buckingham? 'Twas I politically over-threw the young Buckingham') whilst from the left fired the squibs of the artillery, with some grape-shot composed of small parables of scanty wit and low ridicule.[276] To close the scene, appeared the triple qualified orator with motions, resolves, precedents, and statutes tied up in good pennyworths, to be disposed of as hereafter may be – whilst the more necessary requisites of solidity, wisdom, and love of the constitution were absorbed in democrati-cal ideas of rewards, and midnight festivity. If moderate ambition had grati-fied these gentlemen, and the public affairs prospered, surely there never was a more laughable administration; but the vineyard was too narrow, and the grapes too few for the sons of expectation; therefore a wider field of ambition appeared more suitable for the purpose of entrenching deeper in administration, upon a more solid foundation, and of administering sweets more profusely to the friends of the honourable coalition – in short, to render Parliament democratical, and themselves the head of that democracy. For this purpose England was too exhausted in her revenues to give such douceurs as were necessary. Ireland too touchey, recent in her tears and resentment for the loss of her beloved and patriotic viceroy, Lord Temple[277] – America lost, and the plains of Hindostan, and the wealth of the East the only luxuriant morsels that could be sliced and disposed of. Many a fragrant pine has been cut up in imaginary expectation of the fruitful prospect; and without many compliments to Mr Fox's rare abilities, few Secretaries with such temptations in his power to divide and to dispose of, that would not find a majority in Parliament to become the tenantry, the occupiers of. This is the cement which combines that great body, which we find now bursting open the constitution, and committing a rape on her chastity, by fostering in her a brat of the most frightful complection. This is the *imperium in imperio* of the Right Honourable Secretary's grand principle, which he well knows if he departs from, his edifice, like that built of cards, will soon tumble, and each tenant anxiously look out for a new habitation. What a wonderful portion of tenderness and Christian humanity the Right Honourable Secretaries express for the poor Gentoos,[278] and for the unfortunate prince wandering in Asiatic deserts, whilst their humanity appears totally callous to the unfortunate prince of St. James's, whose exchequer they have locked up, whose hands they have attempted to tie up, whose prerogative they have denied, and whom they have marked with derision and treated with scorn.

However, to follow up the inquiry I have demanded relative to the salutary measures of their ministry, where are those visionary phantoms which so oft appeared to the Right Honourable Secretary Fox, presenting to his hands a crown of laurels to place on Britannia's head? Where are those radical cures that were to come from his abilities to the constitution? We find a peace was ratified on the very basis of the preliminary articles,[279] and a vote of thanks presented to the king for giving us those blessings of peace, for which Lord Shelburne's administration was damned. Where is the treaty of peace with the Dutch? Where is the treaty of a reciprocity of commerce with America? Where are the funded millions? How is the public credit supported? Where are those salutary taxes that were to be substituted for the obnoxious ones of the Youth of the Exchequer? These taxes we shall find, after trying every path to taxation, laid on the old jades of finance, the Customs and Excise. Where, then, are those benefits that should endear the ex-ministry to our popular confidence? Behold their last will and testament! Behold their expiring contrition, by strangling an enquiry of indefatigable labour and utility, instituted by the former ministry against an Eastern defaulter for peculation and fraud, and nobly to tell us that a charter is a piece of parchment, with a bit of wax dangling at its tail![280] Sirs, what inferences are we to draw from such insolent language? Does not democracy, or something more portentous, stare us in the face under such a doctrine, and J—n L— tell us, *Go, you tools*, you have no rights but what the omnipotence of the Commons is pleased to give you?[281] Dreadful the prospect, and alarming the black game yet to be played!

Having thus endeavoured to give my readers a short political history of the two last administrations, by a just and impartial statement of facts, for the purpose of their fair investigation – for the purpose of separating loyalty, and a just regard for the constitution, from speculative prejudices and fanatical delusions, which our minds adopt until our passions hurry us into party, party into faction, faction into imbecility, till we become a prey to our enemies, and the mock and derision of every well-governed people. On this ground I shall close this letter, with a few observations on the melancholy aspect of our present situation.

In all controversies, whether religious or political, a principle must be granted to argue upon. The deist in religion, and the sophist in politics, get rid of this principle, by denying the authority of law, and bewilder reason in the chaos of uncertainty. On these premises Mr Fox rears his standard; therefore futile it would be to endeavour to refute such an argumentator, who sets law at defiance, and with a sufficient force at his back to support him. How fortunate the man, who can find positions and solutions for every disposition of his mind! Cromwell could neither find law nor statute in the universe to sanctify his taking off the head of King Charles; yet he found a very civil, and, no doubt, great and just Parliament, to sanctify the holy deed.[282] However, three grand points are indulgently given up by Mr Fox, as rights of the prerogative, namely, to dissolve Parliament, nominate a ministry, and to dismiss himself and his *cara sposa*, who, no doubt, are the only political apostles, under heaven, to preach, teach, and save the constitution. Yet, in the same instant of allowing the rights of prerogative, they are to be suspended, and the sovereign told, that he has no right to exercise it but for the good of the people; and though his people pour blessings on His Majesty for exercising his royal prerogative so justly as to turn out the late ministry, the voice of the people is turned into ridicule, and the act of sovereignty considered as baneful, and private influence.

Had Mr Fox those delicate sensations which he expects to find in others; had he this mighty reverence for the constitution which he affects, why not retire, with his rejected brat in his hand, when he found he lost the confidence of the lords, of the people, and of his sovereign? Who, possessed of pride, or of honour, would force himself upon His Majesty, to embitter his life, and to distract his councils, when so many other statesmen are equally well qualified to conduct the business of the legislature? However, Sirs, it becomes your duty to interfere; your voice is the life of the constitution, the origin and dernier resort of the legislature; therefore, whoever (though decorated with stars and ribbons) derides and scoffs that voice, nay, even the signature, the mark, of the poorest burgess of Taunton, or freeholder of Westminster, will find his popularity is short-lived, and his power of trivial importance. Sirs, in such a period, will you disgrace yourselves, and place an indelible stain on your posterity, by handing over your sovereign, immaculate as virtue, and without a fault, to the taunts, to the menaces of an exasperated faction, to be scourged and whipped by political Pontius Pilates? Forbid it, Heaven! There is a nobler generosity in the British soul, that disdains oppression, and bids each man to be tried by his jurors upon specific charges. Shall His Majesty and his servants be denied the rights of Englishmen, and his prerogative, his ministers, nay, perhaps, something more dear to him, be taken away, without one proof of guilt, or violation of the constitution, but what rumour, and the false and invidious suggestions of a disappointed party point out? Come forward, therefore, ye sons of liberty, and testify your feelings by dutiful and loyal addresses to the throne; be cautious in your future choice of representatives; give to the Senate men of known honour and virtue; dread declaimers as you would the syren's song, which captivates to destruction; promote, if possible, harmony in our councils, which alone can give strength and efficacy to the constitution, and blessings and prosperity to the people!

To enter into a discussion of the various topics which are now the object of parliamentary rage and debate, would require a much larger folio than the compass of a letter to define; therefore I shall conclude by transposing some of those pathetic expressions which Mr Fox applied to the feelings of the people – 'O foolish and deluded party! O ambitious and aspiring dictator! who have made the greatness and dignity of the Commons consist in struggles against your sovereign and the constitution, by an endeavour to establish a democratical power! You have taken from the lustre of the Crown, and shewn its imbecility, its inoperative function, to all the powers of Europe: You have dictatorially desired your sovereign to dismiss his minister; a minister whose virtues shine superlatively bright, and whose fortitude stands as a pillar of strength between you and the constitution; a minister, whose name and integrity draw respect from all the power of Europe; a minister, above deceiving the public by assurances that he has American plenipos in his pocket, and Dutch burgomasters in his fob, with humiliating offers of peace; a minister, combined with a cabinet of men of exalted integrity and spotless virtue! These men are to be made a sacrifice to your ambition, or to be purged of those evils communicated to them by the royal nomination. Such are the modest requests of your dictatorial victory, such the fruits of your triumph, to embarrass the subject, to distress the fair trader, to lock up the revenues, and to disgrace the nation!'

Sire,

The voice of the million is with you; appeal to your people, who will build you a tower of strength, not to be overcome by faction: a love for your subjects and the constitution has endeared you to their confidence; yet it behoves you to stand firm on constitution ground, and to combine royal fortitude with legislative prudence, in support of your Crown and dignity. The masque is taken off, and the champions of democracy are ready to assail and overturn the sons of the constitution.

COMMON SENSE

Thomas Paine proved to be a turncoat, definite in his opinion this way or that.

As Moncure Daniel Conway noted of Paine's letter to Thomas Walker, Paine, 'this supposed purblind enemy of thrones was found in 1789 maintaining that the monarch, however objectionable, was more related to the people than a non-representative Parliament ...'. Neither Conway nor other commentators on Paine were aware of the *Letter from Common Sense Addressed to the King and People*. It appears here for the first time since publication.

10 OCTOBER 1793

Written just five days after the introduction of the new French revolutionary calendar, six days prior to the execution of Marie Antoinette and a matter of weeks before his own arrest as a foreigner in Paris, this letter to Thomas Jefferson, first Secretary of State of the United States, made no mention of the heights to which the Terror had risen.[283] Paine instead wrote of the Siege of Toulon when the Anglo-Spanish fleet occupied the city and its fortifications for four months.

Paris Oct. 10th 1793
2nd year of the Republic

My dear Sir,

As far as my judgement extends I think you cannot do better than send commissioners to Europe; and so far as the freedom of commerce may become a subject of conference it ought to be done. It may be a means of terminating the war for it is necessary that some power should begin. England is in a wretched condition as to her manufactures and her public and private credit. The combined armies make no progress. My opinion is that they cannot agree among themselves, and that the object of the English is to get possession of both sides the channel which certainly cannot be consented to by the Northern powers. It is not the English alone that has possession of Toulon, the Spaniards have landed more troops than the English as if to keep an eye upon them. Holland does nothing. She must wish to be out of the war. If you send commissioners Holland will be the best place for them to arrive at – they can there make known their credentials to all the resident ministers. It will not do to appoint Gou. Morris upon that business – his appointment here has been unfortunate – he has done more harm than good – all the Americans will give you the same account. I wish much to be in America were it only to brief the sundry commissioners – I think it is a plan on which all parties among you will unite. Were you to appoint two or three Comsrs. from America and direct them to call Mr Pinckney to their councils, I think it would have a good effect.[284] I suppose you know the person that wrote the enclosed American letter.[285] The contents state there are many subjects for conference that does not appear at first sight – it either has or will be published in London in a few days. Remember me to the President and all my friends.

Yours affectionately
Thomas Paine

Thomas Jefferson
Secretary of State
United States of America[286]

On the top right corner of the second page Jefferson endorsed the letter as received 31 March 1794; it was then too late to consider or act on Paine's advice, as was also the case with a further letter from him dated 20 October.[287] Jefferson had resigned his position of Secretary of State three months earlier on 31 December 1793 to take time out from politics until he was elected vice president to John Adams's presidency in December 1796.

The 'combined armies' of which Paine wrote did make progress and the Anglo-Spanish fleet succumbed to the military acumen of the young Napoleon on 19 December 1793.

12 NOVEMBER 1795

Described by a recent writer as 'an anonymous pamphlet',[288] the following piece is indubitably the work of Thomas Paine. Signed 'Common Sense', the name no other would dare assume, it followed soon on the heels of part two of *The Age of Reason*. It was written while Paine resided in Paris with James Monroe, then American Minister to France, who one year earlier had secured Paine's release from the Luxembourg Prison. From the then safe haven of France, he wrote what no Englishman of the time would have hazarded. Just eight days before, the king had proclaimed against public meetings; six days earlier Lord William Grenville, Foreign Secretary, and Prime Minister Pitt introduced bills proposing what have since become known as the 'Gagging Acts' or the 'Two Bills'. These were the Treasonable and Seditious Practices Act and the Seditious Meetings Act. The first was designed to prevent the meeting of more than 50 people in any one place for other than official reasons; to prevent the encouragement of foreigners to invade Britain or its possessions; and to prevent expression of criticism of Parliament by speaking, writing or publishing such criticism. The second was a tightening of the first. Any meeting of more than 50 people had to be sanctioned by a magistrate on receipt of notice. Rooms where lectures regarding public matters were to be held required licensing by two magistrates. Even if deemed lawful by the magistrates, such meetings could be dispersed if the magistrates considered them seditious. Resistance to the magistrates' decision to disperse a gathering was a capital offence.[289] Paine proffered the following pamphlet which named no place of publication; readers conversant with the path and chronology of events of Paine's life will realize that the place of publication was Paris.

Ten Minutes Advice to the People of England, on the Two Slavery Bills Intended to be Brought into Parliament the Present Sessions[290]

People of England!

The day is at length arrived, when you must either listen to the voice of reason, or surrender, through your supine obstinacy, every boasted privilege, which you have so long enjoyed as Englishmen! You have been long enough deluded! When the death-blow is struck at your liberties, you are called upon by the imperious summons of duty to yourselves, and to your posterity, to recollect the character of your country, and to approve yourselves deserving of the blessings transmitted to you by your immortal ancestors!

To neglect the preservation of our security from despotism, nay our very existence, is absurdly criminal. There are subjects on which it is unpleasant to address you, but to be silent in the season of danger, and of alarm, when every heart is beating with anxiety and apprehension, is to be subdued by false delicacy, and tends to promote that criminality. Permit me then, my countrymen, to claim your attention to a consideration of this new Convention bill proposed to parliament by Lord Grenville, and are our tongues to be forbidden to discharge their wonted functions, and the liberty of the press be utterly destroyed, to warn you, if this bill passes into a law, of the destruction you have permitted to be brought upon yourselves.

The chief object of this bill is to check the communication of opinions, and to restrain the freedom of the press. On recollecting the late attempts to crush sedition (for so it was said), on recollecting the various prosecutions for seditious language, to which every class of individuals have been exposed, and the unprecedented punishments, which have been inflicted on conviction of those modern offences, it is astonishing that the legislature should all on a sudden think it necessary to make further provisions against the progress of this newly invented crime. Have offences of this nature increased? No. We never hear of them now. Is not the confinement of Holt and Winterbottom in Newgate the one for publishing, the other for preaching,[291] what has been pronounced, seditious opinions, sufficient examples to deter us from disloyalty, and the use of disaffected sentiments? Have we forgotten poor Muir, and Palmer, and Gerrald, and the other Scotch Patriots?[292] Yet notwithstanding the severities with which the law is already armed against the seditious, notwithstanding the appalling examples before our eyes of pillory, four years imprisonment, and fourteen years transportation to Botany Bay, punishment is to be invested in more sanguinary robes, and a new law is to be enacted, the disgrace of those who bring it forward in Parliament, and the ruin of this country if the people suffer it to be carried into force.

People! Are you aware of the privileges which will be torn away from you by this new law? Are you aware that it will degrade you to a level with the most abject slaves under the vilest tyrannic government? Are you aware that it will tear to pieces your Magna Charta, the great charter of your liberties of which your forefathers were so patriotically jealous, that they in the reign of one prince had it recognized at twenty different periods?[293] By this law that illustrious charter will be sacrificed – perhaps for ever! You dare not speak, you dare not communicate, either by conversation or the press, your sentiments. You dare not assemble together to complain against abuses, or to petition for redress! You must bear in silence every insult, every contumely, and every oppression; for your governors by this law will arrogate to themselves the power of arbitrarily tyrannizing over you, to the extent of their ambition, and all consolation they leave to you will be, the privilege of receiving your patience in enduring, and your charity in forgiving, the calamities and wrongs their inhumanity may inflict on you.

People! This is not to be borne! We must not so be defrauded of our rights, of our inalienable rights! You, I am convinced, would never yourselves make this surrender! Suffer not then your unworthy representatives to make this surrender for you! From their virtue you have nothing to expect. From their complaisance to Mr Pitt and Lord Grenville, you have every thing to dread. It is to your own firmness, and patriotism that you have to look for justice, and support, do not desert yourselves. Be no longer deluded.

The liberty of petitioning for relief from oppression is the keystone on which this constitution rests. The constitution was never intended to support alone the prerogatives of the Crown, it was established for your happiness, and to confirm that happiness, the king was placed on the English Throne. Deny us the privilege of remonstrating against the wickedness of unprincipled ministers (and the ministers of every prince are too frequently unprincipled), and instantly the chief magistracy assumes the most horrid complexion, and becomes the engine of the most grading despotism. The subjects are trampled under its blood-stained feet with unfeeling barbarity, and its decrees written in blood, are enacted. Not to punish guilt, and to protect innocence, but to satiate a thirsty, and cruel appetite of administring torture, and death, instead of the blessings of benevolence, philanthropy, mercy and humanity!

Shall we then, Britons, endure to be so vilely treated? Shall we brook such indignities to our national character? Shall we, O Hampden and Russell, so disgrace your names, and render ourselves so undeserving of your spirited and pure exertions?[294] No, let us tell ministers that they are the enemies to the constitution, while they call us its enemies. It is they, O people, who are overturning the constitution, at the very moment that they are laying the charges at our doors. Who have done that constitution the more fatal injury, they or you? They who have attacked it in every part – they who have so encroached upon our rights, that scarcely one right remains to us unviolated – they who have introduced into this country *foreign troops* without the consent of parliament – they who have built barracks in every county in the kingdom – they who have made us an armed nation, and attempted to over-awe opinions by the sword, the musket, and the bayonet – they who are now on the eve of passing into a law this most detested bill, which in more honest, and braver days would have sounded through this nation the deadly trumpet of insurrection and rebellion – or you, illustrious and undaunted *few*, who amid persecution and peril, have held an unshaken course, and have panted in your career of patriotism, and of glory for that reform, which is to restore the constitution to its primitive purity, which is to stop the overwhelming stream of corruption, and which is to make your fellow-subjects honest, industrious, contented, happy, and flourishing.

You must all remember that attacks have been recently made, and with the consent of many of you, on your liberties, under the imposing pretext that it was necessary a part of your freedom should be given up for the preservation of the remainder. You were *then* told that a conspiracy did exist against the existing government of this country, and the protecting Habeas Corpus Act was smuggled away from you.[295] That falsehood the voice of three honest juries manifested, and developed – you are *now* told, that a conspiracy exists against the life of the sovereign, and to avert the intended, and meditated danger, your lips are to be closed, and the press to be put under a ministerial inquisition. Thus will ministers be permitted to pursue their profligate course without molestation to goad you with persecutions – to overwhelm you with taxes and burthens – to spill your blood, and squander away your honest and hard-acquired earnings in subsidizing foreign despots, and carrying on a state of unjust and unprofitable warfare, while you will be insulted without being told, that this is improving your situation, promoting your prosperity, and preserving the blessings conferred on you by your celebrated constitution! This will be called the preservation of the constitution itself!

People! the natural rights of man (and such are the liberty of speech and exercise of reason) can never be attacked but by tyrants. They are the gifts of God. They were given to mankind to consent together the bonds of society, by intercourse of sentiments, and communication of opinions. They were given him too for his protection. Rob him of them, and in dignity you degrade him with the beast. You enslave him. You revive in him the exploded doctrine of divine right, and passive obedience, and you render him the easy slave of tyrants. History tells us but for the free exercise of these blessings, the rights of man would never have been ascertained and claimed, despotism would never have been understood, 'for which Sidney bled in the field, and Russell on the scaffold'.[296] As liberty is the offspring of them, so when they are snatched away from us, liberty must follow in their train. There never was, there never can be a nation, which enjoys the unviolated exercise of its rights, on which silence is imposed, and to which discussion is denied. Ignorance is sister of slavery, and whenever a tyrant wishes to abandon himself to the lust of dominion, his first step is to reduce and degrade his subjects to a state of ignorance; and he can accomplish this alone by cutting off that social intercourse, and unrestrained exchange of opinions, from which all knowledge, all information is derived, and from whence flows the consciousness of the dignity, and rank of human nature.

To conclude – I love order, and I am a friend to peace. I am an enemy to every violent effort, and I never wish to see a change even of abuses, but by a system of mild and unoffending innovation – I disclaim the appellation of an incendiary, tho' I am attached to the happiness and rights of human-kind – I would not prevent opinions to my fellow creatures on the point of a bayonet tho' I wish them to shake off that fatal delusion, by which men themselves have been so long reduced from their senses, and their interest. This detested bill has not hitherto passed —— —— —— [illegible] therefore the power remains to me (and it will remain to me but for a short while longer, unless your timely exertions, O people of England, shall preserve it)! I will conjure you not to desert yourselves, but to display the honest indig-nation of Englishmen at the most audacious, the most profligate, the most diabolical assault that was ever made on your existence as a free commu-nity, and will reduce you, unless firmly resisted, to servitude and despair. The inhabitants of this country have been often compelled by tyranny to speak in the language of remonstrance to the throne, and when they have spoken in the manly tone of insulted freemen, their voice has been heard, and their demands have been granted. The nation which deserts itself, will be deserted by its governors. We must therefore be true to ourselves; and since we are driven to imitate the example of our forefathers, let us imitate it with an intrepidity worthy of their children.

Let us all therefore with one voice protest against this bill. Let us address the prince who sits on the English Throne, to dismiss from his council ministers who were infernal to propose for the disgrace of his reign so wicked a law! Let us assure the prince that this law can be imposed upon us on the terms only of all his subjects impatiently praying for his death; for by his death alone the terrors of this bill will terminate, and our liber-ties will be restored to us! Let us represent to him that the foundation of the constitution, is the liberty of speech, the liberty of the press, and the privilege of complaining against corruption and oppression! Let us tell him, that all these blessings by this one law are torn away from us! Let us remind him that he himself has sworn to preserve the English constitution unviolated.

Let us thus, my countrymen! thus firmly, but with due respect, address the chief magistrate of Great Britain, and let us console ourselves with this reflection, that if our petitions are unheard, or rejected, that we are Englishmen at heart, and that the power remains with ourselves to be free.

COMMON SENSE

12th November 1795

The conclusion to this inflammatory pamphlet clearly intimates that the king's life would be endangered if no heed were paid to Paine's advice. His words can be seen not only as a threat of revolution throughout the land, but also as a threat beyond the Crown to the man himself.

10 MAY 1798

This piece reveals Thomas Paine's abhorrence of the state of affairs in Britain at the time and of its colonization of far-off lands in the past. Nevertheless, it discloses a gentle, caring side to the man of whom history knows little. Serving a double purpose, it was a song of love, in response to a woman's request for his views on a French invasion of England, and a song of hope, written in the fullness of spring in the French countryside.

The two-page manuscript, which is held at the Pierpont Library, New York, is here transcribed in full. It would seem that Paine wrote out a copy for himself, noting the circumstances of its writing, probably as material for the collection of his own works, which he hoped to publish some time in the future,[297] or for an autobiography. The manuscript must have been Paine's own or given as a gift to another. The song has never been printed in full, although two different verses were published in works of the late twentieth century.[298]

Criel near Chantilly 21st Floreal 6th year[299]

Breakfasting one morning at Criel (it was the 21 Floreal) at the house of Madame Gibert, a most amiable friend and companion, the conversation turned on the Descent upon England, and upon my going with it, and she asked me to make her a song in English as a keep-sake. At dinner I gave her following:[300]

On the Descent upon England
Written at the desire of a Favourite

Blow soft ye breezes o'er the wave,
Soft as the thought that Love inspires,
And safely bear, to Angleterre,
The fleet that takes my heart's desires.
Ye gentle fates, if such there be,
Who watch o'er human hopes and fears;
O! land it safe, and let me see
The friends that share my anxious cares.

The world in tumult long has liv'd
A stranger to the voice of peace,
And longer still will it be griev'd,

Till Britain's crimes be made to cease.
Look round the globe from east to west,
Or cast a glance from pole to pole
'Tis Britain bars the world from rest,
'Tis Britain harrows up the soul.

See Afric's wretched offspring torn
From all the human heart holds dear,
See millions doomed in chains to mourn,
Unpitied even by a tear,
See Asia and her fertile plains
Where once the Brahmin dwelt serene,
Now ravaged by the thirst for gain,
Till Famine ends the dismal scene.

It is to bind the tyrants hands,
To give the tortured world repose,
That France sends forth her chosen bands
To meet her friends, or seek her foes.
'Tis then, and not till then, that we,
A better world may hope to view,
'Tis then that man will happy be,
And nations *love as I love you.*[301]

Thomas Paine

Over Paine's signature, which is now barely visible, at some time in the past a detractor has signed heavily in black ink 'Thomas Blockhead', demonstrating the loathing in which many held him on his return to the United States in 1802.[302] A librarian or custodian has marked the manuscript '? Copy – Not in Paine's autograph'. The handwriting, however, is certainly Paine's. The provenance of the manuscript is unknown.

29 MAY 1798

Elbridge Gerry, to whom the following letter is addressed, had been one of the signers of the American Declaration of Independence.[303] In 1797, President John Adams
had sent him,[304] together with John Marshall and Charles Cotesworth Pinckney, to
France in an endeavour to improve America's relations with France.[305] The mission
failed when three French agents, known only as X, Y, and Z, suggested a huge bribe
be paid to Charles-Maurice de Talleyrand, the French Foreign Minister, and a loan
be made to France. Marshall and Pinckney refused and returned to America, but
Gerry thought he might be able to manage the matter. He could not, and the incident
became known to history as the XYZ Affair. War was averted, but relations between
the two countries were strained until settled by the French Convention of 1800. This
letter to Gerry was written during that time of unrest.

Prairial 10 – 6 year[306]

Sir,

I sent you the enclosed paper this morning by Mr Barlow but as you were
not at home he returned it to me.[307] I send it you again but with the injunc-
tion that you return it tomorrow morning at farthest as I intend to send it
afterwards to Revellier le Peaux.[308] Whether it was prudent in John Adams to
make the information it contains public is a matter I leave to your own judgment; or whether it was prudent in the commissioners to hold conference
with unauthorized persons in which the character of the Directory is impli-
cated I also leave you to judge of. The persons who employed themselves in
this business are concealed under the cyphers W.-X-Y.X, but they ought to be
known in order that the suspicion may not fall on other persons.

Yours ... [illegible]
Thomas Paine[309]

It has not been possible to ascertain the nature of the contents of the 'enclosed
paper' or whether it survives, but it would appear that Paine knew something
that Gerry, one of the commissioners, did not. The letter was obviously written as a matter of urgency; the handwriting is not Paine's best. At the time,
he was conspiring with Napoleon on a plan to invade England, the so-called
Descent upon England, a cause to which he donated 100 livres.[310] In the event,
Talleyrand had deceived Gerry by leading him to believe that his staying in
France would prevent war between the two countries. Eventually, with his reputation tarnished, he was recalled to America by President Adams.

PUBLISHED 1801

The following pamphlet, entitled *Compact Maritime*, noted by editors and commentators on Thomas Paine as having been part of a seventh letter addressed 'To the Citizens of the United States', has not seen the light of day in English since it was first published in Washington by Samuel Harrison Smith in 1801. The piece was, prior to that, translated into French by Paine's friend Nicolas Bonneville and printed by Paine and his friends Fulwar Skipwith, the American consul, and Joel Barlow. They presented it as a gift to all foreign ministers of neutral nations then resident in Paris.[311]

Under the title *Maritime, addressé aux nations neutres par un neutre*, the work in its entirety was published by Bonneville in Paris in 1800. All that has ever been included in the English language Paine canon is the third 'head' of this 24-page booklet; that section has, where included in collections, been worded differently from the following transcription of Smith's 1801 publication.

In a letter to Thomas Jefferson of 1 October 1800,[312] Paine enclosed three parts of *Compact Maritime*, with no mention of a fourth. The first, he wrote, was written as a result of a question put to him by Napoleon. He told of the third piece being the sequel of the second and 'digested in form'. He suggested that 'pieces 2, 3, may go to the press', as they would make a small pamphlet to which he would like his name given as the author. The manuscripts of those two pieces were on their way to England where they were to be published; the first enclosure was merely for the amusement of Jefferson and his friends.[313]

The second piece, Paine told Jefferson, was 'written when the English made their insolent and impolitic expedition to Denmark, and is also an auxiliary to the politic of No. 1'.[314] It had been translated and published in French by Nicolas Bonneville as a separate pamphlet,[315] which might explain its being known as a piece in itself without the other parts, despite the fact that Jefferson made sure that the articles appeared in the papers and as a pamphlet.[316]

In a note to Jefferson of 6 October, Paine enclosed an 'introduction to two other pieces already sent'.[317] The final piece, *Observations on some Passages in the Discourse of the Judge of the English Admiralty*, followed in a letter of 16 October.[318] As all these letters were sent by a frigate delayed in its departure from Le Havre by 'the wind at one time and the tides at another',[319] Jefferson obviously received all pieces at the same time and sent them as a whole to the papers and the Washington publisher.

Compact Maritime,
Under the Following Heads:

I. Dissertation on the Law of Nations
II. On the Jacobinism of the English at Sea
III. Compact Maritime for the Protection of Neutral
Commerce, and Securing the Liberty of the Seas
IV. Observations on Some Passages in the Discourse
of the Judge of the English Admiralty

Dissertation on the Law of Nations.
Respecting the Rights of Neutral Commerce and the Liberty
of the Seas

* * * * * * *

In treating of the law of nations, respecting the rights of neutral commerce
and the liberty of the seas, I mean not to follow any thing which Grotius,
Puffendorf, Vattel, or others, have written upon the subject. I shall begin
with first principles, and shew, in the first place, that no such law exists as
a law of nations, and that it is necessary to form one.[320]

Nations in their original state are, with respect to each other, like individuals in a state of nature. From their original state they proceed to form treaties, and the treaty or treaties so formed between any two of them become a
law to the parties forming them, and no more. They have no operation over
other nations, neither do they make any part of a general law of nations,
unless all treaties were formed on one and the same common principle:
And it has been by confounding the law of treaties with the idea of a law of
nations that has given rise to the error of a law of nations existing.

Grotius, Puffendorf, Vattel, and some others have written much, and in
many things, wisely upon the subject; but their writings are not *laws*, but *opinions* upon what ought to be laws, or rather the principles upon which laws
ought to be established. Those men were not authorized by the several nations
of Europe, any more than I am, to draw up a code of laws for the whole. They
could do no more than state cases and give opinions. Consequently no such
thing as a recognized law of nations exists in their writings.

It is equally evident that a general law of nations cannot be drawn, or
extracted from, or founded upon the law of treaties; because treaties, besides
being partial things, are in many instances contradictory to each other. For

example, the treaty of commerce concluded between France and America in the year 1778, says that *neutral ships make neutral property*; and the treaty of commerce concluded between America and England, 1794, says directly the contrary. The same contradictions, and others similar thereto, are to be found among the treaties of other nations; and consequently no general law of nations can be drawn from treaties.

The only thing that has any pretension of right to be called and considered as a law of nations is the convention proposed and patronized by Russia during the American war, and known by the name of the *Armed Neutrality*. That convention was signed and ratified by a large majority of the maritime commercial nations of Europe. The principle it took and established was that, *neutral ships make neutral property*.

It is customary with some politicians to call this the *modern* law of nations, as if there existed an ancient law on a contrary principle authoritatively recognized as this has been; whereas there exists no such thing, nor ever did. Consequently there is either no law of nations in existence, or if there be, it is, that neutral ships make neutral property; from whence it follows, that all treaties made contrary to this principle, and adjudged by that law, are a violation of the general law of nations.

This pretended right is altogether a thing set up by assumption. It is not founded upon any thing that can be called, or considered, a law of nations; nor yet upon the law of treaties. It is a considerable time since I perused the collection of treaties published by Jenkinson, president of the board of trade and plantations in England;[321] but I believe my memory serves me sufficiently to say positively, that none of them recognizes the right of a belligerent power to make any such visit; and consequently the right to make it does not exist.

It is customary in forming treaties, especially treaties of commerce, to introduce an article under the head of *articles contraband of war*, because the same are not contraband in peace. The list of articles called contraband differs in almost all the treaties I have seen, some making them more and others less numerous.

If we search the etymology of the word contraband, it will assist us in getting precise ideas upon the subject. The word *contraband* being compounded of two words, *contra*, against, and *ban*, law, edict, or proclamation, carries, from the etymology, its own signification. Articles, therefore, become contraband, not from any thing in themselves, but because they are prohibited by law from being exported.

The legal sense therefore of any such article in a treaty is, that the contracting parties mutually engage themselves to prohibit by law, edict, or proclamation, the article in the treaty respecting articles contraband of war is completely fulfilled, and the belligerent nation has no right to visit or molest any of its vessels. It is to take the faith of the government it contracted with, as full to all the purposes stipulated for. Treaties between governments can act only between governments, and not reciprocally by one government upon the individuals of the other government. Among the numerous wars that have desolated the world there are very few that had any justifiable pretence, and there is no reason that because two or more nations run themselves into war, that the individuals of the peaceable world are to be molested in their traffic on the ocean. If the contracting party that shall be neutral finds that any of its citizens or subjects have transgressed the prohibition, it should proceed to punish them; or if the minister of the belligerent power residing at the neutral nation have knowledge of any such transgression, he should complain that the offender may be proceeded against according to law. But nothing is more unnatural and unjust in theory and practice, than that the government of a neutral nation should delegate to the belligerent nation, the right of controul and judgment over its own citizens or subjects traversing peaceably the ocean.

The pretended right therefore of the British government to visit neutral vessels is in every view of the case unfounded and piratical.

There remains now only to concert measures for preventing belligerent nations from usurping this pretended right. This with respect to such nations as those of Barbary would be difficult, because they are not commercial; but with respect to a nation like England it becomes practicable and easy, because she lives by commerce; and the commerce with neutral nations, on which she depends, contains the means of its own protection, in spite of fleets and navies. This makes the subject of the following pieces.

* * * * * * *

N.B. Since the foregoing piece was written, the author has seen the excellent official note of the Danish minister Bernstorff to the British minister Merry, relative to the seizing and detaining the Danish frigate by the English in the Straits of Gibraltar, whilst serving as convoy to some Danish merchant vessels.

When men of different nations, unknown to each other, and unknowing what the opinions of each other are, unite in one and the same opinion, or so nearly so, that a little explanation makes them the same, it is correspondent evidence the opinion is well founded.

The principles in the Danish official note and in the foregoing piece are alike, with this difference only, that the official note seems to admit that the armed ships of a belligerent nation can visit neutral vessels *not convoyed*, for the purpose of being assured they are *neutral*, and of the regularity of their papers; after which the note comes to the same point with the foregoing piece, to wit, that the ship of the belligerent nation is to take the faith of the government of the neutral nation in all other matters. The words in the official note are:

'La visite exercée par les corsaires ou vaisseaux de guerre des puissances belligerantes a l'gard des batimens neutres allant sans convoi, est sondée fur le droit d'en reconnoître le pavillon et d'en examiner les papiers. Il ne s'agit que de constater leur neutralité et la regularité de leurs expeditions. Les papiers de ces batimens étant trouvés en règle, aucune visite ulterieure ne peut regalement avoir lieu; et c'est par consequent l'autorité du gouvernement, au nom duquel ces documens ont été dressés et delivrés, qui procure à la puissance belligérante la sûreté requise.'

['The right to identify the flag and to examine the documents was the basis for the visit by the fighting powers' privateers or warships to the neutral ships travelling without convoy. It was simply a way of ascertaining their neutrality and how often they carried out their expeditions. The ships' documents were found to be in order, meaning that no further visits could legally take place. It was therefore the government that drew up and issued the documents that provided the fighting powers with the required security'.]

With respect to neutral vessels *convoyed* by a ship of that neutral government, the note is decisive that no visit of any kind, or under any pretence, can be made. The words are:

'Mais le gouvernement neutre, en sesant convoyer par des vaisseaux de guerre les navires de ses sujets commercans, offre par la même aux puissances belligerantes une garantie plus authentique, plus positive encore que ne l'est celle qui est sournie par les documens dont ces navires se trouvent munis; et il ne fauroit, sans se deshonorer, admettre a cet egard des doutes on des soupçons, qui seroient aussi injurieux pour lui qu'injustes de la part de ceux qui les conserveroient ou les manifesteroient.'

['However, the neutral government arranged for their merchants' vessels to be escorted by the warships, thereby giving the fighting powers a stronger guarantee, better than that of the documents possessed by these vessels. No doubt or suspicion should be held against this government, as such doubts would be insulting to the government and unjust on the part of those harbouring or presenting them'.][322]

From these two cases, that of neutral vessels *with* convoy, and *without* convoy, result a third case that unites the two in one point, which is, that the *convoy*, strictly and properly speaking, *is the flag* under which the neutral merchant vessel sails; for the government ship, under the protection of which, against pirates, the neutral merchant vessel sails, is, at the same time a *visible attestation at first sight* to the ship of the belligerent nation, that the flag of the merchant vessel is neutral. Consequently the belligerent ship has no business with the neutral ship but to be assured of its flag which being assured of, it has no business with its papers or its cargo. The faith of the government, under the flag of which the neutral merchant vessel sails, is to be taken for all other matters. It is the flag, and not its cannon, that is to be respected.

On the Jacobinism of the English at Sea, and the means of preventing it: Addressed to the Neutral Nations, by a Neutral

* * * * * * *

The tyrannical and insolent injustice of the English on the seas in all parts of the world, and against all nations, is risen to a height that provokes universal abhorrence. But the evil is capable of redress, and I go to point out the means.

France is the only nation capable of balancing the power of the English at sea. It is because the French navy is, in a great measure, destroyed, and the balance of naval power destroyed with it, that England dares to act this insolent injustice. All the commercial nations suffer by the loss of the French navy.

England amuses the world with the danger of, what she calls, Jacobinical principles, and that at a time when no such principles exist in France. But the Jacobinical principles of England on the ocean are every day increasing; the rights of commerce are every day invaded, insulted, and destroyed.

When the Emperor Paul arrived at the government of Russia, a great and glorious object lay before him.[323] That object was the protection of neutral commerce and the universal liberty of the seas. But contrary to his character, which disposes itself to great enterprise, he exchanged this great object for a little one. He entered into a coalition with England, whose policy was to make use of him for her own advantage, and to employ him as an instrument against himself. His frankness and want of suspicion, prepared the trap into which he fell. Had that coalition succeeded, and France been conquered, the importance of Russia, as a maritime power, would have been absorbed in it. Her navy would have been of no use to her, and Paul might as well have given it at once to the English government. That government would have taken care that the French navy should never revive, and in that case, the inferior navies of the North would have been like prisoners guarded at view.

All the commercial nations of Europe, and even of the world, are now interested in supporting France against the Jacobinism of the English on the ocean. It is not only their interest, but their honor that calls on them to do this. France wants no aid for herself; she is able to defeat all the coalitions that can be brought against her, and as often as they chuse to repeat it. But there lies in the background of this scene of combat, the great object I am speaking of, *the rights of commerce and the liberty of the seas.* These are so involved with the fate of France, that they must stand or fall with it.

Were the government of France to conclude a treaty of peace with England, without stipulating in that treaty some principle with respect to the rights of commerce in future and the liberty of the seas, the nations who now suffer in their commerce by the infractions of the English, would dispose themselves to murmur. Let then those nations contribute their aid, while the opportunity continues, to obtain the object so necessary to their interest.

England is to be considered in a two-fold point of view: First, as a great commercial nation: Secondly, as a great maritime power. The second depends upon the first, and the first depends upon the will or consent of other nations to permit her to trade with them. This consent is in their power to grant or to withhold; and consequently England is, in fact, a nation dependant upon other nations. The greatness of France is internal and inherent; that of England depends upon external circumstances not in her power to command.

Were the neutral nations of Europe, together with the United States of America, to enter into an association to suspend all commerce with any belligerent power that molested any ship belonging to that association, England must either lose her commerce, or consent to the freedom of the seas.

During the American war an armed neutrality was formed in the North, under the patronage of Russia. It happened that the navies of France and Spain were then in full activity, and the armed neutrality derived consequence from that state of things. But the balance of naval power being now destroyed between France and England, an armed neutrality is not a thing that will make much impression upon England. It is only when the navies of France and Spain are capable of balancing the English navy, and detaining it in the Channel, or elsewhere to the Southward, that an armed neutrality in the North can command respect. Prussia, from her situation, can command respect to her own flag, and though she is not a maritime power, can throw great weight into an armed neutrality. George knows that Prussia can seize upon Hanover.

But in the present state of things, and even in any state, it is an unarmed neutrality, that is, a commercial association, as before spoken of, that will impress England the most. It is through her commerce that she is vulnerable. It is to her the heel of Achilles.

The commerce of the Northern nations is important to England; she can scarcely subsist without it; but they can subsist without her. Consequently those nations have it in their power to make their own *law of nations*, and not permit England to dictate to them what the law shall be. The protection that commerce can give to itself by means of a commercial association (especially if Hamburg be included in it, which she cannot refuse) is at least of equal weight with an armed neutrality; but the two together would be capable of giving the law, or, at least, of controuling the tyranny of England, till the French navy be capable of restoring the balance of naval power. It is then that a general law of nations might be formed; a work that will immortalize the French republic in the commercial world.

Hitherto the nations of Europe, and especially those of the North, have been amused with the cry of religion, Jacobinism, and every other clamour which hypocrisy and concealed design could invent. But it is necessary that those nations view this war, so far as respects England, in its true light, that is, as a *war of monopoly*.

France, great within herself, is not naturally possessed of the spirit of monopoly. She has a vast field for internal improvement open before her, that will demand all her care and attention for many years to come. Monopoly can make no part of her policy; her interest lies in extending the rights of commerce, not in monopolizing it. She has it now greatly in her power to benefit the world of commerce jointly with herself, and I go to point out the means.

The English government by imperiously refusing its consent to the treaty of Al-Arisch, has compelled the French army to remain in Egypt.[324] It is not difficult to see that the policy of the English government was to detain the French army, that she might assist in the unconditional capture of it, and make that a pretence for establishing herself in its place, at the head of the

Red Sea. She would then have occupied both passages to India, to the exclusion of the rest of the world. It is consistent with her spirit of monopoly.

But the case has happened otherwise, and it opens a great field to the commercial world. As England has seized the Cape of Good Hope, it will be policy to keep, with the consent of Egypt, possession of the head of the Red Sea, and to permit the Northern nations to traffic to the Eastern world through that channel. Holland, in particular, will be indemnified by this means for the loss of the Cape.

This is one of the advantages the commercial world will derive from the French Revolution and through the medium of its power. Whereas from England they can look for nothing but monopoly, oppression and insult. Egypt would be benefitted by this establishment. It is England only that is interested in opposing it; and whatever is her interest, is in opposition to the rest of the world.

It is time that nations awake from their lethargy and attend to their interest. As to coalitions, there is something in them mean and despicable; they begin by intrigue and end in disgrace. The little and paltry states of Germany, that can be bought and sold like cattle in a fair, as they were in the American war, may plead their meanness as their excuse. But Russia ought to have felt herself above such traffic – the great Peter would have scorned it; he would have been struck with admiration at the efforts that France has made, and instead of combining against her, would have stood and wondered. Why has not Paul, who attempts his character, done the same?[325]

The majestic spectacle of a nation standing against all the coalitions of Europe, has a claim to the respect, at least to the admiration of the world. To borrow a metaphor from a Jewish fable, we see France like the burning bush, not only unconsumed, but erecting her head and smiling above the flames. She throws coalitions to atoms with the strength of thunder – combat and victory are to her synonymous.

Compact Maritime of an Association of Nations for the Protection of the Rights and Commerce of Nations that shall be Neutral in Time of War Addressed to the Neutral Nations by a Neutral

* * * * * * *

Whereas, the inconvenience and injuries to which the commerce and rights of neutral nations are exposed, in time of maritime war, render it absolutely necessary that a *Law of Nations* be formed to prevent a continuation or repetition of those injuries in all times to come, and to secure to neutral nations, during the time of such war, the exercise of their just rights, We, the undersigned powers enter into the following association and compact, establishing thereby a law of nations with respect to the sea.

ARTICLE I
Definition of the rights of neutral nations

That the common rights of nations, such as are exercised by them in time of peace, in their intercourse with each other, are, and ought to be, the rights of neutral nations *at all times*: because they are not forfeited by them, and cannot, of right, be lost to them in consequence of war breaking out between any two or more nations. Such war being altogether the act of the nations *making it*, and not of the neutral nations, cannot in itself, or in its consequences, affect the rights of the nations neutral and continuing in a state of peace.

II

That the ships or vessels of nations that may be neutral during such war have a right to pass unmolested on the seas as in time of peace (it being peace with them) and to proceed to, and enter the port or ports of any of the belligerent powers, with the consent of that power, uninterrupted, unvisited, and unsearched by the party or parties with which that nation is at war.

III

For the maintenance of the aforesaid rights, We, the undersigned powers, declare, and for the performance thereof, bind ourselves in honor to each other, that if any belligerent power shall seize, or molest, or search, any ship or vessel belonging to the citizens or subjects of any of the powers composing this association, shall cease to import, and will not permit to be imported, in any ship or vessel whatever, any goods, wares or merchandise, of what kind soever, from the nation so offending against the law of nations hereby established.

IV

That all the ports appertaining to the powers composing this association, shall be shut against the flag of the offending nation.

V

That no remittances in money, goods, or bills of exchange, shall be made by any of the citizens or subjects of any of the powers composing this association, to the citizens or subjects of the offending nation for the term of one year, or until reparation be made; the reparation to be ____ times the amount of the damage received.

VI

When any ship or vessel belonging to any of the citizens or subjects of any of the powers composing this association, shall be seized by any ship or vessel of any belligerent power, or be forcibly prevented entering the port of her destination, or be seized or molested in coming therefrom, or forcibly prevented entering the port of her destination, or be seized or molested in coming therefrom, or forcibly prevented proceeding to the place to which she is next bound, or be searched, or visited, by any person coming on board such ship, the executive government of the nation to which the vessel so seized or molested belongs, shall, immediately on ascertaining the fact, make proclamation of the same, and send a copy thereof to the executive of each of the powers composing this association, who shall publish the same through his dominion, and proclaim, that at the expiration of ____ days after the date thereof, the execution of the penal articles against the offending nation shall commence.

VII

If reparation be not made within the space of one year, the proclamations shall be renewed for one year more, and so on.

VIII

The association establishes a flag for itself, to be carried by the ships and vessels of every nation composing this association, in addition to its proper national flag. The flag to be a pennant at the head of the main-mast, composed of the same colours as compose the rain-bow, and arranged in the same order as they appear in that phenomenon.

IX

And whereas it may happen that some one or more of the nations composing this association may be, at the time of forming it, or in some future time, in a state of war, the ships and vessels of such nation shall omit carrying the flag of the association at the mast head, but it shall be bound round the main mast, to denote they are members of the association, and respecters of its laws.

See Art. X. – Contraband

* * * * * * *

We, the undersigned powers, declare these articles to be a law of nations *at all times*, or until a congress of nations shall meet to form some law more effectual.

And we do recommend, that immediately on the breaking out of war between any two or more nations, whether members of this association or not, to meet in congress in some central place, to take cognizance of any violations of the rights of neutral nations by the belligerent powers.

* * * * * * *

It may be judged proper, for the order of business, that the association of nations have a president for a term of years, and to pass by rotation through all the parties composing the association. In that case, and for the sake of regularity, the first president to be the executive of the most northerly nation composing the association, and his deputy, or minister, at the congress, to be president of the congress – and the next most northerly, to be vice-president, who shall succeed at the expiration of the term, and so on – the line determining the geographical situation, to be the latitude of the capital of each nation. If this method be adopted, it will be proper that the first president be nominally constituted, in order to give rotation to the rest. In that case the following article might be added to the foregoing. The constitution of the association nominates the Emperor Paul, first president of the association of nations for the protection of neutral commerce and securing the liberty of the seas.

* * * * * * *

X
Articles Contraband.

And whereas it is contrary to the moral as well as the political principles of neutrality, that any neutral nation should supply the belligerent nations, or either of them, with the means of warring against each other, we, the powers composing this association, declare, that we will, each for himself, prohibit, by law and proclamation within our several dominions, all and every of the citizens or subjects thereof, from supplying or carrying to the belligerent powers, or either of them, any kind of military stores or articles, including thereby gun-powder and fire arms of all sorts, and also all sorts of steel and iron weapons used in war, and excluding therefrom all kinds of steel and iron tools and instruments used in civil or domestic life, and also all articles that cannot be used in the immediate state they are in for the purpose of war.

Having thus declared the moral and political motives of this article, we declare also the civil intention thereof, to wit – that as the belligerent nations have no right to visit or search any ship or vessel belonging to a neutral nation, and under the protection of the laws and government thereof; and as all such visit or search is an insult to the nation to which such ship or vessel belongs, and to the government of the same, we will take the right of prohibition upon ourselves, to whom it properly belongs, and by whom only it can be legally exercised, and not permit foreign nations, in a state of war, to usurp the right of legislating for any of the citizens or subjects of the powers composing this association. It is, therefore, in order to take away all pretence of search or visit, which by being offensive, might become a new cause of war, or of quarrel or dispute, that we provide laws, published by proclamation, each in his own dominion, to prohibit the supplying or carrying to the belligerent powers, or either of them, the military stores or articles before-mentioned, annexing thereto a penalty, to be levied or inflicted upon any person or persons transgressing the same. And we do invite all persons, as well of the belligerent nations as of our own, or of others, to give information of any knowledge they have of any transgression against the said law, that the offenders may be prosecuted.

By this conduct we restore the word *contraband* (*contra* and *ban*) to its true and original signification, which means against law, edict or proclamation, and none but the government of a nation can have, or can exercise, the right of making laws, edicts, or proclamations, for regulating the conduct of the citizens of subjects thereof.

* * * * * * *

Observations *on some passages in the Discourse of Sir* William Scott, *Judge of the Admiralty in England, in the affair of the Swedish vessel the* Maria *captured by the English*

The Judge, after stating the fact of the capture, proceeds as follows: 'Having now exhibited the fact, I ought to establish the right. I go, in consequence, to research what is the rule, or in other terms, what the neutrals are subjected to by *the law of nations*. To this effect I will lay down some principles that I hold to be incontestable'.[326]

My remark upon this passage will be concise – It is a logical maxim, that *a false position must end in an absurd conclusion*; and this maxim applies itself to this introductory passage of Scott; for, in the first place, there is no such thing as a *law of nations*, and consequently his position is false; and, secondly, nothing can be more absurd than to draw conclusions from *non existence*, and then call them incontestable principles.

He then proceeds: 'The right', says he, 'to visit merchant vessels in open sea, whatever may be the vessels, their cargoes, or their destination, is a right *devolved incontestably*, to the cruisers commissioned by a belligerent nation – I say, whatever may be the vessels, their cargoes, or their destination, because, before they are visited, it cannot be known what vessels they are, nor what their cargoes, nor to what ports they are bound'.

I might, as a general answer to this, say – Sir, *you have no right to know: The peaceable world ought not to be disturbed in consequence of your quarrels.*

But though this answer might very justly be given to such a dogmatical assertion, I will shew the fallaciousness of it by another process, which is, that reasoning by deduction or implication, though it is admitted in conversation, and among controversial writers (because they have no rule of law for their guide) cannot be admitted as law in a court of law, nor as legal testimony upon oath, and a judge ought always to remember he is upon oath.

Morality and neutrality have dictated the principle, that neutral nations ought not to supply belligerent nations with military stores; but in doing this, the neutral nations did not surrender their several flags to be suspected nor insulted, nor their vessels to be visited, overhauled, and controuled by any belligerent power. The faith of the government of the neutral nation (as I have several times repeated) is to be taken upon the whole of the case, and the *not taking it* is a national insult to the neutral nation, and to all neutral nations, and an act of hostility. It is by deduction and implication that this judge argues, and he calls this deduction and this implication, which he makes himself, the law of nations.

I will put a ridiculous case to this judge, that will shew, upon a small scale, the absurdity of his reasoning upon a larger scale. If two judges had quarrelled, and were to fight a duel about which of them should have most powder in his wig (for you know, Sir, that great wigs are great things with English judges) and if Scott, as a third person, neutral, impartial, and independent (as you know, Sir, a judge ought always to be, though they are not always so) had engaged that he would not supply either of the quarrelling judges with wig-powder, gun-powder, pistol or ball, does this engagement on his part, give a right to the individuals that compose the families of the quarrelling judges, or either of them, to stop and search the pockets of any and all of the individuals of Scott's family, to know if they have any wig-powder, gun-powder, pistol or ball, and to open and read the papers and letters they are entrusted with? Yet the right (pardoning the abuse of the word) to do this, follows by deduction and implication in the same manner, and raises itself on the same ground as what he calls his *incontestable principles*.[327]

Every thing in this judge's discourse is on a false principle. If there were such a thing as a general law of nations, which there ought to be, and which I hope there will be, that law, to be on a right principle, must be the reverse of what this judge says. It must be a law to restrain and controul the belligerent maritime powers, and protect the neutrals against their depredations. Laws are made for those who break the peace, not against those who keep it. But according to this belligerent judge, his law of nations is to subjugate the peaceable neutrals to the controul of the belligerent powers, and the belligerent powers to act uncontrouled by any law of nations. *Rights*, according to his doctrine, are all on the side of those who quarrel, and subjection and restraint are for those who are peaceable. When a nation runs itself into war, it breaks the general peace of the world, and it is absurd and vicious to suppose that such a nation shall acquire an addition of rights in consequence of an act by which it merits punishment.

THE END

It is interesting to note that these combined articles were written at a time when Paine wished to return to the United States, but was prevented from so doing for fear of capture by the British, whose ships patrolled about the ports of France; his return to England would have led to his certain execution. He was obviously fearful of the perceived law of nations as defined by Sir William Scott; freedom of the seas would have ensured his safe crossing of the Atlantic.

PUBLISHED 11 APRIL 1801

Prompted by a letter in an earlier issue, Paine asked that an extract of a critical commentary on the Declaration of Independence be inserted in *The Port Folio*, a Philadelphia paper edited by Oliver Oldschool.[328] Written from France, where Paine was still resident until the end of 1802, it was published in Philadelphia on 11 April 1801. Signed 'Common Sense', Paine expressed his unwavering concern with rights, but his motive for writing the piece and publishing it with the extract from an English paper, if any beyond literary criticism, is difficult to conceive.

Over all his years of political penmanship, Paine revealed his constant awareness of affairs on both sides of the Atlantic; he frequently remarked in his private correspondence on his need for, and receipt of, American and British newspapers. His friends, one of whom must have inserted the letter here presented, accommodated him. As with an earlier piece, Paine's footnote, marked with an asterisk, is placed at the end of his contribution. Both the introductory letter and extract follow.

For the Portfolio

Mr Oldschool,

I have often thought, that the reading of the instrument, called the *Declaration of Independence,** on every anniversary of the American republic, an improper act; as it tends to prolong, in the minds of an ignorant, and brutal mob, animosity and hatred, against a nation, with which we are united, by a similarity of language, laws, religion, customs, habits: and with which, we reciprocate a large and lucrative commerce. I was, therefore, pleased, to see, in *The Port Folio*, some sprightly strictures, on the introductory paragraph, of this American manifesto, written by the pen of an acute philologist. The criticism, is just and seasonable; and ought to put the Americans, of the present day, on thinking, how far it may dishonour their character, or injure their interest, to prolong the credit of a declaration, which contains so much nonsense and untruth.

Our independence requires not such a rotten prop. From the peace, of '83, to this hour, Great-Britain has never manifested a wish unfriendly to our independence and self-government. It is not her interest, and it would be absurd policy so to do. The danger, if any exist, is from another quarter: from our own squabbles, and the treacherous friendship of France;[329] and against these, the annual declaration of war against England, can afford no security whatever. Indeed, it may have a contrary effect; it may render us less attentive to the quarter, from which danger really threatens: and this, peradventure, is the design of some men, in perpetuating this hostile manifesto. On looking over some old papers, I met with another criticism, on the same subject, to which, as you sometimes admit of extracts, I request you will give a place in your paper.

'The Declaration is, without doubt, of the most extraordinary nature, both with respect to sentiment and language; and, considering that the motive of it, is to assign some justifiable reasons, of the colonists separating themselves from Great-Britain, unless it had been fraught with more truth and sense, might well have been spared, as it reflects no honour upon either their erudition or honesty.

'We hold (they say) these truths to be self-evident: that all men are created equal. In what are they created equal? Is it in size, strength, understanding, figure, moral or civil accomplishments, or situation in life? Every ploughman knows, that they are not created equal in any of these. All men, it is true, are equally created; but what is this to the purpose? It is certainly no reason, why the Americans should declare themselves independent, because the people of Great-Britain are their fellow-creatures, *i.e.* are created, as well as themselves. It may be a reason, why both should continue united; but none, why they should separate. They therefore, have introduced their self-evident truths, either through ignorance, or by design, with a self-evident falsehood: since I will defy any American, or any of his patriotic retainers, here in England, to point out to me, any two men, throughout the world, of whom it may with truth be said, that they are created equal.

'The next of their self-evident truths is, that all men are endowed, by their Creator, with certain unalienable rights (the meaning of which words, they appear not at all to understand) among which are life, liberty, and the pursuit of happiness. Let us put some of these words together. All men are endowed, by their Creator, with the unalienable right of life? How far they may be endowed with this unalienable right, I do not yet say; but sure I am, these gentry assume to themselves, an unalienable right of talking nonsense. Was it ever heard, since the introduction of blunders into the world, that life was a man's right? Life, or animation, is of the essence of human nature, and is that, without which, one is not a man; and therefore, to call life a right is to betray a total ignorance of the meaning of words. A living man, *i.e.* a man with life, hath a right to a great many things, but to say, that a man with life, hath a right to be a man with life, is so very novel, that I believe the texture of no other brain but the author's will admit the idea. Whatever it may be, I have tried to make an idea out of it; but own I am unable. Prior to my having any right at all, as man, it is certain, I must be a man: that is, I must have life; and therefore, if it be said that I have no right to life, then the word *I*, must signify something without life, and consequently, something without life must be supposed to have a property, which, without life, it is not possible it can have.

'Well, but they say, all men have not only a right to life, but an unalienable right. The word unalienable signifies that which cannot be alienated; and that which is not alienable, is what cannot be transferred so as to become the property of another; so that, their unalienable right, is a right which they cannot transfer to a broomstick, or a cabbage-stalk; and because they cannot transfer their own lives from themselves to a cabbage-stalk, therefore, they think it absolutely necessary that they should become independent: and out of a decent respect to the opinions of mankind, allege this is one of the reasons why they have separated themselves from the British Empire.

'The next assigned cause, and ground of their independence, is, that every man has an unalienable right to *liberty*; and here, the words, as it happens, are not nonsense, but then, they are not true: slaves there are in America (particularly in Virginia;) and where there are slaves, there liberty is alienated.

'If the Creator hath endowed man with an *unalienable* right to liberty, no reason in the world will justify the abridgment of that liberty; and a man hath a right, to do every thing that he thinks proper, without controul or restraint; and upon the same principle, there can be no such thing, as servants, subjects, or government, of any kind whatsoever. In a word, every law, that hath been made in the world, since the formation of Adam, gives the lie to this self-evident truth (as they are pleased to term it) because, every law, divine or human, that is, or hath been in the world, is an abridgment of man's liberty.

'Their next self-evident truth, and ground of independence, is, that they have an unalienable right to the pursuit of happiness. The *pursuit* of happiness an unalienable right! This surely is outdoing every thing that went before. Put it into English: the pursuit of happiness is a right with which the Creator hath endowed me, and which can neither be taken from me, nor can I transfer it to another. Did ever any mortal hear of taking a pursuit of happiness from a man? What they possibly can mean, by these words, I own, is beyond my comprehension. A man may take from me a horse, or a cow, or I may alienate either of them from myself, as I may, likewise, anything I possess; but how that can be taken from me, or alienated, which I have not, must be left for the solution of some unborn Oedipus'.

* Supposed to be written by Thomas Jefferson, esq. of Virginia.

COMMON SENSE

Signed 'An Englishman', the original of the article Paine quoted appeared in the *St James's Chronicle or the British Evening Post* of 7 September 1776. He neither sourced nor quoted it faithfully; it was heavily edited with much added punctuation and change of wording. For instance, where Paine has used the word 'independence' or its forms, the original uses forms of 'rebellion'. It was he who inserted the parenthetical remark 'particularly in Virginia'. The extract here transcribed and edited is from the Paine version.

10 OCTOBER 1803

The letter offered here has been published previously. The addressee was Elisha Babcock of Hartford, Connecticut, editor of the *American Mercury* and printer of the laws of the union,[330] The letter was last transcribed and published by Richard Gimbel from the original manuscript for the *Yale University Library Gazette*.[331] As with the few Paine items he published, it is little known. It is here transcribed and edited afresh.[332]

Stonington, Connecticut

Oct 10 1803

Dear Sir

During my absence from Bordenton your friendly letter arrived there which I received on my return, and as I then intended coming on to the eastward I had hopes of making my thanks to you personally, but the fever at N. York obliged me to go by Long Island which threw me out of my intended course.[333] I left Joel Barlow in good health at Paris. Mrs B was but indifferent.[334] He is always talking of coming home, but he waits to sell a house which he bought about four years ago, and for which he expects eight or nine thousand pounds sterling. I was lucky in passing the Atlantic between the storms of the last war and this, but America is not the same agreeable country as when I left it. This federal faction has debased its politics and corrupted its morality.

I have seen Uriah Tracy's publication and also some other pieces in Green's paper in answer to the Republican Address.[335] They all deny the charge of plotting to overthrow the Constitution and establishing a monarchy, and I do not suppose the charge is true against them as a whole party, for though one in a thousand might be advanced by such a system, hundreds of thousands of them must be sunk by it, and become hewers of wood and drawers of water to support the pomposity of the few,[336] and they must be fools indeed not to see this. But the charge is true against their leaders, or at least against some of them, and this is the only way in which the charge has been made. It is true, I believe, against your leading man in Connecticut, Oliver Ellsworth.[337] Star Chester of Groton, a Justice of the Peace and a very respectable man, told me a few days ago that he was in company with Ellsworth and about twelve other persons, about a year ago, *and that Ellsworth there declared himself to be a monarchist.* Major Smith of New London was with Mr Chester when he related this declaration of Ellsworth.[338] As a fact that can be established is sometimes of more effect than a great deal of argument I put you in the way of satisfying your-self with respect to Mr Ellsworth's anti-republican principles. Perhaps you[r] correspondent David can find a stone in his scrip for this Philistine.

I shall stay at this place about three weeks and as your paper is preferable to any in this part of the country I will be obliged to you to favour me with it. Direct to me at Stonington point, Connecticut. Present my respects to your correspondent David.[339]

Yours in friendship
Thomas Paine

Thomas Paine, as will be seen, was dabbling in party politics, possibly at the invitation of Elisha Babcock.

20 NOVEMBER 1803

Addressed to Anthony Taylor, Bordenton, New Jersey, this letter was mentioned by Alfred Owen Aldridge, but has not been reproduced until now.[340] It is here transcribed from a copy of the original held in the United States.[341]

New Rochelle, State of N. York, November 20 1803

Dear friend

I am just arrived here. I received your friendly but afflicting letter announcing the death of Col. Kirkbride in whom Bordenton has lost its patron and I my best friend.[342] When I saw a letter from Bordenton not in Col. Kirkbride's handwriting I suspected the cause of it. Had I known that his last moments were approaching I would have come to have paid to him my last respects. I feel the more grief at his death because he died at the moment when, had he lived, he would have rejoiced at the triumphant success of the last elections.[343]

I am told, for I have been out of the way of seeing news-papers, that your assembly have appointed a committee to enquire into the cause of the riots at Trenton and report thereon.[344] I will be obliged to you to inform me what is done upon that subject. Remember me in friendship to Mrs Kirkbride and Mrs Wharton, and to your father and family.[345]

Yours in sincerity
Thomas Paine

PS
Your letter being directed to me at N. Haven did not come to hand till three weeks after date.[346]

PUBLISHED 2 AUGUST 1804

Unlike most states, Connecticut did not quickly drop its English charter but held on to that granted by Charles II. On 15 September 1803 the *Republican Address to the Free Men of Connecticut* was published in the *American Mercury*.[347] It stated that the Federalists were really monarchists whose plans were to overthrow the Constitution of the United States in order to establish a form of monarchy or perpetual presidency. The matter was addressed at the National Festival in Hartford, on 11 May 1804, when Abraham Bishop, Collector of the Port of New Haven, delivered an *Oration, in Honor of the Election of President Jefferson, and the Peaceable Acquisition of Louisiana.* It began:

> We are not convened to do homage to a tyrant, nor to parade the virtues of *a President and Senate for life,* nor to bow before a First Consul, nor to bend the knee before a host of privileged orders; but we have assembled to pay our annual respects to a President, whom the voice of his country has called to the head of the freest and happiest nation on earth.
>
> While Providence is giving to Britons a solemn commentary on the burning of our towns and the murder of our brethren, we are enjoying the fruits of a glorious defence against the passive obedience, which her insatiate court attempted to impose on us, as a punishment for the high misdemeanors of having descended from themselves, of having sought liberty of mind and conscience in this new world, and of having resolved to be free.
>
> While France is learning, under awful impressions, the danger of delegating power without limit, and of trusting to ambition and the sword what ought to remain in the sacred deposit of peace and legislative counsel, the people of most of our states enjoy the full benefit of free elections, and derive from them all the blessings, which the best state of society admits.[348]

The essence of the piece may be gathered from its introduction.

Thomas Paine, the champion of just constitutions, became interested in the politics of Connecticut, a state where he spent considerable time towards the end of his life. The article, which follows, was published by Richard Gimbel in *The Yale University Library Gazette*.[349] It first appeared on 2 August 1804 in the *American Mercury* from which the transcription given here was made.[350]

To the People of Connecticut,
on the Subject of a Constitution

It was not generally known, until Mr Bishop's excellent Oration of last May appeared, that the State of Connecticut had not a constitution. Congress, some time in 1775 or the beginning of '76, recommended to the people of the several provinces (as they were then called) to take up and establish new governments; but the Legislature of Connecticut, disregarding this recommendation of Congress, assumed the power of enacting that the form of government contained in the Charter of Charles the II of England, should be the civil constitution of Connecticut. This was an unwarrantable act of assumption of the Legislature of that day. The right of forming a constitution belongs to the people in their original character, and cannot be exercised by any body of representatives unless they are chosen expressly for the purpose.

The people of Connecticut have now to exercise the right they ought to have exercised before, for it may be doubted, whether in their present condition, not having an authorized constitution, they have any legal government of their own. The Legislature which enacted that the form of government contained in the Charter of Charles the Second should be the civil constitution of the state could not derive the right of so doing from the Charter itself, because the Charter could not give the right of changing the authority from whence it issued and under which that legislature was then sitting. The only source from whence such a right could proceed was the authority of the people, but this the legislature was not possessed of because they were not invested with it, nor elected, as conventions in other states were, for the express purpose of forming a constitution. The act therefore which changed the name of charter into that of constitution being an unauthorized act, is in itself a nullity.

Neither have the present Legislature any right in the matter otherwise than as individual citizens because the right of forming and establishing constitutions belongs, as before said, to the people in their original character, and cannot be assumed or exercised by any body of men elected for the ordinary purposes of legislation.

It is evident, from the nature of the case, that the first step towards bringing this business forward must be voluntary, for in all cases where rights are equal, though any one may propose or recommend, none can have authority to command in the first instance.

Let then, in the first place, the people of the several towns elect Town Committees and let the elections be made by persons subject to military or militia duty or who pay taxes.

Secondly, let the committees thus elected be authorized to appoint deputies to meet in conference with deputies from the other towns.

Thirdly, let the deputies thus met in conference form a plan for the election of a convention, which shall be authorized to form and propose a constitution to the people.

Fourthly, when the constitution is proposed let it be voted for by *yeas* and *nays* by all the people of the several towns who were entitled to vote for the Town Committees in the first instance.

It is not difficult to foresee that when the constitution shall be before the people for their consideration, there will be those who will be proposing alterations or amendments, some will do this from a good motive, and others from no other motive than that of embarrassing and preventing the matter coming to a conclusion, like the Connecticut members in Congress to prevent the repeal of the internal taxes.

As a constitution should contain within itself the means of amending any part thereof as time and experience shall shew necessary, and as it is to be presumed the Convention will discuss every article they adopt, more effectually than men thinking individually can do, it will be best to vote its adoption or rejection simply to *yeas* and *nays*, unincumbered by conditions. There has been so much experience on the principles and manner of forming constitutions since the Revolution began, that no material error can now take place. This was not the case at first. The legislature that affirmed the power of re-enacting the Charter knew so little about constitutions that they arrogated to themselves the right of establishing their illegitimate offspring through all generations.[351] There is no article which provides for the amendment. They dethroned Charles and then put themselves in his place, and to display their sovereignty they uncharted the Charter to charter it anew. The whole matter therefore must now begin as it ought to have begun at first, on the authority of the people in their original character.

Governor Trumbull, in his speech to the Legislature in May last, informed them of the proposed amendment to the Constitution of the United States, by designating the persons to be voted for as president and vice-president, and he made this the occasion of speaking against the policy of altering constitutions on '*speculation*'. This word was very injudiciously applied to the case; because it is not on *speculation* but *experience* had at the last presidential election that the amendment was proposed.[352] Something therefore, must have been in Governor Trumbull's mind, besides the case itself, to have led him so far and so erroneously from the merits of it. He could not but know that Connecticut, though it has a form of government, has not a constitution, and that the thing patched up in the place of one (and that by those who had not authority for the purpose) has no declaration of rights prefixed to it, nor any article in which it provides for its amendment. It was therefore consistent with the policy of the party to which Governor Trumbull adhered to keep all considerations on the subjects of constitutions and amendments as distant as possible from the minds of the people. It might occur to that party, that if we (the Feds) agree to amend the Constitution of the Union, it will suggest the idea of looking into our own, and in that case the firm of Moses and Aaron, and the beast with SEVEN HEADS*, will fall like the dagon of the Philistines.[353]

A Friend to Constitutional Order[354]

* See the account in Mr Bishop's Oration about the seven lawyers who govern the state.[355]

PUBLISHED 23 AUGUST 1804

Again, only once printed previously by Richard Gimbel, this item was revealed by him as being by Thomas Paine from the item dated 27 August 1804, the next offered. It was, as will be seen, described by Paine as 'a burlesque on a piece in Lang's paper and on Mason's Oration on Hamilton'.[356] Alexander Hamilton, one-time statesman, second in command of Washington's army, and, at the time, Secretary of the Treasury, died in a duel with his political enemy, Aaron Burr, who had been the Republican candidate for vice president in the 1800 election; he won the same number of votes as Thomas Jefferson. Early in 1804, Burr was nominated for the governorship of New York, but Hamilton sent out denigrating letters about him, which led to his being defeated. Paine's 'burlesque', signed Comus, is here newly transcribed and lightly edited from the Philadelphia *Aurora* of Thursday, 23 August 1804.

For the *Aurora*
Nonsense from New York

The following absurd and extravagant publication entitled 'Reflections', is copied from Lang's *N. York Gazette*, of July 27. I send it you, accompanied with some remarks.[357]

'The loss of Gen. Hamilton (says this writer) cannot be considered by those who knew his extraordinary worth in any other light than as a *severe judgment upon the United States*. This being the case (it happens not to be the case) it becomes every one seriously to reflect on the *cause of the displeasure* and the only method for its removal. (Now for it.)

'The primary source, says he, of all the evils appears to be *the conduct of the citizens at the last presidential election*. From that moment, *discontent, division and confusion* began to take place; and unless a speedy remedy be applied more *afflicting scenes may be expected*. Mr Jefferson and Mr Burr were elected, each having an equal number of votes. (Burr was not voted for with the idea of his being president.) The public are now dreadfully convinced (*this is another severe judgment*) that the election of Mr Burr was improper; and they have seen fall by his hand their *first citizen* and one of the most *enlightened* and *honest* statesmen in the world. Language *fails* to express (that is, the writer has not wit enough to do it) the extent of his *talents*, and of the *services* which he has rendered.

'But the principal error was the election of Mr Jefferson, and what the nation has the greatest reason to fear is his re-election. *The objections to him are well known and need not be repeated.* If in opposition to former warnings, and the calamities which have been felt, the electors *will* vote for him, then ruin *will* most probably ensue; embittered with consideration that the people have drawn it down upon themselves.

'It is understood that Mr Jefferson and Mr Clinton are to be the candidates, at the next election. If there should be no other candidate the preference ought *clearly* to be given to Mr Clinton for president, though a more suitable man than either might be found, yet of the two the election of the latter would avert *those frowns of Heaven under which the country labours.* Every serious and reflecting person should look forward with anxiety to the event.' (The writer signs himself)

INVESTIGATOR.
[He means *Instigator* or *Infestigator.*]

* * * * * * *

Remarks on the foregoing publication

The poor unfortunate feds of New York, appear to be drawn from folly to insanity, and the foregoing piece is a proof of it. The meaning of the first paragraph, if the writer was capable of having any meaning, is that God, to shew '*a severe judgment*' upon the United States had Alexander Hamilton *shot in a duel!*

He then goes on. 'The primary source says he, of all this appears to be the conduct of the citizens at the last presidential election. From that moment (O terrible to tell!) *discontent, division,* and *confusion* began to take place,' (among the feds he must mean, for the republicans are contented and happy at the event of the last presidential election, and united for the next) and 'unless, (says he) a speedy remedy is applied *more afflicting scenes* may be expected.' That is, all the feds will certainly *shoot one another.* This will be a *severe judgment!* upon the republicans, for they will have to bury them!!!

But the principal error, (continues our unfortunate author, for he is quite *beside himself*) was the election of Mr Jefferson, and what the nation has most to fear, is his *re-election,* (Yes, it will be the death of the feds!) The objections to Mr Jefferson, continues he, are well known, and need not be repeated. Yes, we know what the objections are. He turned some of them out of office that were not fit for it, and broke up a gang of blood-suckers that were living by useless offices on the public, of which, most probably, our unhappy author was one.

'It is understood', continues he, 'that Mr Jefferson and Clinton are to be the candidates at the next election. If there should be no other candidate the preference ought *clearly* be given to Mr Clinton for president'.[358] (This quackery-monger might have the manners to let the electors make their own choice.) 'Though', says he 'a more suitable man than either might be found', (he means *more suitable* to his own purpose) yet, says he, 'of the *two* the election of the latter would avert *those frowns of Heaven under which the country labours*'!!!

Can this whining hypocrite suppose that this sort of *cant* will have any influence? To pretend to write, and have nothing to say, is the worst of nonsense, because nonsense ingeniously done, may afford a momentary amusement, but there is something in this *hypocritical cant* that is tinctured with impious ingratitude. We have been favored with a fine season, with plentiful crops of grass, grain, and fruits, for man and beast; we are blessed with peace abroad and at home; we have acquired Louisiana by negociation, without bloodshed, and without the addition of any new tax; no symptoms of the yellow fever have appeared at New York, nor elsewhere in our country that is publicly known; we have every cause to be thankful; yet this murmurer of discontent and ingratitude talks of the '*frowns of Heaven under which the country labours*' because the poor feds were defeated at the last presidential election, and because Alexander Hamilton, though a man of some private merit, has died, '*as a fool dieth*', 2, Sam. chap.3, v.33.

Another writer of Rodomontade (one Mason) has made his appearance in a funeral oration on Hamilton; to let you know it is a *catch-penny*, the copy right is secured. No man who writes from principle, and wishes that principle to spread through the world, secures a copy right for small works. It is only in large and expensive undertakings, and to prevent other printers committing robbery, that this is prudent to be done.

'When Washington was *taken*', (says our wild goose orator!)[359] 'Hamilton was *left* – but Hamilton is *taken* and we have no Washington, *we have not such another man to die*'. This might be true if we had no better men than our orator. 'Bereaved America!' (cries he) '*Thou art languishing beneath the divine displeasure.*' The orator has certainly got a crack in the brain; a touch of what they now call in England the *King's Evil*, or he would not rave thus. This short specimen of our orator's work will serve to shew what this catch penny oration is, of which, to catch every penny, the copy right is secured. It is a mean and despicable trick. He might think himself well off if people would read his wild goose nonsense gratis.

Should no yellow fever afflict New York this summer, and we hear of none at present, the New York clergy, if they do as they did the year before last, will have to return thanks to heaven for its bounty to New York. Our revered orator will then have to unsay all that he now says. We shall then hear of nothing but the smiles of heaven.* Now we are told of its frowns and '*divine displeasure*'.

There is a marked inconsistency in every thing the feds undertake. Their praise of Hamilton is a satire on themselves – they extol his wisdom, now he is dead, and they despised his advice when he was living; for he strongly opposed putting Burr in nomination for the governorship of the state of New York, and the duel in which he fell, grew out of that circumstance. They are themselves the *cause of the loss they deplore*, and their manner of deploring it is an additional disgrace. '*We have not*' (says our orator) '*such another man to die*'. Then they have nobody left they can put up for President at the next election. This is a good reason for declaring off, and we give the orator *credit for the truth* of it, for it is the *only truth* his oration contains. It is however an ill bird that befouls its own nest.

COMUS

* The summer before last, Philadelphia was afflicted with the fever and New York escaped. The New York clergy advertised a public thanks-giving for this; and the triumphant manner in which it was done, had the appearance of a commercial advertisement, to inform people at a distance and vessels of commerce, that it was safer to trade to N. York than to Philadelphia. This was the light in which it was considered by great numbers of thinking people. Let every man thank God in his own heart, but let not men assume to be mediators with heaven.

27 AUGUST 1804

This letter to Elisha Babcock, also published by Richard Gimbel, confirms the previous item and that of 2 August 1804 as having been by Thomas Paine under the formerly unknown pseudonyms of 'Comus' and 'A Friend to Constitutional Order'. It is here newly transcribed from a copy of the original manuscript.[360]

New Rochelle, New York State,
August 27 1804

Fellow Citizen

I have received three of your papers. The first wherein you announce for publication of the piece I sent to Mr Bishop signed *A Friend to Constitutional Order*.[361] The next, in which the piece is published; and the last (August. 23). The papers of the two preceding weeks have not arrived. In Duane's paper (the Aurora of the 8th Inst.) is a piece of mine signed Common Sense, on Gouverneur Morris's foolish Oration on Hamilton[362] I desired Duane to send you one in case he was not in the habit of doing so; and in Duane's country paper of the 23 and 24, and in his daily paper of one of those dates, is a piece of mine signed *Comus* and entitled *Nonsense from New York*. It is a burlesque on a piece in Lang's paper and on Mason's Oration on Hamilton.[363]

Mr Bishop, in his answer to me (20 July) after receiving the piece says, 'I have submitted its contents to our general Committee, who consider it rather as a valuable chapter of texts, from which we may preach for a long time, than as an essay for publication'. But as it was better to publish it first, and *preach* about it afterwards, I was glad to find they had changed their mind and sent it to you.

From what I could learn, the republicans of Connecticut were endeavouring to reform their legislature for the purpose of obtaining a constitution. This round-about way, besides the tediousness and uncertainty of it, was fundamentally wrong, because as a constitution is a law to the legislature, and defines and limits its powers, it cannot, from the nature of the case, be *the act* of the legislature; it must be the act of the people *creating a legislature*. The right way is always a strait line, and a strait line is always shorter than a crooked one. A law, enacted by a legislature, binds the citizens individually; but a constitution binds the legislature collectively.

I see by your last paper there is to be 'a meeting of the Republicans at New Haven, *not to form a constitution*, but to consider the expediency of proposing this measure to the people'. I much question if the feds had any idea of being taken upon this ground, and therefore as long as they could keep a majority, according to the present state of election rights, they felt themselves secure; but this cuts them up at the root. I know not what is the qualification to entitle a man to vote according to your rechartered Charter, but be it what it may it cannot become a rule for electing a convention, because conventions for forming constitutions being of American origin cannot be under the controul of an English charter. The people when they elect a convention, and the convention when elected, can know of no such authority as Charles the Second, nor of any such instrument as the Charter.

I suppose I shall see in your next paper some account of the meeting at New-Haven, and if there is any thing you can inform me of by letter I shall be glad to receive it.

The last paragraph in the first page of this letter beginning with the words – *From what I learn*, and ending on this page with the words *legislature collectively*, you may, if you please, put in the *Mercury* as, *Extract of a letter from a Republican in a Neighbouring State*. The paragraph is concise and the idea clear, and is of that kind that serves to put thought in motion.

I am now settled on my farm at N. Rochelle where I intend to reside. It is a healthy pleasant situation about ten miles from the Connecticut line. The southern and eastern posts pass through every day. It is not my intention to publish any pieces or letters on the ensuing presidential election, because I think there will be no occasion for it; but if any champion of the Feds whether priest or musqueteer throws the gauntlet I hold myself in reserve for him.[364]

Yours in friendship
Thomas Paine

The extract appeared in Babcock's paper of 6 September 1804, edited and under a different title from that requested by Paine. It was titled *Extract of a letter from a gentleman, to his friend in this city, dated Aug. 17, 1804*. Here Paine declared himself a Republican but, as noted by Gimbel, on several occasions he had written of his not being a member of any political party.[365]

11 SEPTEMBER 1804

In this previously unpublished letter to Elisha Babcock, here transcribed from a copy of the original manuscript,[366] Paine acknowledges receipt of a pamphlet which, apparently, Babcock had sent him as preparatory reading material for an article the newspaperman wished him to write for his paper.[367] To better acquaint the reader with a later writing by Paine, the reading matter with which he was provided, although protracted, is transcribed verbatim at the end of this piece.

New Rochelle September 11 1804

Citizen

I received a copy of the Address of the Delegates from Ninety Seven Towns. It is a good beginning, and as it is always more difficult to start a loaded cart than to keep it going afterwards or to increase the motion of it, I can have no apprehension but you will go well on. I see you have inserted the paragraph from my last.[368]

This letter is accompanied by a packet containing a small pamphlet. I have added a short introduction to it addressed to you which will explain the occasion of its being written and my motive in sending it. There is not a passage in it that is unsuitable to the circumstance you are in, and much that is as direct to the purpose as if it was written for it.[369] Every page of it answers to the title, and therefore it is not like poor John's *Defence of the American Constitutions* where every page contradicted the title.[370]

If you change papers with the *Courant* I should be glad you would send me that paper or that some of your friends would. It is always of use to know the ground an enemy occupies. I have sometimes a leisure hour in which I might give a little auxiliary aid, but I am not enough informed of what is going on to do it.

Yours in friendship
Thomas Paine

I wrote to you last summer from Stonington and informed you of what Mr Star Chester told me of Mr Ellsworth declaring himself a monarchist.[371]

The pamphlet sent to Paine by Babcock, which was printed in his paper of 6 September, reported the outcome of a meeting of Republican constitutionalists who were concerned that the State of Connecticut, unlike other states of the Union, retained the charter of Charles II, whereby citizens of that state did not enjoy the same privileges as those of states that had drawn up their own constitutions following independence. The meeting resolved to print 10,000 copies of the proceedings of the meeting. The following is transcribed from a copy held at the Library of Congress.

On the 29th of August, a meeting was holden in New-Haven, from which the following Address issued, copies of which were dispersed through the State.

At a meeting of Delegates from ninety-seven towns of the State of Connecticut, convened at New-Haven, on the 29th day of August, 1804.
WILLIAM JUDD, Esq. in the Chair.
HENRY W. EDWARDS and LEMUEL WHITMAN, CLERKS.

Whereas it is the unanimous opinion of this meeting, that the people of this state are at present without a constitution of civil government, – resolved, that it is expedient to take measures preparatory to the formation of a constitution, and that a committee be appointed to draft an Address to the people of this state on that subject, and make report thereof to this meeting.

The committee appointed in pursuance of the foregoing resolve, reported the following

ADDRESS
TO THE PEOPLE OF THE STATE OF CONNECTICUT.

'We hold these truths to be self-evident – that all men are created equal – that they are endowed by their Creator with certain unalienable rights – that among these are life, liberty and the pursuit of happiness. That to secure these rights governments are instituted among men, deriving their just powers *from the consent of the governed*: that whenever any form of government becomes destructive of these ends, it is the right of the PEOPLE to alter or to abolish it, and to institute a new government, laying its foundation on such *principles* and organizing its powers in such *form*, as to them shall seem most likely to effect its safety and happiness.'

Since that declaration the *people* of New-Hampshire, Massachusetts, New-York, New-Jersey, Pennsylvania, Delaware, Maryland, Virginia, the two

Carolinas and Georgia have formed constitutions. The four new states added to the thirteen, are governed under constitutions formed by the *people*. Throughout the Union Rhode-Island and Connecticut are the only states, which still recognize the charter of King Charles as the basis of civil government. This shews that the formation of constitutions by the people has been, without any influence of party, regarded essential to political safety. It has been considered indispensable that the rights of man, however unalienable in their nature, should be guarded from alienation by positive contract, not alterable by the few, who may be in power, but by the *people* who are to be governed.

No one of the constitutions thus formed has changed the rights of persons or of things in respect to the time past, but all of them have defined and guarded the important civil and religious rights of man. They have separated powers, which, if connected, might be dangerous to each other or to the public. They have limited the bounds of each department of government and have established first principles, not to be changed by the consent of the people. They have left to legislators the application of these principles, to judges the impartial construction of laws and to executive officers the power of effecting the objects of government.

In a perfect state of society (where such possible) we should need no constitution, but universal experience has shewn the insecurity of trusting mere men to set bounds to their own power and to remove the land marks at pleasure. Private interest, ambition, or temper may tempt the legislator to sudden and dangerous exercises of power, but a constitution is to the people a permanent shelter and defence. As our situation now is, what one legislature does may be revoked by the next, but what *the people do in their collective capacity* is done permanently for every man and cannot be revoked in haste or without the full consent of the people.

If a constitution shall declare *taxation and representation inseparable*, the legislator cannot separate them with his breath.

If a constitution shall declare all men free in the exercise of religion according to conscience, so far as it can be done without violating public order, the legislator cannot bind over one denomination to another.

If a constitution shall give permanence and independence to judges, the legislator cannot make judges annually dependant on his will.

If a constitution shall establish the qualifications of a freeman, the legislator cannot change them.

If a constitution shall separate the legislative, executive and judicial powers, the legislator cannot unite them in his own person.

It has been said that every thing has gone well in Connecticut. Supposing this were true, yet who will ensure that this shall be the case with the next generation or even for the next year? Men's zeal for popularity and for retaining their places is some guaranty for political safety, but not a permanent one, yet no other have we had since 1776, for the conformity of our laws and establishments to the will of the people. What prudent farmer among us is contented with the abundant crops of his farm, while he has no title deed on record or while his evidence of title is defective? He leaves his plough and his field to establish his title for the benefit of himself and children. If a vessel should happen to perform a good and safe voyage without rudder or compass, the mariners might be complimented on their success, but the owner would never send her to sea again in such condition.

On the subject of government, which involves a concern with all our lands, our labors and pursuits, prudence demands most loudly our vigilant care that nothing be left to hazard which can be made perfectly safe. The people of the other states did not leave all their political concerns to the vague contingence of things going well or ill; but they asserted *the power to be in themselves*, and established rules, which should control all the departments. The old congress did not declare the old confederation to be the constitution of the United States. They did not proceed to organize a government: but the sovereign people appointed delegates to a general convention, which proposed a constitution to conventions of the people of the states.

If all things are now right, let the voice of the *people* establish them as they are. If any amendments are desirable, let the people have opportunity to make them.

Excellent as may appear the government of Connecticut to those, who have administered it, and to their favorites, yet to us, who belong to the majority of the Union, it has been and is an unequal government, constantly tending to the increase of aristocracies and to the consequent humiliation of men and principles, friendly to our revolution. The government is indeed good for those who have enjoyed all power and privileges under it, but to us it has been and is a bad government, because legislators, who are opposed to their own former professions, who are opposed to the general government and to us, have not over their conduct any control, which they cannot remove at pleasure, and have no restraint from making laws favorable to their own perpetuity in power and our perpetuity in subjection.

It is to us a bad government, because judges appointed by such legislators and hostile to us as their makers, have the uncontrolled decision of all our rights, and are annually dependant on our political opponents for continuance in office.

It is to us a bad government, because men thus uncontrolled have concentrated in themselves, the few, that power of the many, which all wise governments have separated.

The grounds, on which we call the government bad, are referred to the very nature of the government, to the construction of courts and to the unavoidable operations of party and passion; hence we shall be excused a detail of the numerous wrongs, which have arrived to us under this government. The same wrongs would arrive to the opposite party, provided the same dangerous unlimited power was to be placed in our hands. In *seasons of party a constitution is an invaluable instrument.*

The federalists claim all greatness and goodness, and refer us to these as security for our enjoyment of equal rights. We recognize no evidence of these exclusive attributes, but in the frequent repetitions of the claim, and these repetitions have been all our consolation and all our redress, when from time to time we have complained of evils, which, defying all human greatness and goodness will be perpetually breaking forth from the corrupt source of human passions.

At the close of our revolution this state stood high in name and in honor among the States of the Union. Under the management of our federal statesmen we are thrown into a minority and have lost our weight in the general scale. Contrary to their policy the president and all the officers of government have been appointed, the amendment of the Constitution has been sanctioned by 13 states and by the people of a 14th, and nearly all the general measures carried. To this condition are we driven by men, who pointedly oppose the measure of a state constitution. Perhaps the same imperious necessity, which yielded to France a Consul and an Emperor, has impelled our rulers to hold their unlimited powers till this time and to refuse relinquishing them to the people: but whatever impediments to forming a constitution might have existed in July 1776 or at the close of the war in 1783 or at the establishment of our national government in 1788 or at any time since that period, no such impediments now exist. The general government is in a train of successful operation, approving its principles and measures to the judgment of a vast majority of our people: thousands in this state are dissatisfied with our want of a constitution; parties are not exactly balanced, but *we have no fear that a constitution will be formed on party principles*: the good sense of the people will never lead them to the establishment of principles, injurious to their own rights and liberty. The interests of a legislature in power and those of the people may be at variance; but the interests of a convention and those of the people are the same.

We will not pretend to decide what a constitution formed by a convention and submitted to the people, will or ought to be; but we take the liberty of expressing what it probably will not be. It will not be an instrument full of innovations, nor will it be a departure from what the experience of other states and of our own has proved to be useful. You will have no new experiments to try; all this business has been made intelligible in our country as the art of ship-building.

If it be a fact that the people of Connecticut are their own worst enemies; if they are ignorant and unable to discern their true interests; if amidst the blaze of light on the subject of free government, which has been all about them, they are able to discover no political safety but in reliance on men of high passions, powerful interests, and wholly uncontrolled, then indeed we may as well proceed on the charter of King Charles; but in the quiet habits of our people we discern no such humility of character. We have been uniformly told by the federalists, that the people of this state are highly intelligent, firm and honest; therefore that they approve the present state of things. We wish to hear from this intelligence, firmness and honesty, *directly*, and not through their self-appointed organs. Never since the settlement of our country has it been submitted to our people to decide explicitly on a form of government. The power of Charles passed directly over their heads to the men then in place, and these made laws for passing it to their successors in office. Thus no part of our independence has ever arrived among the people. We deem it high time that they should take rank among the people of other states, who having lived under free, equal governments of their own choice, have acquired no habits hostile to the principles and operations of such a government throughout the union.

Opposed to our wishes on this subject are the interests of all the men in high office and of most of their dependants. Opposed to us are all the argument, eloquence and influence of federalism. Opposed to us are some public attacks, many private suggestions, and all the phantoms of danger, which the cunning of men can conjure up to alarm the people. Our object will be combated by all, whose interest it is to combat a state constitution.

But among the body of the people can any one see fifteen of the seventeen states enjoying constitutions formed by the *people*, and not reflect that this fact must have resulted from an extended impression of their expediency and necessity? Can any one reflect on the constituent parts of all these constitutions and not discern this impression in favor of separating powers, which are now united in this state?

Does any one believe that all things are now right and is he not willing to establish them as they are and thus to silence our complaints?

Does any one doubt the perfection of the present state of things and is he not willing to apply a constitutional remedy?

Are any persuaded that the government is unequal in its operations, are they not willing to balance it by a constitution?

Do any discern in the leading federalists a strong reluctance to submit this subject, and do these discover in this reluctance no argument in favor of the measure? Could this reluctance exist, if there were a full persuasion that the *people* would sanction the present government in all its parts? Could men in power be unwilling to be strengthened by a constitutional force, can those who claim to have all talents and all virtue, fear that they will fail of influence with an enlightened people, habituated to obey them? Could this reluctance in fact exist, if all things were now right?

Can the people see this state lost in the republican scale of the Union and not seek for the cause in the aristocratic habits, engendered between the charter of King Charles and the pride of rulers, resolved not to descend to the level of the people?

Can any doubt that this is to us a bad government and are such unwilling to give a fair chance of making it equally good for all?

To gain a fair standing among the free nations of the earth we feel that in addressing ourselves to the people, we submit to a safe and judicious tribunal the important question,

Whether we will have a State Constitution?

Tedious as has been the season, and long as have been the details of our wrongs, we ask no sudden redress. Our wish is that men of all classes would cooly examine this subject in all its parts and would decide under a full conviction of its importance. *By their votes will be known their decision.* If a constitution appears desirable, they will vote for men, who are in favor of it. Previous to voting for men, who oppose the measure, let them weigh carefully the motives of such opposition, let them decide that a free, intelligent people are unfit to form a constitution for themselves, and in this decision let them recollect that they abandon the cardinal principle of our revolution and that they exhibit a character of Connecticut, such as it has been unwilling to wear in view of the world. Are we in fact an intelligent people, let us, if we dare risque it, assert this publicly, by establishing the charter of King Charles, as our form of civil government.

People of Connecticut, you are careful respecting titles to your estates, you are careful in your contracts and in your last wills. Can you deliberately reject the only season, which will probably be lent you on earth for establishing a constitution, which shall give validity to the past and the future, which shall quiet all men in their rights, which shall secure you a government of sound principles and perpetuate such a government to the latest generations?

We ask men of all parties to attend punctually at proxies and to continue a contest of votes, till the great question,

Whether this state shall have a CONSTITUTION, be settled finally and forever – ingloriously, (if such must be the effect of invincible prejudice) – but *gloriously*, we trust, for we are persuaded that on our part we have truth and reason, which must sooner or later impress all ingenuous minds beyond the power of opposition.

The foregoing Address having been read –

Resolved, *that the same be accepted, and that ten thousand copies thereof be printed and distributed.*

Signed by order of the meeting,

    WILLIAM JUDD, Chairman.
      H. W. EDWARDS,
      L. WHITMAN, Clerks

The use to which Paine put this pamphlet will become clear in the penultimate article of this book; it provided the background necessary to enable him to 'increase the motion' of his 'cart' and 'keep it going afterwards'.

21 SEPTEMBER 1804

Discovery of the following letter was significant in that it led to the finding of a further work, which follows under the date of 27 September 1804.[372] As Paine revealed in his letter to Babcock of 11 September, Babcock had asked him to comment on the then ongoing controversy of Connecticut never having adopted its own constitution but retaining the old English Charter. Unsure of the laws relating to voting rights in Connecticut, he provided the alteration necessary in the event of his not having pertinently argued his case.

New Rochelle near N. York Sep 21 1804

Citizen

I received Jonathan Steadfast's pamphlet and send you some observations upon it. I know not exactly what is the qualification required by your laws to entitle a man to vote at elections. Do occupiers of land vote as well as land owners? If so, one of the expressions in the piece requires an addition to it. It is that opposite this mark $\times$ on the first page, viz 'and in order to sell the lands, thus obtained, at a higher price they excluded all persons from the right of voting but those who purchased or proposed landed property' – the addition required will be, they excluded all persons from the right of voting but those who purchased or possessed landed property, or occupied it to the amount of ____ here mention the sum.

I expected you would, at least, have informed me of your receiving the pamphlet I sent you, Dissertation on first principles of Government. *I object to any use being made of it but that of publishing it as it is.*[373]

Yours in friendship
Thomas Paine

This is the last letter (being the third) you will receive from me till you acknowledge the receipt of those already written.

The pamphlet Babcock had sent to Paine was *Count the Cost: An Address to the People of Connecticut, on Sundry Political Subjects, and Particularly on the Proposition for a New Constitution*, by Jonathan Steadfast,[374] the pseudonym of Daniel Daggett.

Paine's suggested alteration to the text of material he had already sent to Babcock clearly identified him as author of the next article, 'Jonathan Steadfast and his Book'. The previous two letters he mentioned were those of 27 August and 11 September, which, together with his article published on 2 August and the next writing, comprise a self-explanatory series in their own right.

27 SEPTEMBER 1804

This article, a response to Daniel Daggett's *Count the Cost* with which Babcock had furnished Paine, appeared in Babcock's *Mercury* on 27 September 1804 under the pseudonym 'An Enemy to Monopolies and Inconsistencies'. Confirmation of the work being by Paine, shown in the foregoing letter of 21 September, offered an additional pen name to those proved to have been used by him.

Jonathan Steadfast and his Book

Jonathan has taken up his gray-goose weapon and gone to war, in his way, without 'counting the cost'. There is not a case asserted or assumed in his book but may be overthrown.

One of the first things he attacks is what he calls *universal suffrage*, that is, the right of every man to vote at election who pays taxes, or contributes by personal service, towards the support of government; and he calls on his readers '*to notice his remarks with attention*', I also call on them to notice my counter remarks with the same attention.

'*No community*' says he, '*can be safe unless the power of election resides specifically with the great body of the land-holders*'. This is no more than a *say so* of Jonathan Steadfast, who says it because it suits him to say it. A manufacturer might also say, no community can be safe unless the powers of election reside principally with the great body of the manufacturers. A lawyer might say that the *sanctuary* of the law cannot be safe unless the power of election resides principally with the great body of the lawyers and quill-drivers; and a printer might say that neither the freedom of the *people* nor the freedom of the *press* can be safe unless the power of election resides principally with the great body of the printers. The truth of the case is, that no community is safe where a monopoly of rights is claimed and exercised by any one description of men over the rest.

Jonathan, to maintain his *say so*, says in the next paragraph, that 'such influence had this principle' (that is, this *say so*, for there is no principle in it) 'on those *wise men* who formed our laws' (which, I suppose, were the same *wise men* who formed the Blue-laws and hanged the Quakers) 'that a mere trifle in real property gives a right of suffrage while a man may be excluded who is the proprietor of personal property to a large amount'.[375]

Jonathan, in speaking of his *wise men* (and Jonathan is but a short-sighted politician himself) ascribes to their *wisdom* what ought to be charged upon their *injustice*; or, if you please, their selfish cunning. The men who applied for, and received the Charter from Charles the 2d, and who are mentioned in the Charter, might be useful men in their day for certain matters, but they were land jobbers and speculators. They had by various means (which are set forth in the Charter) gotten possession of a large tract of country from the Indians, and in order to sell the lands thus obtained at a higher price they excluded all persons from the right of voting but those who purchased or possessed landed property. They sold the land and right of voting together. These are the men whom Jonathan calls *wise men*, and I will not dispute the title he gives them if he will confine it to mean that they were *as wise as serpents*.

But whatever apology might be made for the injustice then, none can be made for it now. Commerce and manufactures, at that day had scarcely any existence. They are now rising into consequence, and it is necessary to encourage their liability by doing them that justice they were deprived of before. There are two classes of men in Connecticut, *Fishermen* and *Manufacturers*, who bring money into the state, and tho' many of them may not hold landed property, because they have other employment for their money, are of as much consequence, and are as worthy of the same rights, as if they did. Benjamin Franklin says, '*Every man that draweth a fish out of the water findeth a piece of silver*'. Connecticut abounds with fishermen; the state is benefited by the riches they bring in; and yet without landed property they have no rights in the state. It is time this shameful and dangerous monopoly, which generates discontent and throws the state into distraction, should end; and that the rights of citizenship be established by a *constitution*.

When this be done we may hope to see Connecticut restored to her proper rank in the Union of the States. At present she appears like a cypher with a blot over it. Her members attend Congress to bring home six dollars a day, and expose themselves and the state by ridiculous wrangle, and senseless opposition. They boast of economy in their state government, and oppose every motion for economy in the general government. But their folly is too visible to do mischief, and it is only the character of the state that suffers by it.

An Enemy to Monopolies and Inconsistencies.

The matter of Connecticut staunchly holding to the Charter remained contentious for several years and occupied much space in Babcock's paper. There was no change until 1818, and then little.[376] Until now, it has not been generally known that Paine entered the fray of that state and its constitutional status.

17 JUNE 1806

Apart from being a new addition to the Paine corpus, this letter shows that, contrary to belief, Paine's well-known essay on the cause of yellow fever was written in 1805, not 1806.[377] The essay was enclosed with the following letter to De Witt Clinton, Mayor of New York and president of the Board of Health. Part of a special collection of the New York City Municipal Archives, the original manuscript is titled *On the Cause of the Yellow Fever, and of the Means of Preventing it in Places not yet Infected with it.* The reason for delay in its publication is revealed in the letter's postscript.

To De Witt Clinton Mayor of New York and
President of the Board of Health

I send you an essay on the Cause of the Yellow fever addressed to the Board of Health.

I have shown it to Doctor Miller this Morning who has paid me some compliments upon it and advises the publication of it.[378]

I leave it to your own choice whether you will present it to the Board before publication, or publish it first.

Yours with respect
Thomas Paine

June 17th 1806

PS
The enclosed essay was written last Summer at New Rochelle but the fever breaking out in the city prevented my sending it for publication. It is only this morning that I have seen Dr Miller's publication.[379] I sent to him for it yesterday and he brought it me this morning when I showed him my own essay. I am not well enough to go out or I would wait on you.[380]

Paine's rationalist friend William Carver, with whom he was staying in New York, took the letter and accompanying work to the mayor.[381] The essay was read to the Board of Health on 20 June 1806 and ordered to be published. It first appeared as a four-page pamphlet and was later published in the *American Citizen*, a newspaper in which Paine had published several pieces.[382]

NOTES

1. Philip S. Foner, ed., *The Complete Writings of Thomas Paine*, 2 vols (New York: Citadel Press, 1969).

2. Non-digitized sources were *The Times*; *New York Times*; *Early American Imprints, Series I: Evans, 1639–1800*; and *Early American Imprints, Series II: Shaw-Shoemaker, 1801–1819*. Databases used were American Memory; APS (American Periodicals Series) Online; Archive of Americana; The Burney Collection; ECCO: Eighteenth Century Collections Online; EEBO: Early English Books Online; and The Times Digital Archive.

3. More will be said of Paine revealing his identity in the body of this work.

4. Board of Excise Minute, 8 April 1774, in Moncure Daniel Conway, *The Life of Thomas Paine*, 2 vols, vol. 1 (New York: G. P. Putnam's, 1892), p. 29.

5. Originally titled *Case of the Officers of Excise; With Remarks on the Qualifications of Officers; and on the Numerous Evils Arising to the Revenue, From the Insufficiency of the Present Salary, Humbly Addressed to the Hon. and Right Hon. the Members of Both Houses of Parliament*, the petition was published by J.S. Jordan of London in 1793 under the short title of *The Case of the Officers of Excise*. Jordan had earlier printed both parts of Paine's *Rights of Man*, the work posterity proved to consider his most praiseworthy.

6. Paine is said to have later added the *e* to his name in America. See Francis Oldys, *The Life of Thomas Pain, The Author of the Seditious Writings Entitled Rights of Man: With a Defence of His Writings* (London: John Stockdale, 1791), p. 2.

7. The government of the day engaged the services of Chalmers to write a denigrating biography of Paine following publication of *Rights of Man*. See Thomas Clio Rickman, *The Life of Thomas Paine, Author of Common Sense, Rights of Man, Age of Reason; Letter to the Addressers, &c. &c.* (London: Thomas Clio Rickman, 1819), p. 2. Within a few pages of the opening of his chronicle, Chalmers clearly demonstrated the diligence with which he earned the £500 paid to him by Lord Hawkesbury to discredit Paine to the satisfaction of the former's ministry. Hereafter in the text, but not in notes referring to his biography, Francis Oldys will be referred to as George Chalmers.

8. Thomas Paine, *Rights of Man*, pt 2, 2nd edn (London: J.S. Jordan, 1792), p. 91.

9. *The Age of Reason* (Paris: Barrois, 1794), p. 77 (or p. 37 of another print of the same year).

10. The name of Paine's teacher was first provided by Oldys, p. 5.

11. Thomas Martin, *The History of Thetford, in the Counties of Norfolk and Suffolk, from the Earliest Accounts to the Present Time* (London: J. Nichols, 1779), p. 233. The roll of headmasters kept by Thetford Grammar School confirms the date given by Martin. Personal communication, Phil McGahan, Bursar, Thetford Grammar School, 7 December 2001.

12.   See W. P. Courtney, 'Mingay with the Iron Hand', *Notes and Queries*, series 11–8:186 (1913) 41.
13.   Thetford Grammar School, which traces its history to 631 AD, with the earliest existing document concerning the school dated at 1114 (D. Seymour, *Thetford Grammar School: An Outline History* [Thetford: Thetford Grammar School, 1991], unpaged pamphlet), holds no record of Paine's attendance; the school historians have relied solely on Paine's footnotes. Personal communication, Phil McGahan, Bursar, Thetford Grammar School, 5 November 2001.
14.   *Rights*, pt 2, pp. 91–2.
15.   *Rights*, pt 2, p. 92. The *King of Prussia* left London for a planned six months on 17 January 1757, and berthed at Dartmouth, Devon, on 20 August. See *The London Chronicle*, 18–20 January 1757, and Alyce Barry, 'Thomas Paine, Privateersman', *The Pennsylvania Magazine of History and Biography*, 101 (1977) 458–50. Obviously having read Paine's *Rights*, pt 2, Chalmers noted the seafaring stories and, in his later editions, quite correctly argued that the date Paine gave did not correspond with the age at which he told of first attempting to go to sea.
16.   William Cobbett, the English pamphleteer and reformer, published Chalmers's book with his own virulent and scurrilous attacks on Paine inserted. See Peter Porcupine [William Cobbett], *The Life of Thomas Paine, Interspersed with Remarks and Reflections* (London, n.p., n.d. [1796?]).
17.   Oldys, p. 6.
18.   Oldys, pp. 7–8.
19.   Richard Solly served as mayor in 1738 and 1749. He was to serve a third term in 1778. Personal communication, Bob Solly, descendant of Richard Solly, November 1999.
20.   Listed as Item 1050, in *The Thomas Paine Collection at Thetford* (Norwich, n.p., 1979), unpaged catalogue.
21.   Canterbury Cathedral Archives, U3/12/1/7. The entry was reproduced for the first time in Hazel Burgess, 'The Disownment and Reclamation of Thomas Paine: A Reappraisal of the "Philosophy" of "Common Sense"' (doctoral thesis, University of Sydney, 2002), p. 30.
22.   Margate is 10 miles from Sandwich.
23.   Oldys, p. 18. By the time he published his tenth edition, Chalmers had also found that Paine's wife was not living in the workhouse of St George's, Southwark, as newspapers of the 1790s had reported (p. 14). With the wealth of facilities now available to researchers, searches conducted for this work of the records of all London lying-in hospitals of the time showed no records of a Mary Pain, Paine or Lambert. Lying-in hospitals were introduced in London in the mid-eighteenth century. These hospitals were intended for the 'wives of poor industrious Tradesmen or distressed House-keepers' and wives of soldiers and sailors. See *Records of Patients in London Hospitals*, London Metropolitan Archives Information Leaflet, no. 15 (London, 1999), pp. 3–4.
24.   Francis Westley, *The Life of Thomas Paine* (London: Francis Westley, 1819), p. 9; Thomas Clio Rickman, p. 36; W. T. Sherwin, *Memoirs of the Life of Thomas Paine, with Observations on his Writings* ... (London: R. Carlile, 1819), p. 8.

25. *Baptised 1760* and *Buried 1761* (Canterbury Cathedral Archives, U3/19/1/5). For reproduction of the entries, see Hazel Burgess, 'A Small Addition to the Writings on Thomas Paine', *Thomas Paine Society Bulletin and Journal of Radical History*, 5:3 (2001) 8.

26. Sherwin, pp. 9–10.

27. Sherwin, p. 10.

28. '... the great Academy in Lemon-street, Goodman's fields' and 'a reputable school at Kensington'. Oldys, pp. 20–1.

29. Jared Sparks, ed., *The Works of Benjamin Franklin; Containing Several Political and Historical Tracts Not Included in Any Former Edition ...*, 10 vols (Boston and Milwaukie: A. Whittemore & Co., 1856), vol. 8, pp. 137–8.

30. Thomas Paine to Benjamin Franklin, 4 March 1775, Foner, vol. 2, pp. 1130–1.

31. In early America, it was usual to publish a proposal 'soliciting the kindly regard of all persons interested in the "preservation" and "encouragement" of the noble estate of literature' prior to launching a new magazine. Lyon N. Richardson, *A History of Early American Magazines: 1741–1789* (New York: Thomas Nelson, 1931), pp. 1–2.

32. Thomas Paine to Benjamin Franklin, 4 March 1775, in Foner, vol. 2, p. 1131.

33. Frank Luther Mott, *A History of American Magazines: 1741–1850* (Cambridge, MA: The Belknap Press of Harvard University Press, 1957), p. 40.

34. Frank Smith, 'The Authorship of an Occasional Letter on the Female Sex', *American Literature*, 2 (1930–1) 276–80.

35. Mr [William] Russell, *Essay on the Character, Manners, and Genius of Women in Different Ages*, 2 vols (London: G. Robinson, 1793).

36. Conway, vol. 1, pp. 45–6.

37. Foner, vol. 2, p. 34. See Frank Smith, 277–80. See also James Cheetham, *The Life of Thomas Paine, Author of Common Sense, The Crisis, Rights of Man, &c* (Delmar, NY: Scholars' Facsimiles & Reprints, 1809), pp. 34–5. Benjamin Rush, a physician, became a member of the Continental Congress in 1776. He also served as Surgeon-General in the Continental Army.

38. See Moncure Daniel Conway, coll. and ed., *The Writings of Thomas Paine*, 4 vols, (New York: G. P. Putnam's, 1894), vol. 1, p. 1.

39. Cheetham, pp. 34–5. Cheetham noted the wrong date given by Rush; Paine himself told of arriving in America on 30 November 1774. See Thomas Paine to George Washington, 30 November 1781, in Foner, vol. 2, p. 1203.

40. See William C. Kashatus III, 'Thomas Paine: A Quaker Revolutionary', *Quaker History*, 74:2 (1984) 51.

41. A. Owen Aldridge wrote of the likelihood of the piece not being by Paine. See *Thomas Paine's American Ideology* (London: Associated University Presses, 1984), p. 290.

42. The men named were 'Dr. Ames, Baxter, Durham, Locke, Carmichael, Hutcheson, Montesquieu, and Blackstone, Wallace, etc. Bishop of Gloucester'. Conway, *Writings*, vol. 1, p. 4, n.

43. Thomas Paine to James Cheetham, 21 August 1807, in *Complete Works of Thomas Paine* (London: E. Truelove, n.d. [1878?]), p. 719. A. Owen Aldridge claimed to have reprinted this letter to Cheetham in full for the first time; he

was unaware of the rare book published by Truelove. See 'Thomas Paine and the New York *Public Advertiser*', *The New York Historical Quarterly*, 37 (1953) 376.

44. The date of publication is usually given as 10 January 1776, but from an advertisement in *The Pennsylvania Evening Post* of 9 January it is clear that the pamphlet was published on that day. See Moses Coit Tyler, *The Literary History of the American Revolution 1763–1783* (New York: G. P. Putnam's, 1897), p. 469.
45. 'The Influence of New York Newspapers on Paine's *Common Sense*', *The New-York Historical Society Quarterly*, 60:1/2 (1976) 53.
46. Thomas Paine to Henry Laurens, 14 January 1779, in Foner, vol. 2, p. 1165.
47. Foner, vol. 1, p. 50.
48. Paine became friendly with Col. Joseph Kirkbride of Bordentown when he retreated to New Jersey on the fall of Philadelphia in September 1778. He bought a property in the town in the early 1780s.
49. The matter of Paine styling himself 'Secretary for Foreign Affairs' will be addressed as this work proceeds.
50. London: J. Dodsley, 1790.
51. *Rights*, pt 2, p. 174.
52. Thomas Paine, Preface to *Agrarian Justice* (London: T. Williams, 1797).
53. *Agrarian Justice*, p. 15.
54. See Foner, vol. 1, p. 45.
55. See Hazel Burgess, 'An Extended History of the Remains of Thomas Paine', *The Journal of Radical History of the Thomas Paine Society*, 8:4 (2007) 1–29.
56. The toast was proposed at the annual dinner of the Revolution Society in London on 4 November 1791 in response to one thanking Paine for his defence of the rights of man. It was reported in *The Morning Chronicle* [London], 5 November 1791, shortly before publication of *Rights*, pt 2.
57. The letter was printed in Charles Isham, ed., *The Deane Papers, 1774–1790*, 5 vols (New York: The New-York Historical Society, 1887–90), vol. 3, pp. 101–2.
58. See A[lfred] Owen Aldridge, *Man of Reason: The Life of Thomas Paine* (London: The Cresset Press, 1960), p. 64; John Keane, *Tom Paine: A Political Life* (London: Bloomsbury, 1995), p. 172; Arnold Kimsey King, 'Thomas Paine in America, 1774–1786' (doctoral dissertation, University of Chicago, 1951), p. 178. Beaumarchais is better known as the author of *The Marriage of Figaro* and *The Barber of Seville*.
59. Thomas P. Abernathy, 'Commercial Activities of Silas Deane in France', *American Historical Review*, 39 (1934) 484–5.
60. Audrey Williamson, *Thomas Paine: His Life, Work and Times* (London: Allen & Unwin, 1973), pp. 91–2.
61. Worthington C. Ford et al., eds, *Journals of the Continental Congress, 1774–1789*, vol. 11 (Washington, DC: Library of Congress, 1904–37), pp. 799, 802, 826.
62. Ford et al., vol. 11, p. 1206.
63. Thomas Paine to the Committee of Claims, 14 February 1809. The letter is printed in *The Annals of Congress, 10th Congress, Second Session, 1808–1809*, pp. 1780–83. See Foner, vol. 2, pp. 1492–4.
64. The letter was published in the *Pennsylvania Packet* of 15 December 1778. It can be found in Foner, vol. 2, pp. 97–108. It can also be found in Charles Isham, pp. 86–100.

65. See Isham, pp. 101–2.

66. John Dunlap was the publisher of the *Pennsylvania Packet*.

67. 'The elaborate Address to Mr Deane' was a letter addressed to Silas Deane under the signature of 'Common Sense'. It appeared in the *Pennsylvania Packet* of 15 December 1778 as a reply to a piece published by Deane in the same paper on 5 December. Titled 'To the Free and Virtuous Citizens of America', it was both a defence of his character and an accusation against those within the governing body who did not support him of being disposed towards reconciliation with Britain. It led to public knowledge of dissension within Congress.

68. Paine was here alluding to threats of 'extraordinary violence' against himself. The one he believed should not have been party to such a matter was Robert Morris, recently retired from Congress and a member of the legislature. See Thomas Paine, 'The Affair of Silas Deane', in Foner, vol. 2, pp. 97–8.

69. See Paine's statement written on 18 December and published on 21 December 1788.

70. Ford et al., vol. 11, p. 758. Cf Foner, vol. 2, (p. 108, n. 35), who identified 'Plain Truth' as 'Dr William Smith, the royalist clergyman of Philadelphia'.

71. This brief announcement has only once been published since Paine inserted it. It can be found in Isham, pp. 127–8. It is here transcribed from the original publication.

72. See Ford et al., vol. 13, pp. 54, 75–7.

73. This item was transcribed and edited from the original in *The United States Magazine: a Repository of History, Politics and Literature ...*, May 1779, p. 236.

74. Ford et al., vol. 13, p. 75.

75. Newly transcribed from the original for this work, the letter was printed in full in Foner, vol. 2, p. 111.

76. Ford et al., vol. 13, pp. 32–3.

77. See Ford et al., vol. 13, p. 76.

78. For a fascinating insight into Rivington's espionage activities, see Catherine Snell Crary, 'The Tory and the Spy: The Double Life of James Rivington', *The William and Mary Quarterly*, 3–16 (1959) 61–2.

79. Breckenridge's magazine was in print for only twelve months. At one stage, it included a satirical piece on Rivington which was a parody of Psalm 137.

80. By 'Emperor of Germany', Paine was referring to Joseph II, Holy Roman Emperor. At the time of Paine's writing, the name Germany referred to the polity of the principalities of Germanic-speaking peoples of Western Europe, the nucleus of the Holy Roman Empire.

81. New York was occupied by the British from September 1776 until the end of the Revolutionary War.

82. The information was first passed on by Ralph Izard, then commissioner to the Court of Tuscany, in a letter of 16 February 1778, to Henry Laurens, president of Congress. The 'state officer of the first rank of the Prussian court' was the King of Prussia himself. See Paul H. Smith et al., eds, *Letters of Delegates to Congress, 1774–1789*, vol. 9 (Washington: Library of Congress, 1976–2000), p. 605.

83. France, of course, had been the first of the powers of Europe to recognize the independence of the United States of America.

84. The letter quoted was from William Lee, who had recently been appointed commissioner to the courts of Berlin and Vienna, but, unwelcome and unrecognized by them, he was in Paris at the time of writing. It was read at the Continental Congress on Monday, 8 June 1778 and ordered to be referred to the Committee for Foreign Affairs. See Ford et al., vol. 11, p. 576.

85. W. Bodham Donne, ed., *The Correspondence of King George the Third with Lord North from 1768 to 1783*, 2 vols (London: John Murray, 1867) vol. 2, pp. 145, 363, 380–1, 384. Reprinted by Da Capo Press, New York, 1971. Page references are to the 1971 edition. Cf. Isham, 'Biographical Notice', p. xiii, who wrote of Deane's heirs being paid $37,000 in 1842.

86. Donne, p. 363.

87. Further items are to be found in Foner, vol. 2, pp. 96–186.

88. The follow-up letter was reproduced by Foner, vol. 2, pp. 173–6.

89. See Conway, *Writings*, vol. 3, p. 151, n. 1. The religious grounds on which the Boston Museum refused the painting were based on Paine's opinions of revealed religions as expressed in the two parts of his *Age of Reason* published in 1794 and 1795. In 1854, the private collector who bought the painting acquired it for $6.50. Gary B. Nash, *First City: Philadelphia and the Forging of Historical Memory* (Philadelphia: University of Pennsylvania Press, 2002), pp. 220–1.

90. One work containing the portrait was William M. Van der Weyde, ed., *The Life and Works of Thomas Paine*, 10 vols (New Rochelle, NY: Thomas Paine National Historical Association, 1925) vol. 6, frontispiece. The original print copy is held at the Smithsonian Institute, Washington.

91. Foner was aware of this letter, but did not reproduce it. See vol. 2, p. 173, n. 60. It was mentioned by David Freeman Hawke, *Paine* (New York: Harper & Row, 1974), p. 98.

92. Foner, vol. 2, pp. 173–6. The item is transcribed anew from the original source, the *Pennsylvania Packet* of 31 July 1779.

93. Charles Thomson was secretary of Congress. William Carmichael was secretary of the American Commission of Silas Deane, Benjamin Franklin and Arthur Lee in their quest for French aid.

94. For Paine's piece of 16th February, see Foner, vol. 2, pp. 151–62.

95. Samuel Wharton, an American businessman in London, was closely connected with British members of parliament. See J. Kent McGaughy, *Richard Henry Lee of Virginia: A Portrait of an American Revolutionary* (Lanham, MD: Rowman & Littlefield, 2004), p. 154.

96. Whitehead Humphreys was a Philadelphia iron and steel merchant who wrote under the pseudonym of Cato. Paine had sought from the printer the identity of his antagonist, but the printer refused to name him.

97. Thomas Paine, 'To the Public', in Foner, vol. 2, pp. 173–6.

98. Aldridge, *Man of Reason*, pp. 75–6.

99. The King's House, once a palace of James I, now houses the Thetford Town Council and a valuable library bequeathed to the town by a former owner of the house. The original letter is held in The Peter Force Papers at the Library of Congress, Washington, DC.

100. Peabody was later confined to a debtors' prison for about 20 years and seems to have died in ignominy. See *Sketch of the Life and public Services of the Hon. Nathaniel Peabody* (Concord: Jacob B. Moore, 1824), p. 13.

101. Keane (p. 572, n. 47) mentioned the letter as being to Baron de Miklazaire. He gave no source. King (p. 240, n. 80) gave its location as the 'Library of Congress, United States Revolution MSS, March 11 to November 19, 1779', and named the addressee as 'Baron Mehlazane'.
102. Ford et al., vol. 15, p. 1400.
103. It is described by the Norfolk Record Office as 'a black and white photograph of a portrait of Paine, with underneath what is presumably a copy of his signature and the date "November 23 1779"'. Personal communication, Jenny Watts, Senior Archivist, Norfolk Record Office, 23 January 2008. The exercise book in which the picture is pasted is a volume compiled by W.G. Clarke, titled *Notes on the Thomas Paine Centenary, 1909*. It is part of a collection of newspaper articles and a manuscript copy of a letter from W.G.C. [Clarke] to F.H. Millington and Millington's reply of September 1907. The collection, boxed as 'MS 120' should not be confused with F. H. Millington, *The Paine Centenary* (Thetford, Norfolk: privately printed, 1909) in which the photograph does not appear. Clarke's collection was not published.
104. See introduction.
105. The National Portrait Gallery, London, purchased Dabos's portrait, where it is now on display.
106. The National Portrait Gallery, London dates the portrait circa 1791.
107. Conway, *Life*, vol. 2, p. 474.
108. Conway, *Writings*, vol. 3, p. 151, n. 1.
109. Catalogue of *The Thomas Paine Exhibition, at South Place Institute, Finsbury*, 3–4 December 1895, item 318, p. 20.
110. Conway, *Life*, vol. 1, pp. 156–7.
111. William Reed, *Life and Correspondence of Joseph Reed*, 2 vols (Philadelphia: Lindsay and Blakiston, 1847), vol. 2, p. 202.
112. Thomas Paine to Blair McClenaghan, end of May or early June, in Foner, vol. 2, pp. 1184–185.
113. Thomas Paine, 'Dissertations on Government', in Foner, vol. 2, p. 385. For an interesting discourse on the various media of exchange at this time, see Farley Grubb, 'Creating the U.S. Dollar Currency Union, 1748–1811: A Quest for Monetary Stability or a Usurpation of State Sovereignty for Personal Gain', *The American Economic Review*, 93 (2003) 1778–98.
114. Paine, 'Dissertations on Government', in Foner, vol. 2, p. 385.
115. King, p. 248, n. 107. It is not possible to say whether Paine actually subscribed. The original source was sought for this reference, but was nowhere available.
116. The article was mentioned but not transcribed by King, p. 250. For use in this work, it has been lightly edited.
117. Paine's use of the expression 'set the river on fire' is interesting in its being something of a foretaste of an experiment he was to conduct with Washington three years later. Together they did indeed manage to set the river on fire at Rocky Hill, New Jersey. See 'The Cause of the Yellow Fever' in Foner, vol. 2, p. 1062.
118. Thomas Paine, 'Memorial to Congress', October 1783, in Foner, vol. 2, p. 1235.
119. Thomas Paine to George Washington, in Foner, vol. 2, pp. 1202-4. The manuscript of this letter is not held in the Washington Papers at the Library of Congress, as sourced by Foner, but forms part of the Gratz Collection at the Historical Society of Pennsylvania. At the time it was first transcribed by

Moncure Daniel Conway for inclusion in his *Life of Thomas Paine*, it was in the possession of Mr Simon Gratz of Philadelphia.

120. Thomas Paine, 'Memorial to Congress', October 1783, in Foner, vol. 2, p. 1236.

121. 'Agreement with Robert R. Livingston and George Washington', in E.J. Ferguson et al., eds, *The Papers of Robert Morris: 1781–1784*, vol. 4 (Pittsburgh: University of Pittsburgh Press, 1975), p. 201.

122. Robert Morris, 'Memorandum on Thomas Paine', February 1782, in Ferguson et al., vol. 4, p. 328.

123. Thomas Paine to Gouverneur Morris, in Ferguson et al., vol. 4, pp. 258–9, and Foner, wrongly dated 4 March, vol. 2, p. 1211.

124. See Ferguson et al., vol. 4, p. 259, n. 1. The manuscript is held in the Rare Book Room of the Manhattanville College Library. It was reproduced in an article by Elizabeth O'Connor, R.S.C.J., *Manhattanville*, Spring, 1976, 26–7. *Manhattanville* is the alumni magazine of Manhattanville College.

125. The first instalment appeared in the *Pennsylvania Packet* of 19 February, and the second in the *Pennsylvania Gazette* and the *Pennsylvania Journal* of 27 February. The *Pennsylvania Journal* of 23 February also carried the first instalment, and the *Pennsylvania Packet* of 28 February, the second. Both appeared in the *Freeman's Journal* of 27 February. See Ferguson et al., vol. 4, p. 259, n. 1, and Eric Foner, *Thomas Paine: Collected Writings* (New York: The Library of America, 1995), pp. 873–4, n. Paine's piece was republished for the first time in Eric Foner's book (pp. 187–95). It has frequently been printed as part of *American Crisis Number X*, which did not appear until March.

126. The letter to Robert Morris of 13 March has never been published within Paine collections, but was printed in Ferguson et al., vol. 4, p. 409. It is here transcribed from the original manuscript.

127. It seems that the following day, 14 March was not suitable to Morris as he did not record a meeting with Paine in his diary until 16 March when he wrote 'Mr Ths. Paine made me some proposals for rendering a Public Service on which I promised to Speak to the Commander in Chief'. Ferguson et al., vol. 4, p. 413.

128. This letter is here transcribed from a copy of the original manuscript. Thomas Addis Emmet Collection, Manuscripts and Archives Division, The New York Public Library, Astor, Lenox and Tilden Foundations.

129. Ferguson et al., vol. 4, p. 409, n.1.

130. Ferguson et al., vol. 4, p. 201.

131. Under the title of 'A Motion of Thomas Paine', the transcribed manuscript was first and last published in Van der Weyde, vol. 8, p. 248. See also 'The Will of Thomas Paine', in Philip S. Foner, vol. 2, p. 1499.

132. Conway, *Life*, vol. 1, pp. xx–xxi.

133. Personal communications, Jason D. Stratman, Missouri Historical Society, Library Assistant – Reference, 2 August 1999 and 16 February 2002, in response to requests for information.

134. Robert Morris, 'Diary', 25 March 1783, in Ferguson et al., vol. 7, p. 631.

135. 'Agreement with Robert R. Livingston and George Washington', in Ferguson et al., vol. 4, p. 201.

136. Elizabeth M. Nuxoll and Mary A. Gallagher, eds, *The Papers of Robert Morris* (Pittsburgh: University of Pittsburgh Press, 1995), vol. 8, p. 39. The letter is here

transcribed from a copy of the original manuscript. Morris and Stark Papers, bound volume at New Hampshire Historical Society, pp. 139–40.

137. Nuxoll and Gallagher, vol. 8, p. 38, and p. 39, n. 1.

138. Keane, p. 242.

139. Nuxoll and Gallagher, vol. 8, pp. 95–100. It is here transcribed from a copy of the original manuscript. Morris and Stark Papers, bound volume at New Hampshire Historical Society, pp. 131–8.

140. Nuxoll, and Gallagher, vol. 8, p. 100, n. 1. New York had been occupied by the British from late 1776 until the end of the Revolutionary War in 1783.

141. Nuxoll and Gallagher, vol. 8, p. 100, n. 1.

142. Thomas Paine to George Washington, 30 November 1781, in Philip S. Foner, vol. 2, pp. 1202–4.

143. James Duane served in Congress from 1774 to 1784 when he was appointed Mayor of New York. He is suggested as a possible recipient of the letter because when, as requested of the addressee, the matter was put before and considered by a committee appointed by Congress, Paine, unhappy with their decision, wrote to the committee informing them that he did not wish to be appointed to the position he had heard they were likely to offer him. The manuscript of that communication, an enclosure with a letter from Thomas Paine to George Washington of 2 October 1783, is with the papers of James Duane at the New York Historical Society. See Philip S. Foner, vol. 2, pp. 1224–6. Beyond this fact, on 3 December, Paine wrote to Duane referring to conversations they had had regarding his financial problems which would seem to link him to the matter. See Philip S. Foner, vol. 2, pp. 1244–5.

144. See Nuxoll and Gallagher, vol. 8, p. 100, n. 2.

145. Paine was referring to Congress, whose members were unaware of the secret agreement under which he had been working.

146. Paine's mention of conversation suggests that the letter might have been addressed to Robert Morris himself. As already mentioned, they met on 13 May, but Paine might equally well have had an unrecorded meeting with James Duane.

147. Paine's *Letter to the Abbé Raynal, on the Affairs of North America: in which the Mistakes in the Abbé's Account of the Revolution of America are Corrected and Cleared Up*, published on 21 August 1782, was his longest work to that date. It was intended that the pamphlet 'should reach Europe, and by obtaining a general reading there, put the affairs of America and the revolution in the point of light in which they ought to be viewed'. See Paine's 'Memorial to Congress', October 1783, in Philip S. Foner, vol. 2, p. 1236. Paine circulated free copies of his *Letter to the Abbé Raynal* but its writing was subsidized by both the French and his secret service allowance. He had earlier borrowed Morris's copy of Raynal's *Révolution de l'Amérique* with which he found many faults and extracted excerpts for his notes. See Nuxoll and Gallagher, vol. 8, p. 100, n. 3, and Paine's letter to Morris of 26 November 1781 in Philip S. Foner, vol. 2, pp. 1201–2.

148. Paine was referring to the Holy Roman Emperor Joseph II.

149. Paine later wrote: 'Such was Col. Laurens's passionate attachment to me ... that his importunities for my returning with him were pressing and excessive, and he carried them to such a height, that I felt I should not be very easy to myself

do which I would; and as he would have had nobody with him on the passage if any misfortune had befallen him, I gave into his wishes and accompanied him back.' Thomas Paine, 'Memorial to Congress', October 1783, in Philip S. Foner, vol. 2, p. 1234.

150. At the time of which Paine was writing, 1781, Benjamin Franklin was serving as Minister Plenipotentiary to the Court of France.

151. The letter to Ralph Izard has not been found. See Nuxoll and Gallagher, vol. 8, p. 100, n. 4.

152. Paine was suggesting an extremely close relationship between himself and John Laurens who was later killed in a minor skirmish in the last days of the war.

153. Paine quoted the letters from both General Greene, to whom he had been aide-de-camp early in the war, and John Laurens in his sixth piece written under the pseudonym of 'A Friend to Rhode Island and the Union', published in the *Providence Gazette and Country Journal* of 1 February 1783. See Philip S. Foner, vol. 2, pp. 362–6. Each letter lauded Paine's generosity, with Greene lamenting the shameful neglect with which he had been treated, and Laurens offering his all for sharing with his friend. It is possible that Paine solicited such letters from his friends because Greene was certainly aware of the agreement under which he had worked for Washington, Morris and Livingston. Before the agreement was signed, Joseph Reed, a former governor of Pennsylvania, had written to Greene informing him that Paine had proved to be the mercenary his enemies had thought him to be. See Joseph Reed to General Greene, January 1782, in Dennis M. Conrad, ed., *The Papers of General Nathanael Greene* (Chapel Hill, NC: University of North Carolina Press, 1998), vol. 10, p. 200. In order to gain support in his quest for reward, Paine probably sent the letter from Greene to Robert Morris as evidence of the esteem with which he was held. It should be noted that Paine wrote his unaddressed letter at a time when he had been accused of being a mercenary writer by many who objected to his articles addressed to the citizens of Rhode Island, pieces that appeared in the *Providence Gazette and Country Journal*. Those articles were an endeavour to persuade the Rhode Island Assembly to reconsider accepting a federal impost which the other states had passed on all imported goods. Shortly after the second rejection by Rhode Island, other states revoked their grants.

154. The person in Market Street has not been identified. Christopher Ludwick was Superintendent of Bakers, and Director of Baking in the Continental Army. See Ford et al., vol. 7, p. 323.

155. As he wrote this sentence, between the lines prior to mentioning 'the sum of five or six thousand Guineas', Paine had written the figures '65' which he probably intended to, but did not, delete.

156. David Rittenhouse, an astronomer and patriot famous for his observations on the transit of Venus in 1768, was a friend of Paine. At the time Paine wrote this letter, Rittenhouse was State Treasurer of Pennsylvania.

157. As already intimated, Paine's writings had not been welcome in Rhode Island where he was seen as a mercenary writer promoting the cause of Congress in threatening the sovereignty of the state.

158. Kirkbride welcomed Paine into his home, first at Bellevue Farm, in Bucks County, Pennsylvania, then at Bordentown after the farm was burned by enemy

forces. In 1783, due to his impecunious circumstances, Paine moved in with the Kirkbride family. There, in a workshop on the property by the Delaware River, he worked on his invention of an iron arch bridge.

159. Thomas Paine to General Greene, 10 September 1781, in Philip S. Foner, vol. 2, p. 1191.

160. Ford et al., vol. 24, pp. 512–13.

161. It was about 1783, when this letter was written, that Paine purchased his property at Borden Town, now known as Bordentown, New Jersey.

162. See Philip S. Foner, vol. 2, p. 1244.

163. The short letter introducing the piece was vaguely mentioned by Jack Fruchtman, Jr, *Thomas Paine: Apostle of Freedom* (New York: Four Walls Eight Windows, 1994), p. 464, n. 33, and p. 504, and Nuxoll and Gallagher, vol. 8, pp. 100–1, n. 5.

164. The letter to Washington of 22 July 1783 was included in Philip S. Foner, vol. 2, p. 1222, but mistakenly dated August 1783.

165. Some few words were crossed out by Paine.

166. Paine refers to an 'Address of the Citizens of Philadelphia and the Liberties Thereof' which was referred to a committee for consideration. The address followed a disturbance on 21 June 1783 when disgruntled Pennsylvania soldiers mutinied against the rejection of their pay claims by the state's Executive Council. Annoyed by the affair, Congress moved from Philadelphia to Princeton. The purpose of the address was conciliatory. It was a petition urging Congress to return, and a testimony assuring the gratitude of Philadelphia's citizens to 'that Union which so happily succeeded in accomplishing the freedom and independence of America'. It assured Congress that the situation of Philadelphia was returned to composure and nothing would occur to disturb deliberations. It bore 800 signatures. See Varnum Lansing Collins, *The Continental Congress at Princeton* (Princeton, NJ: The University Library, 1908), pp. 88–9. On 28 July the committee reported favourably: 'Resolved That the President inform the citizens of Philadelphia, and its liberties, in answer to their respectful and affectionate address, that the United States in Congress assembled have the highest great satisfaction in reviewing the spirited and patriotic exertions which have been made by the government and citizens of Pennsylvania, in the course of the late glorious war; and that they are highly pleased with the resolution expressed by the citizens of Philadelphia, to aid in all measures which may have a tendency to support the national honor and dignity'. See Ford et al., vol. 24, p. 444, n. l:l, and p. 452.

167. As an ally of France, Spain had entered the War of Independence in 1779, but did not enter into a formal alliance with the American revolutionary forces. Early in 1783, Spain recognized the United States of America as an independent entity and, as a result of the peace treaties, was ceded Florida.

168. Letter transcribed and edited from *The George Washington Papers*, Library of Congress, Manuscript Division.

169. The *Pennsylvania Packet*, 22 July 1783. Washington's circular letter, written from his headquarters at Newburgh on 18 June 1783, was addressed to the governors of the states. It appeared as a broadside, *His Excellency General Washington's Last Legacy*. In a sense, with the country independent and at peace, it might be read as a State of the Union address.

170. In 1776, George Mason had drafted the Virginia State Constitution, and authored the Virginia Declaration of Rights.
171. The *Richmond Virginia Gazette* of 7 June 1783 proved unavailable. It is thought that the original manuscript, which was sought for citation in this book, was probably used as the printer's copy and then discarded. See Kate Mason Rowland, *The Life of George Mason, 1725–1792*, 2 vols (New York: G. P. Putnam's, 1892), vol. 2, pp. 782.
172. It has not proved possible to identify with certainty the 'friend in Fairfax, in Virginia'.
173. A printer's error occurs in this sentence; the word 'as' which precedes the word 'honorable' is printed as 'sa', thereby reinforcing the suggestion that the piece was intended to have been introduced by 'C.S.', not 'S.C.' Note also spelling of the word 'meer' which follows five paragraphs on.
174. See Rowland, p. 781. Ship money was a tax imposed by Charles I as a means of funding for a possible war. It was declared illegal in 1641, seven years after its introduction.
175. The enclosure sent for Thomas Willing's 'perusal' was, most likely, a rough outline of Paine's forthcoming *Dissertations on Government, the Affairs of the Bank, and Paper Money.*
176. The 'Memorial' was Paine's *Dissertations on Government, the Affairs of the Bank, and Paper Money.*
177. Robert Whitehill was a radical representative of Cumberland County who had complained that the bank was incompatible with public welfare as its loan period was limited to forty-five days, not long enough for the farming community to benefit from their loans. Besides, he argued, the notes issued by the bank suffocated the credit and circulation of Pennsylvania's paper money. Bray Hammond, *Banks and Politics in America, from the Revolution to the Civil War* (Princeton: Princeton University Press, 1991), p. 55.
178. Thomas Willing's brother-in-law, Tench Francis, was the first cashier of the Bank of North America, and Blair McClenachan accumulated riches as a privateer during the Revolutionary War. He subscribed thousands of pounds to supply the army. After the war, he became a successful merchant and ship owner. Attempts to locate Paine's letter to McClenachan for inclusion in this collection have not been successful; it is possible, in that Paine seemed to wish it back in his own hands, that it was recovered and destroyed. Likewise, no letter to Francis has been located.
179. This letter to Thomas Willing was transcribed and edited from a photocopy of the original supplied by the New-York Historical Society. The letter is held in the Gilder Lehrman Collection at GLC 6276.
180. In July 1785, the legislature of Massachusetts passed an act that imposed a duty on advertisements placed in newspapers. Isaiah Thomas, publisher of a paper known as the *Massachusetts Spy*, in protest against the tax, astutely abandoned the folio form of his paper in favour of small octavo, thereby avoiding the tax that was not imposed on periodicals. Publication of the *Spy* ceased for the two-year period the act was in force, but, in its physically different form, virtually continued under the name of the *Worcester Magazine*. The tax was rescinded in April 1788 and the *Spy* was resumed immediately. See Mott, pp. 92–3.

181. Paine here refers to Cicero who was born at Arpinium, the Italian town now known as Arpino. The reference to the Earl of Chatham, William Pitt the Elder, is odd, because he was born in London. Paine might have confused him with his son Pitt the Younger, who was born at Hayes, Middlesex, in 1759. At that time, Hayes was a small village, but, with the building of the Grand Junction Canal in 1796, it became industrialized.

182. At the time of Paine's writing, Benjamin Franklin was serving as the sixth President of the Supreme Executive Council of Pennsylvania. He was born in Boston, Massachusetts, the tenth son of a tallow tradesman. John Adams, born the son of a militiaman and deacon at Braintree, Massachusetts, was the Minister Plenipotentiary representing the United States at the Court of St James.

183. Paine here refers to Jonah 4.

184. Paine was to embark on a voyage to Europe the following month and needed capital to promote the proposed erection of his iron bridge.

185. The letter is here transcribed by courtesy of Bauman Rare Books.

186. On 3 October 1785, Congress resolved that Paine be paid $3,000 for his war-time services. Ford et al., vol. 29, pp. 779, 796.

187. Morellet was an academic and encyclopaedist. Benjamin Franklin possibly provided Paine with a letter of introduction to him prior to his departure for Europe.

188. Three days after the death of the prime minister, the Marquess of Rockingham, the Marquess of Lansdowne was appointed First Lord of the Treasury. He negotiated the Treaty of Paris that brought the War of Independence, as it became known, to an end.

189. This letter was discovered following enquiries of the Royal Commission on Historical Manuscripts. First read on microfilm at the Bodleian Library, University of Oxford, in 1996, on learning of its sale, a discretionary approach was made to the new owner through the auction house, but a response did not come to hand; the owner's right to privacy is respected. The transcription given is from a catalogue: *Important Autograph Letters from the Historical Archives at Bowood House*, Christies, London, 12th October 1994, with permission of the Book Department of Christies, London.

190. Lewis Morris was an aristocratic landowner and a signatory of the Declaration of Independence.

191. David Freeman Hawke, *Paine* (New York: Harper & Row, 1974), p. 180.

192. Paine refers to *Prospects on the Rubicon*.

193. When he first built a model of his bridge, Paine intended it as a crossing over the Harlem River for use by Lewis Morris, but, in letters to George Clymer of 19 November and Benjamin Franklin of 6 June 1786, he noted its potential as a bridge suitable for spanning the Schuylkill River at Philadelphia. Made of iron, unlike a timber bridge supported by piers, its strength would withstand the force of melting river ice. See Philip S. Foner, vol. 2, pp. 1258 and 1027–8.

194. In a letter of 1789 to his friend Kitty Nicholson Few, who had written to Paine of her marriage, Paine asked after the girls of Bordentown. He wished for more information on 'my favorite Sally Morris, my boy Joe, and my horse Button'. See Philip S. Foner, vol. 2, p. 1275. The words 'my boy' imply a master–servant relationship.

195. For a brief, general account of slaveholding in Philadelphia at the time, see Jean R. Soderlund, *Quakers and Slavery: A Divided Spirit* (Princeton, NJ: Princeton University Press, 1985), p. 64.

196. 1 (1929–30) 170.

197. Apparently, 250 lines of the poem were written by Day and 186 by Bicknell. See James Keir, *Account of the Life and Writing of Thomas Day* (New York: Garland Publishing, 1970), p. 143.

198. Thomas Day and John Bicknell, *The Dying Negro, a Poem. To Which is Added, a Fragment of a Letter on the Slavery of the Negroes by Thomas Day, Esq.* (London: John Stockdale, 1793), p. 51.

199. Day and Bicknell, pp. 51–2.

200. Day and Bicknell, pp. 51–3. 1776 was, of course, the year when *Common Sense* was published, and when America declared its independence from Britain.

201. Day and Bicknell, p. 51.

202. Keir, p. 114. By the time Day's letter was published, John Laurens, who was well acquainted with him in London, had been killed in the last stages of the War of Independence. Day and Bicknell, n., pp. 55–6.

203. In the account of his life, there is no mention of America in the travels undertaken by Day. See Keir, pp. 32–4.

204. David Duncan Wallace, *The Life of Henry Laurens: With a Sketch of the Life of Lieutenant-Colonel John Laurens* (New York: Russell & Russell, 1967), p. 190.

205. Day and Bicknell, pp. 55–6.

206. Day and Bicknell, p. 57.

207. Thomas Day died in 1789 aged 41. It is probable that he asked for publication to be delayed until after his death.

208. Day and Bicknell, p. 52.

209. Day and Bicknell, pp. 16–18.

210. Day and Bicknell, pp. iv–v. The editor wrote between the time of the prosecution being laid against the publisher of *Rights of Man*, pt 2 on 14 May and Paine's trial on 18 December 1792.

211. Day and Bicknell, pp. 57–61.

212. George S. Brookes, *Friend Anthony Benezet* (Philadelphia: University of Pennsylvania Press, 1937), p. 163.

213. Paine wrote to Lewis Morris, 16 February, to George Washington, 28 April, and to General Irwin, 27 November. Philip S. Foner, vol. 2, pp. 1245, 1248, 1249.

214. Thomas Paine to Thomas Jefferson, 15 January 1789, in Julian P. Boyd et al., *The Papers of Thomas Jefferson*, vol. 14 (Princeton, NJ: Princeton University Press, 1958), p. 454.

215. Paine refers to the English ballad that tells the story of the vicar of Bray who easily changed his creed to Catholicism when James II ascended the throne.

216. Thomas Walker was a bridge-builder who had undertaken to build a bridge to Paine's design.

217. Thomas Paine to Thomas Walker, 26 February 1789, in Philip S. Foner, vol. 2, pp. 1279–80. One writer on Paine, who elsewhere alluded in his article to political matters, apparently found the letter so confrontational that he cut it short in the quoting, signing Paine off at the point where the quotation here

begins. See W.H.G. Armytage, 'Thomas Paine and the Walkers: An Early Episode in Anglo-American Co-operation', *Pennsylvania History* 18 (1951) 20–21.

218. Keane, p. 52.
219. A. Owen Aldridge, 'The Poetry of Thomas Paine', *The Pennsylvania Magazine of History and Biography*, 79 (1955) 96.
220. There were four Walker brothers, Samuel, Joshua, Joseph and Thomas. Armytage, 19.
221. The letter is here transcribed and lightly edited from an unpublished manuscript letter, Gouverneur Morris Papers, Rare Book and Manuscript Library, Columbia University.
222. Although this piece was published in 1791, it will become obvious that it was ready for publication in June 1790, before Edmund Burke's *Reflections on the Revolution in France* appeared in November of that year. It is well known that Paine's *Rights of Man* was a response to that work and was published on 22 February 1791.
223. Thomas Paine to William Short, 24 and 25 June 1790, in Philip S. Foner, vol. 2, p. 1310.
224. As is evident from the writings collected in this book, Paine was a wily, devious character, who would have been well aware of the passionate reaction that such a pamphlet was likely to arouse in Britain. *Rights of Man* had created a sensation, provoking dissent and division even within families as they argued for and against the issues raised in the work, and it seems that Paine wanted to test British tolerance with the pamphlet before embarking on *Rights of Man, Part the Second*. In the end, publication of *Rights of Man, Part the Second* led to the issue of a warrant for Paine's arrest, news of which is said to have been imparted to him by William Blake. Paine fled to France and, as noted earlier, was tried *in absentia* and found guilty of seditious libel, a crime punishable by execution. Paine seems to have waited several months on publication of this pamphlet in France. Had he been able to publish it subsequent to French publication and as a translation from the French, he might have hoped that English readers would have been persuaded that the freedom of expression enjoyed across the Channel could be theirs as well, if only they would heed his advice. However, Paine was known for his vanity, and had the work been published in France the fact would certainly have been mentioned on the title page. It was not.
225. The fact that it was Miller's publication that attracted review in the *Monthly Review* of June 1791 (pp. 226–228) suggests that it followed the piece with a shorter title, here transcribed. The impartial, concerned reviewer recommended the 'ample performance' to the 'attention of the public; as we would the sentiments of every competent and well-intending writer, on subjects of so much consequence to the prosperity of our country'. W. Miller's obituary, which tells of his publishing career, can be found in the *Gentleman's Magazine* of January 1845, p. 102.
226. A copy of the longer title, held by the British Library, is inscribed 'D[uke]. of Grafton 1791'. Most of the many Paine biographies tell of his mother having worked on the estate of the Duke of Grafton prior to her marriage to Joseph Pain in the chapel on the estate.
227. In a piece dated 28 December 1778 addressed 'To the Public', which appeared in the *Pennsylvania Packet* of 29 December, Paine appended his true signature

for the first time in America. He signed the piece 'THOMAS PAINE, Secretary for Foreign Affairs, and Author of all the Writings under the Signature of *Common Sense*'. In disclosing himself, he elevated his trusted position of secretary to the Committee for Foreign Affairs to that of Secretary for Foreign Affairs. He revealed himself during the controversial Silas Deane Affair and, in doing so, made enemies of the pro-Deane faction of Congress and their supporters.

228. See 'The Will of Thomas Paine', in Philip S. Foner, vol. 2, p. 1500.

229. In the event, 127 years were to pass before universal suffrage was introduced for all men, at the same time that the vote was given to some women. This pamphlet is addressed specifically to men.

230. Paine here refers to the church.

231. Paine's reference is to the pope.

232. The Indian war was the theatre of the Seven Years' War in which Britain fought both the French and American Indian forces in North America.

233. Paine was telling the British that the French economy was on the rise following the upheavals of the Revolution, and that Britain would lose out on the French market they had enjoyed of recent times. As it happened, matters in France were to deteriorate.

234. 'Justicia gallies' were old ships that had been converted into floating prisons to accommodate convicts awaiting transportation.

235. Following American Independence, Britain sent prisoners convicted of serious crimes to a penal settlement on the east coast of Australia. It was intended that the settlement be at Botany Bay, but the area on its shores was deemed unfit for farming so the colony moved a few miles north to Port Jackson, now known as Sydney.

236. These words bear comparison with the opening sentence of Paine's Introduction to *Common Sense*: 'Perhaps the sentiments contained in the following pages, are not *yet* sufficiently fashionable to procure them general favour; a long habit of not thinking a thing *wrong*, gives it a superficial appearance of being *right*, and raises at first a formidable outcry in defense of custom.' Philip S. Foner, vol. 1, p. 3.

237. Paine refers to the body of laws enacted during 1597–98 whereby relief for the poor was administered through parishes. With changes, some mentioned in following pages, they remained in force until after the Second World War.

238. According to Greek legend, Hydra was an enormous monster with many heads, one immortal. It was one of the labours of Heracles to destroy the beast, but as soon as one head was cut off, two grew in its place. It was only by burning out the roots of the heads with firebrands that the central head was severed.

239. For this and the other Elizabethan Poor Law mentioned in the appendix of this work, see Sir John Comyns, *A Digest of the Laws of England*, vol. 4 [Estates – Liberties] (London: Privately printed, 1822), *passim*.

240. Paine refers to Roger Mortimer, 8th Baron of Wigmore, 1st Earl of March.

241. See Judges 17:6, which Paine paraphrased.

242. Paine here refers to Peter Lombard, a great Irish scholar, philosopher and priest, who was appointed by Pope Clement VIII as Archbishop of Armagh in 1601. With the penal laws in force in Ireland, priests who practised their faith were subject to the death penalty. As a Catholic who had welcomed and supported

those involved in the Flight of the Earls following the Tudor reconquest of Ireland, Lombard was unable to return to his homeland, and Armagh was without an archbishop for nearly a quarter of a century; he never returned and died in Italy. James I, who disliked Lombard intensely, attacked him in Parliament. In 1604, he wrote a piece in support of religious freedom for the Irish addressed to James I; it has not yet been edited.

243. It is interesting to note that part, if not all, of Paine's *Reflections* might have been written in the Austrian Netherlands where, for some time, there had been political upheaval and revolution, exactly the conditions attractive to him. The French were to intervene in the following year which might have explained Paine's presence. The Austrian Netherlands were annexed to France in 1795.

244. Paine refers to the Magdalen Hospital, opened in 1758, for the reception of penitent prostitutes. By December 1786, as many as 2,471 women had been admitted. See Thomas Pennant, *Some Account of London*, 3rd edn (London: Robert Faulder, 1793), p. 37.

245. At the time Paine was writing, the country was, as a result of the American Revolution, hundreds of millions of pounds in debt.

246. Paine was, of course, referring to the French Revolution which, at the time he wrote, had not descended into the horrors of the Terror. The Revolution had not 'concluded'.

247. Paine refers to George I of England, the Protestant Elector of Hanover, who succeeded Queen Anne, and the Catholic claimant, James, who came to be known as the Old Pretender. The Act of Settlement of 1701 ensured that James would never rule over England. George was not popular, but survived Jabobite plots to replace him with James, whom they planned to crown in Scotland. The money used by the government 'for its own purposes' was that invested in the money-making scheme known as the South Sea Bubble in 1720. The South Sea Company had loaned £7,000,000 to England to finance the war against France. In return, a bill was passed which assured the company of monopolization in South American trade. Shares in the company soared when it underwrote the national debt which was to be repaid with interest of 5 per cent. People of all walks of life all over the country invested in the many bogus companies that were set up. When the stocks crashed, they lost everything. Hundreds of members of the Houses of Parliament and the king himself were involved. Chaos ensued. It was left to the Chancellor of the Exchequer, Robert Walpole, who had never approved of the South Sea Company, to resolve the problem. By dividing the national debt, that is, the South Sea Company, into three parts between the Treasury, the Bank of England, and the Sinking Fund – for which part of the national income was set aside each year, England ultimately returned to financial stability.

248. See Exodus 5:7.

249. The event mentioned became known as the Midland Revolt, a series of anti-enclosure riots which culminated in the Newton Rebellion. Captain Pouch, one John Reynolds, was the supposed leader of a gang of masked individuals who levelled the fences throughout several Midland counties. Reynolds's uneducated followers were led to believe that in a pouch which hung at his side he carried a charm which would protect them all from danger provided they were well behaved. The rioters, numbering some thousands, were eventually suppressed

and many executed as traitors for opposing the king's men. 'Captain Powch was made exemplary'. When his pouch was opened, it was found to contain nothing but a piece of green cheese. See John Stowe and E. Howes, *Annales, or a Generall Chronicle of England* (London: Richard Meighen, 1631), p. 890.

250. John Millar was appointed to the Regius Chair of Civil Law at Glasgow in 1761. See John W. Cairns, 'John Millar's Lectures on Scots Criminal Law', *Oxford Journal of Legal Studies*, 8 (1988) 364. The Witenagemot (or Wittenagemote as Paine spelt the word) was the advisory council of the Anglo-Saxon kings.

251. Henry I reigned from 1100 to 1135, and was succeeded by his nephew Stephen who usurped the throne from the rightful heir, Matilda. He reigned until his death in 1154.

252. Magna Charta, commonly known as Magna Carta, was sealed by King John, who reigned over England from 1199 to 1216, in 1215.

253. Sometimes referred to as the Bloodless Revolution, the Glorious Revolution of 1688–89 led to the deposition of James II and the accession of his daughter Mary II and her husband, William III, thereby restoring Protestantism to the monarchy. Since then Catholics have been barred from the throne of England.

254. Paine's reference is to Oliver Cromwell.

255. John Wilkes was a licentious character who first entered Parliament in 1757. He was a radical journalist and a supporter of the Americans in their quest for independence. Popular with the less privileged of society, he was twice expelled from Parliament: the first time for criticizing a speech made by the king, and again for publishing an obscene work. He was re-elected to Parliament three times, but the House of Commons invalidated each of his elections. As a champion of liberty, he was elected to the House of Commons in 1774 where he remained as a member until 1790.

256. Having held minor ministerial positions in the ministry of Lord North, Fox was dismissed by George III when he, like Wilkes, was seen to be a sympathiser of the Americans during the War of Independence. He joined the Whig Party and became one of their leading spokesmen. He was to become Foreign Secretary for a short time in the ministry of Lord Rockingham, who returned to power after the fall of North's ministry in 1782.

257. The reference is to rotten boroughs, constituencies of few people but strong representation in government. Paine gave examples in *Rights of Man*: 'The county of Yorkshire, which contains near a million souls, sends two county members; and so does the county of Rutland, which contains not an hundredth part of the number. The town of Old Sarum, which contains not three houses, sends two members; and the town of Manchester, which contains upwards of sixty thousand souls, is not admitted to send any.' Thomas Paine, *Rights of Man* pt 1, 1st edn (London: J.S. Jordan, 1791), p. 57.

258. Paine again refers to Joseph II, Holy Roman Emperor.

259. In 1772, during what history came to call the First Partition of Poland, the country, weakened by civil war, was incapable of resisting its partition by Russia, Prussia and Austria. In an effort to prevent escalation of the Russo-Turkish War, Frederick the Great of Prussia hoped to appease Austro-Russian relations by expanding into Poland rather than Turkish territory. Poland's near-impotent legislature, concerned about further loss of territory to the three

powers, ratified the treaty that deprived the country of nearly one-third of its land and one-third of its population.

260. In 1782, the Parliament of Ireland won freedom from British laws that prevented Roman Catholics from partaking in government. Those laws had been in effect since medieval times. Under the Constitution of 1782, the changes and relative freedom of Ireland from Britain remained in place until the Irish Parliament merged with the British Parliament in 1801. At the time of Paine's writing, America had gained independence from Britain, and his mention of an attempt to purloin the East Indies refers to hostilities between Britain and France, known as the East Indies Campaign of 1778–83, which were in fact a separate theatre of the Revolutionary War.

261. 'Ambitious minister' refers to Fox.

262. Lord North, well rewarded by George III for his services as prime minister during the War of Independence, a war for which he held little enthusiasm, resigned his position immediately on its conclusion. In 1783, to the king's displeasure, he formed a coalition with the Duke of Portland and Fox, both of whom had been in the Whig opposition during North's administration. They won office, under the titular leadership of the Duke of Portland, and governed from April to December 1783. North was Home Secretary and Fox served as Foreign Secretary.

263. Fox and Lord North were known as men of eloquence.

264. Wilkes's first arrest was made under a general warrant, but he was released when Lord Chief Justice Pratt ordered that his arrest was a breach of parliamentary privilege. Wilkes and his supporters entered into proceedings against the government that led to the abolishment of general warrants that did not name the person or persons subject to arrest.

265. In December 1783, Fox had introduced the India Bill to Parliament which proposed that the government would govern India and the East India Company would handle trade. The Bill, which proposed that seven commissioners appointed by the government be appointed for four years and, beyond that, appointed by the East India Company, was passed in the House of Commons. It was found that the proposed commissioners were supporters of Fox and North, and one the son of North. George III made it known to the Lords that any who voted for it would incur his wrath. It was not passed by the Lords. It was then that the king saw the government as inept and dismissed Fox and North.

266. Paine here refers to the rejected India Bill of 1783.

267. The reference is to Warren Hastings, as will become clear.

268. Paine's reference is to the time when William Pitt the Elder, Earl of Chatham, was prime minister, 1766–68.

269. Following his dismissal of the Fox–North coalition, the king asked Pitt the Younger to form a government. Despite being defeated in government shortly after, Pitt refused to resign. In 1784, Parliament was dissolved and a general election returned Pitt to the helm. The matters mentioned here refer to Pitt's continued leadership as prime minister and the heavy taxes he imposed to restore public finances, which had been drained by the War of Independence. See the previous piece, *Reflections on the Present State of the British Nation*, wherein Paine referred to taxes as monies borrowed from the populace.

270. Rockingham died suddenly and the king asked William Petty-Fitzmaurice, 2nd Earl of Shelburne, to form a government. Shelburne held office until William Pitt the Younger was elected in 1784.

271. 'Boy of the Exchequer' refers to Shelburne.

272. See Exodus 7:10.

273. Paine's reference is to his friend Joseph Priestley, who, for his radical opinions, was nicknamed 'Gunpowder Joe'.

274. In introducing the characters of his late seventeenth-century comedy, William Congreve described Maskwell as a villain and pretended friend of another character, Mellefont, both of whom were in love with the same woman. William Congreve, *The Double Dealer* (Ilkley, Yorkshire: A Scolar Press Facsimile, 1973), p. 6 of the text.

275. In Greek mythology Thalia, one of the three daughters of Zeus and Eurynome, was one of the nine Muses, and patron of comedy.

276. Paine here writes of the Marquess of Buckingham, George Nugent Temple Grenville, who represented Buckinghamshire from 1774 to 1779. He was a member of the Privy Council and Lord Lieutenant of Ireland in the Rockingham ministry. For a short time in 1783, he was Secretary of Foreign Affairs and again, in 1787, he was appointed Lord Lieutenant of Ireland.

277. Commonly recognized as resorting to bribery, Grenville was admonished by the Irish Houses of Parliament and resigned in 1789.

278. Gentoo is an archaic expression meaning Hindu.

279. Following the conclusion of the War of Independence, the Preliminary Treaty of Paris, or preliminary articles, was signed in Paris in November 1782 and three further definitive treaties were signed in September 1783.

280. Paine here refers to the India Bill introduced by Fox towards the end of the Fox–North administration. It was indeed adoption of a cause of the preceding Shelburne ministry. An 'Eastern defaulter' describes Warren Hastings, Governor General of British India, who, in 1787, was impeached on charges of corruption; after a ten-year trial, he was acquitted. It was in 1782 when Fox's bill was being debated, that the Attorney General, John Lee, made the quoted remark about the charter of the East India Company; reference to the remark can be found in Edwin Sidney, *The Life of Sir Richard Hill, Bart.* (London: R.B. Seeley and W. Burnside, 1839), p. 324, n. 1.

281. J—n L— obviously refers to the Attorney General, John Lee. Not spelled out, it might have been that Paine feared allegations of libel.

282. Charles I was overthrown by Cromwell and his followers, the Roundheads. Supporters of the king were barred from his trial by Cromwell's parliament. Condemned as a tyrant, traitor, murderer and enemy of the public, Charles was executed outside the Palace of Whitehall in 1649.

283. On 28 December 1793, Paine was incarcerated in the Luxembourg Prison where he remained until November 1794.

284. Thomas Pinckney was the United States minister to Britain from 1792 to 1796.

285. The 'American letter' Paine mentions can be found headed 'A Citizen of America to the Citizens of Europe', in Philip S. Foner, vol. 2, pp. 561–5.

286. This letter to Jefferson is transcribed from the original, which is held at the Library of Congress.

287. The letter of 20 October is to be found in Philip S. Foner, vol. 2, pp. 1333–4.
288. Paul Keen, *The Crisis of Literature in the 1790s: Print Culture and the Public Sphere* (Cambridge: Cambridge University Press, 1999), p. 27.
289. Unaware of the true author, a scholar of recent years described the piece as 'a brief but passionate outcry against these measures'. Don Herzog, *Poisoning the Minds of the Lower Orders* (Princeton, NJ: Princeton University Press, 1998), p. 117.
290. By his use of the words 'slavery bills', Paine was not referring to black slavery, but that which he saw as the submission of loyal subjects to the rule of a tyrannical government.
291. Daniel Holt, a leading radical publisher, was twice tried for publishing seditious libels in 1793 and found guilty on both counts. The Rev. William Winterbotham, also tried in 1793 was convicted of seditious preaching. For full reports of Holt's trials, see T. B. Howell, comp., *A Complete Collection of State Trials and Proceedings for High Treason and Other Crimes and Misdemeanor ...*, vol. 22 (London: T. C. Hansard, 1817), pp. 1189–238, and for Winterbotham's trial, pp. 824–908. (The reader will note that Paine's spelling was often as heard, as was frequently the case at the time.)
292. Thomas Muir, Thomas Fyshe Palmer and Joseph Gerrald were Scottish political reformists convicted of sedition and sentenced to transportation to Australia.
293. Paine's reference is to the reign of James II which led to the Glorious Revolution of 1688 when Parliament peacefully asserted its rights over the monarchy. The resulting Bill of Rights of 1689 formed the basis of the British constitution.
294. John Hampden, in the seventeenth century, became renowned for opposing Charles I over ship money and royal policy in general. He died in a skirmish of the Civil War in 1643 and the reformists of the eighteenth century considered him a martyr. According to his biographer, he was a politician of little significance, who, like Paine, left little in the way of papers or remembered conversation on which to build a life story; possibly because, as he was a chief leader in events preceding the Civil War, all records were destroyed for fear of recrimination against his family. See Lord Nugent, *Memorials of John Hampden, His Party and His Times*, 4th edn (London: Henry G. Bohn, 1860), p. 1. Lord William Russell opposed the kingship of James II and was executed in 1683, allegedly for plotting to murder Charles II and his brother James. George Godfrey Cunningham, ed., *Lives of Eminent and Illustrious Englishmen ...*, vol. 3 (Glasgow: A. Fullarton and Co., 1837), pp. 42–3.
295. The Habeas Corpus Act was suspended on 16 May 1794 because it was feared by the government that revolution such as had occurred in France might happen in Britain. Suspension of the Act was seen as a means of arresting parliamentary reformers. The suspension lasted only fourteen months, but was restored for three years in 1798.
296. Paine misquotes a Whig toast. It was, in fact, John Hampden who 'bled in the field'. Like Lord William Russell, Algernon Sydney (spelt by Paine as 'Sidney') was executed in 1683, for an alleged plot to kill Charles II and his brother. Cunningham, pp. 49–50.
297. See Thomas Paine to Colonel John Fellows, 20 January 1797, in Philip S. Foner, vol. 2, p. 1384.

298. Aldridge published verse three in *American Ideology*, p. 291, and Keane published verse one, p. 441.
299. Paine quickly adapted to dating his letters by the French revolutionary calendar, a system that was soon abandoned. The song was written on 10 May 1798.
300. As Paine breakfasted and dined at the house, it appears that he was staying there.
301. Paine's emphasis.
302. On his return to the United States Paine was publicly reviled on the basis of his having written both *The Age of Reason* and his public attack on President Washington whom Paine perceived as having done nothing to help him while he was imprisoned in France.
303. Elbridge Gerry was to become the fifth vice president of the United States in the second term of the presidency of James Madison, 1813–17. During his governorship of Massachusetts, 1810–11, his administration was noted for dividing electoral districts for partisan political gain, a practice that became known as 'gerrymandering'.
304. John Adams became President of the United States in 1796.
305. John Marshall, a Virginian and long-time military man, became a member of the House of Representatives the following year and was to serve as Chief Justice of the United States for more than 30 years.
306. 29 May 1798.
307. Joel Barlow, an American citizen and friend of Paine with a literary history closely resembling his own, was living in France at the time. He wrote several republican works, one of which, *Advice to the Privileged Orders*, was published a few days before Paine's *Rights*, pt 2. He is best remembered in the United States for his epic poem *The Columbiad*, which was published in 1807.
308. Louis-Marie de La Revellière Lépeaux, a friend of Paine, was the first president of the Directory. Like Paine, he was interested in Theophilanthropy, the idea of establishing a deistic form of religion.
309. The letter to Eldridge Gerry is here transcribed and edited from a photocopy of the original from the collection of the James S. Copley Library, La Jolla, California.
310. See Thomas Paine to the Council of Five Hundred, in Philip S. Foner, vol. 2, p. 1403.
311. Thomas Paine, in Philip S. Foner, vol. 2, pp. 939–40.
312. Thomas Paine to Thomas Jefferson, in Philip S. Foner, vol. 2, pp. 1406–2.
313. Philip S. Foner, vol. 2, pp. 1409–10.
314. Paine refers to what became known as 'the Freya Affair'. On 25 July 1800, the Danish frigate *Freya* was escorting a convoy when a British squadron attempted to search the escort ship. The captain protested and a battle ensued in which Danish and English sailors were killed. The capture of the convoy led to an official protest by the Danish minister in London that resulted in Lord Whitworth being sent to Copenhagen to negotiate; a few days later a British naval squadron appeared off the Danish coast. At first, the Danes considered resistance to the British threat, but finally agreed to accept the return of the *Freya* and the ships of the convoy. A. D. Harvey, *Collision of Empires: Britain in Three World Wars, 1793–1945* (London: Hambledon Press, 1992), pp. 92–3.
315. Philip S. Foner, vol. 2, p. 1409.

316. Letter from Thomas Jefferson to Thomas Paine, 18 March 1801, in Philip S. Foner, vol. 2, p. 946.

317. Philip S. Foner, vol. 2, p. 1417.

318. The manuscript of Paine's letter, held by the Library of Congress, is clearly dated 15 October 1800, but in the first paragraph he wrote of 'a paper of yesterday, 15th October – 23 Vendemaire'.

319. Thomas Paine to Thomas Jefferson, 1 October and 15 October 1800, in Philip S. Foner, vol. 2, pp. 1412, 1428.

320. Hugo Grotius's first published work on international law, *Mare Liberum*, of 1609, argued that it was not within the rights of any nation to claim rights to any part of the open sea; it ran counter to natural law and the law of humanity. In the seventeenth century Samuel Pufendorf (spelt by Paine as 'Puffendorf') published works on the law of nature, and, in 1758, Emmerich de Vattel published *Le Droit des Gens*, or *The Law of Nations*.

321. Paine's reference is to the work of Charles Jenkinson, *A Collection of all the Treaties of Peace, Alliance, and Commerce between Great-Britain and other Powers; from the Treaty signed at Munster in 1648, to the Treaties signed at Paris in 1783*, 3 vols (London: J. Debrett, 1785). Jenkinson, 1st Lord Hawkesbury, 1st Earl of Liverpool, was President of the Board of Trade from 1786 to 1804.

322. Editor's translations.

323. Paul was emperor of Russia from 1796 to 1801.

324. The town of El-Arish on the Sinai Peninsula was taken by Napoleon in 1799. The ineffectual treaty provided for the French evacuation of Egypt.

325. Peter the Great, founder of the Russian Empire, reigned from 1682 to 1725. His reforms, at times ruthless, changed Russia from a poverty-stricken Asian country to a modern Western European power. On the other hand, Paul, son of Catherine the Great, was considered a reactionary. His uncertain foreign policy led to his abandoning a peace policy to join with France during the War of the Second Coalition in 1798 and, in 1800, to side with Napoleon against Britain. He was assassinated in March 1801, the year that Paine's *Compact Maritime* was published in Washington.

326. In 1798, the Swedish merchant ship *Maria* was seized by English naval vessels and became involved in a battle with two Spanish frigates in the Bay of Barcelona. Sir William Scott, Judge of the British Admiralty court, found that the naval ships had acted legally.

327. The remarks within parentheses were probably directed to Thomas Jefferson.

328. Oliver Oldschool was the pseudonym of the Federalist writer Joseph Dennie. *The Port Folio* was an eminent politico-literary weekly journal launched in 1801. In 1805, Dennie was tried for seditious libel as a result of his violent published attacks in the paper on Thomas Jefferson, but was acquitted.

329. As this piece was written, France was under the military leadership of Napoleon; he had approached Charles IV of Spain with a proposal that he cede Louisiana back to France who had ceded lands west of the Mississippi to Spain in 1762. This meant that the American states would no longer enjoy the privilege of storing goods at New Orleans for later shipment. Matters became tense between the United States and France to the point of seemingly imminent war.

330. Babcock proudly displayed his printing status on the front page of his paper.

331. Richard Gimbel, 'New Political Writings by Thomas Paine', *The Yale University Library Gazette*, 30 (1956) 97–8.
332. The letter is here transcribed and lightly edited from a photocopy of the original document, which is held in the Manuscripts Division, Department of Rare Books and Special Collections, Princeton University Library.
333. Paine was to write an essay on the cause of yellow fever in 1805.
334. Paine returned to the United States of America from France in September 1802. In 1774, Barlow, together with Babcock, had founded the weekly *American Mercury*.
335. Uriah Tracy was a Federalist Connecticut representative and senator. He published a pamphlet, *To the Freemen of Connecticut* (Litchfield: Thomas Collier, 1803), in response to the *Republican Address to the Freemen of Connecticut* (Connecticut: General Committee of the Republicans of Connecticut, 30 August 1803). Paine refers to Thomas Green's New Haven paper, the *Connecticut Journal*. See Joseph T. Buckingham, *Specimens of Newspaper Literature with Personal Memoirs, Anecdotes, and Reminiscences*, vol. 1 (Boston: Redding and Company, 1852), p. 313.
336. See Joshua 9:23.
337. Oliver Ellsworth had served in the United States Senate and, in 1796, was appointed by George Washington as Chief Justice of the Supreme Court. At the request of President John Adams, in 1799, he went as a commissioner to France to negotiate a new treaty which, in effect, ended the undeclared war between the United States and France.
338. Star Chester of Groton had been appointed under an Act of Ohio, 15 April 1803, as one of the first directors of a company formed to incorporate the owners and proprietors of a vast tract of land south of Lake Erie. See Salmon P. Chase, ed., *The Statutes of Ohio and of the Northwestern Territory, Adopted or Enacted from 1788 to 1833 Inclusive* ... (Cincinatti: Corey & Fairbank, 1833), pp. 372–3. Researching the background of Major Smith, lacking a forename, has proved close to futile. Despite wide searching and seeking information on a discussion list for historians of Connecticut, there seems to be only one reference to a Major Smith. It is an interesting story of an incident that occurred in 1813, beyond the time restraints of this book. The major found himself in a predicament when, in fear of an attack on New London by two British ships, the residents fled and volunteers rushed to man the guns of the fort. They found themselves desperately short of gun wadding to the extent of rendering the cannons virtually useless. Frantic door-knocking finally found a woman who had remained in her house. On hearing of the volunteers' plight, she let her red flannel petticoat drop to the floor and told the men to 'Give this to the British at the cannon's mouth'. As it happened, the British did not attack and, after lingering for some days in a threatening manner, quietly sailed away. See David E. Philips, *Legendary Connecticut: Traditional Tales from the Nutmeg State*, 2nd edn (Willimantic, CT: Curbstone Press, 1992), pp. 56–7.
339. 'David' regularly wrote to the *American Mercury* and had vehemently denounced Uriah Tracy's address which was published in the paper of 22 September 1803. As noted by Gimbel (98, n. 7), 'David' did not oblige Paine in publishing his charge against Ellsworth. Later editions of the paper were checked during research for this work.
340. Aldridge, *Man of Reason*, pp. 282–3, 339.

341. GLC04281. Thomas Paine. Autograph letter signed: to Anthony Taylor, 20 November 1803. (The Gilder Lehrman Collection, courtesy of The Gilder Lehrman Institute of American History.)

342. As mentioned earlier, Kirkbride and Paine had been friends since the early days of the Revolution. Kirkbride died on 3 October 1800.

343. Paine refers to the controversial election of 1800 in which Thomas Jefferson defeated John Adams.

344. The riots mentioned took place on 18 February 1803. Paine had driven to Trenton from where he intended to travel on to New York. Neither of two coachmen would take him as a passenger due to his being both a deist and a staunch Republican travelling through strongly Federalist territory. A mob gathered and a riot ensued. Aldridge, *Man of Reason*, p. 280. On 3 November, the General Assembly of the State of New Jersey resolved that a committee be appointed to inquire into the cause of the riot and the conduct of the mob. Edwin Robert Walker et al., *A History of Trenton, 1679–1919: Two Hundred and Fifty Years of a Notable Town with Links in Four Centuries*, vol. 2 (Princeton, NJ: Princeton University Press, 1929), pp. 208, 218.

345. Mrs Wharton had briefly rented Paine's house at Bordentown. See Thomas Paine to Mr Hyer, 24 March 1804, in Philip S. Foner, vol. 2, p. 1452.

346. It is clear from his correspondence and writing of 1803 and 1804 that Paine was in Connecticut on business of an anti-Federalist nature.

347. Paine mentioned the address in his letter to Elisha Babcock of 10 October 1803. See edited transcription in this book.

348. Abraham Bishop, *Oration, in Honor of the Election of President Jefferson, and the Peaceable Acquisition of Louisiana, Delivered at the National Festival in Hartford, on the 11th of May, 1804* (New Haven: The General Committee of Republicans, 1804), p. 3.

349. Gimbel, 94–107.

350. The article has also been lightly edited.

351. Beyond what can be seen from earlier writings in this book, Paine made this point repeatedly in several of his works.

352. The reference is to the Twelfth Amendment (1804). The experience of the presidential election of 1800 revealed a defect in the Constitution. Both Jefferson and his Democratic-Republican partner received equal electoral votes. The Amendment introduced separate voting for the position of president and vice president.

353. Mention of 'seven heads' relates to the seven lawyers mentioned in Paine's note to the article. Together with the ten ministers who controlled Yale College, all ardent Federalists, they formed a powerful 'political machine' combining church and state that their opponents of the Republican Party referred to as 'Moses and Aaron'. See Gimbel, 94. For biblical references to Dagon see Judges 16:23; 1 Samuel 5:2–7; and for seven heads see Revelation 12.3, 13.1, 17.3, 17.7 and 17.9. Paine also referred to Samuel and the Temple of Dagon in *Rights*, pt 2, p. 104. He later mentioned Dagon in a letter of 31 July 1805 to his friend, Colonel John Fellows. See Philip S. Foner, vol. 2, pp. 1470.

354. Confirmation of this pseudonym being one of Paine's several will be noted in a later item dated 27 August 1804.

355. The seven lawyers were named in a footnote by Bishop as 'Messrs Daggett, Smith, C. Goodrich, Brace, Allen, Edmonds, and E. Goodrich'. Richard Gimbel summarized the power of this group of men who were, in effect, a supreme court and appointers of the judiciary; they were able to plead cases before courts where they sat, and secured re-election by dubious means.

356. Lang's paper was the *New York Gazette*. From 1795 to 1811, John Mitchell Mason served as a trustee of Columbia University and later became provost. In 1804, he established the first theological seminary of the Union Theological Seminary in New York. His son edited his works in a four-volume series: Ebenezer Mason, ed., *The Complete Works of John M. Mason, D.D.* (New York: Baker and Scribner, 1849). The oration on the late Major-General Alexander Hamilton may be found in vol. 4, pp. 497–523 followed by an appendix, pp. 524–7.

357. All bracketed comments in the quoted material are Paine's remarks.

358. At the 1804 election, George Clinton was elected vice president to Thomas Jefferson.

359. Paine refers to Mason's oration.

360. The manuscript is held in the Andre DeCoppet Collection of the Manuscripts Division, Department of Rare Books and Special Collections, Princeton University Library.

361. An announcement in Babcock's paper, *American Mercury*, of 26 July 1804 read, '"A Friend to Constitutional Order" is received, and shall have a place in our paper of next week. We thank the writer for this Communication, and hope for a continuation of his favors'.

362. For the piece in William Duane's paper, the Philadelphia *Aurora*, see Philip S. Foner, vol. 2, pp. 958–62.

363. John Lang edited the *New York Gazette*.

364. Paine's reference is to the election of 1804; he was confident that President Jefferson would be returned to office.

365. Gimbel, 94.

366. GLC 6330. Thomas Paine. Autograph letter signed: to Elisha Babcock, 11th September 1804. (The Gilder Lehrman Collection, courtesy of The Gilder Lehrman Institute of American History.)

367. See letter of 21 September 1804, edited transcript included in this book.

368. See letter of 27 August 1804, newly edited for inclusion in this book.

369. As will be seen from a later letter to Babcock, 21 September 1804, the pamphlet was a copy of Paine's *Dissertation on First Principles of Government* which was written in Paris early in July 1795. He mentioned the work in a speech translated and delivered on his behalf by a secretary who stood beside him on the Tribune in the Convention of 7 July in which he expressed 'his sentiments on the Declaration of Rights and the Constitution'. Thomas Paine, *Dissertation on First Principles of Government to which is Added the Genuine Speech, Translated, and Delivered at the Tribune of the French Convention, July 7, 1795* (Philadelphia: E. Conrad, 1795), p. 36.

370. Paine refers to John Adams's long work, *Defence of the Constitutions of Government of the United States of America* which was published in 1787.

371. As noted earlier, Babcock's correspondent 'David' did not take up Paine's charge against Ellsworth for favouring a monarchy. In a letter to Babcock of 2 July

1805, Paine complained that Babcock had made no use of his useful intelligence. See Philip S. Foner, vol. 2, p. 1468.

372. The manuscript of this letter, Thomas Paine to Elisha Babcock, 21 September 1804, is held in the James Fraser Gluck Collection, Buffalo & Erie County Public Library, Buffalo, New York.

373. Paine's objection relates to the editing and renaming of the paragraph mentioned in his letter to Babcock of 27 August 1804.

374. Hartford: Hudson and Goodwin, 1804.

375. Blue laws were those that forbade particular activities on the Sabbath. Puritanical in origin, they included such things as work, travelling, trading and sport. The name might have derived from archaic usage of the word blue meaning 'strictly moral'. The state of Connecticut enforces one blue law to the present time; it is illegal to trade in liquor on a Sunday. In New England in the mid-seventeenth century, several Quakers were hanged merely for practising their faith. Without separation between church and state, the Puritans insisted on all attending church. Those who did not were punished under civil law.

376. There is a body of literature on this topic that needs no elaboration here.

377. All writers on Paine who have mentioned the essay have dated it 1806 because that was the year it was published.

378. Dr Edward Miller was the resident physician for the city of New York.

379. *Report on the Malignant Disease, which Prevailed in the City of New-York in the Autumn of 1805* (New York: James Cheetham, 1806).

380. The letter is held in the Gouverneur Morris Papers and the De Witt Clinton Papers, Rare Book and Manuscript Library, Columbia University.

381. The letter was addressed in Paine's hand to 'De Witt Clinton – Mayor of New York, favoured by Mr Carver Cedar Street where Mr Paine is at present'. At the time, Carver was named as a beneficiary in Paine's will, but their friendship came to an abrupt end and Carver did not benefit on Paine's death in 1809.

382. The *American Citizen* was owned by James Cheetham who, after Paine's death, immediately rushed into publishing a denigrating biography of him. The two fell out when Cheetham published a piece by Paine with large omissions. See Aldridge, *Man of Reason*, p. 308.

INDEX

Made in the USA
Monee, IL
30 July 2021